So You Want to Be an Accountant ?

A Youth Career Guide

Kiet Huynh

Table of Contents

Introduction

1.1 Why Consider a Career in Accounting?

When it comes to selecting a career path, accounting may not be the first choice that comes to mind. Some people associate it with dry numbers or a lack of creativity, but accounting is far more dynamic than it may seem at first glance. In fact, a career in accounting offers a wealth of opportunities, from job stability to meaningful contributions to businesses and communities. Let's explore some key reasons why you might consider accounting as your professional path.

1.1.1 The Backbone of Business and Society

Accounting is often called the "language of business." Every organization, whether a small local business or a multinational corporation, relies on accountants to understand and manage their finances. Accountants help track income and expenditures, ensuring that organizations remain profitable, compliant, and prepared for growth. Without accounting, businesses would struggle to make strategic decisions, manage their resources, or even exist in the long term.

Beyond individual businesses, accounting plays a critical role in society at large. Governments rely on accounting to allocate budgets, fund infrastructure projects, and ensure transparency. Nonprofits use accounting to manage donations, grants, and resources to maximize their social impact. Accountants help bring accountability to every aspect of finance, making them invaluable to society.

1.1.2 Diverse Career Paths and Specializations

A career in accounting is far from one-size-fits-all. The field offers a wide range of career paths and specializations, meaning there's something for nearly every interest. Some of the most popular fields include:

- *Public Accounting:* As a public accountant, you could work for an accounting firm providing services like tax preparation, auditing, and consulting to a wide array of clients. Public accountants gain exposure to many industries, learning about different businesses and helping them maintain accurate financial records.

- *Corporate Accounting:* Corporate accountants work within a single company, handling budgeting, internal auditing, and financial planning. This career path offers stability and often involves working closely with other departments to manage company finances.

- *Forensic Accounting:* Combining detective work with financial expertise, forensic accountants investigate fraud and financial misconduct. This specialization is ideal if you have a keen eye for detail and a strong sense of justice.

- *Tax Accounting:* Specializing in tax accounting means helping individuals and organizations navigate tax regulations, reduce tax liability, and stay compliant with the law. Tax accountants often work during "tax season," but they're also needed year-round to advise on tax planning.

- *Government Accounting:* Working as a government accountant involves managing public funds, conducting audits, and ensuring transparency. Accountants in this field contribute to the responsible use of taxpayer money.

The wide array of choices means that accountants can pivot their careers based on interests, strengths, or even lifestyle preferences. This diversity also allows for continued growth and specialization, making accounting a versatile and evolving career.

1.1.3 Job Security and Stability

One of the most appealing aspects of a career in accounting is its stability. Regardless of economic cycles, accountants remain in demand. During times of economic growth, businesses need accountants to handle increased financial activity. In economic downturns, accountants become even more essential for cost-saving strategies, audits, and compliance.

The Bureau of Labor Statistics and various employment agencies consistently rank accounting among the most in-demand professions. As long as businesses and organizations exist, there will be a need for accountants. If you're looking for a career with long-term security, accounting is an excellent option.

1.1.4 Attractive Earning Potential

Accountants can earn competitive salaries, and their earning potential tends to increase with experience, specialization, and certification. Entry-level accounting positions often offer a solid starting salary, and as accountants gain experience or pursue certifications like the CPA (Certified Public Accountant) or CMA (Certified Management Accountant), their earning potential increases significantly.

Additionally, accountants with specialized skills, such as forensic accounting or tax expertise, can command even higher salaries. If you're interested in a career that not only offers stability but also the opportunity for financial growth, accounting provides a clear path toward financial success.

1.1.5 A Global Career with Endless Opportunities

Accounting is a globally recognized profession. The fundamental principles of accounting are similar across countries, which means that skilled accountants can find opportunities anywhere in the world. Many certifications, like the CPA, are respected internationally, allowing accountants to work in global firms, international organizations, or even pursue work in different countries.

As global economies become more interconnected, the demand for international accountants—those who understand global standards and can work with multinational companies—continues to grow. Whether you dream of working abroad or collaborating with global clients, accounting can open those doors.

1.1.6 Building Valuable Skills Beyond Numbers

Contrary to popular belief, accounting is not just about crunching numbers. Accountants develop a suite of valuable skills that can transfer to almost any industry. Here are some key skills you'll gain:

- *Analytical Thinking:* Accountants must analyze data to provide insights and make informed decisions. This analytical approach is useful in all types of problem-solving.

- *Attention to Detail:* Accounting requires a keen eye for detail, as even small errors can have significant consequences. Developing this skill enhances accuracy and professionalism in any field.

- *Communication Skills:* Accountants frequently explain complex financial information to clients, executives, or colleagues who may not have financial backgrounds. The ability to communicate clearly and effectively is a critical skill in any profession.

- *Ethics and Integrity:* Accountants adhere to strict ethical guidelines, as they handle sensitive financial information. This commitment to integrity is invaluable in building trust and credibility in any career.

These skills make accountants well-rounded professionals who can adapt and succeed in various roles and industries.

1.1.7 The Impact of Technology and Innovation

Accounting is far from a static profession. With advancements in technology, accounting is becoming more efficient and precise. Automation, artificial intelligence, and data analytics are transforming how accountants work, allowing them to focus on strategic decision-making rather than routine tasks. As technology continues to shape the field, accountants are at the forefront of integrating innovative solutions to improve business processes.

Learning to work with new tools and technologies is an exciting part of being an accountant today. Those who embrace technology can add immense value to organizations, setting themselves apart as forward-thinking professionals.

1.1.8 Making a Difference

At its core, accounting is about helping people and organizations manage resources wisely. Accountants provide the insights needed to make informed decisions that impact employees, shareholders, and communities. In nonprofit accounting, for example, your work might support a charity's ability to fund important social projects. In government accounting, you might help manage taxpayer money responsibly.

Accounting also plays a crucial role in preventing financial fraud and ensuring ethical business practices. Forensic accountants, auditors, and compliance professionals protect the integrity of financial systems, helping to build trust in financial institutions and markets.

In summary, accounting offers a blend of stability, variety, and growth potential that few other professions can match. Accountants enjoy meaningful work, strong earning potential, and the chance to make a real difference. For young people considering their career paths, accounting provides an excellent foundation, whether you're drawn to the world of finance, driven by ethical considerations, or simply interested in building a versatile and fulfilling career.

1.2 Who This Book is For

This guide is designed for anyone who has ever wondered about a career in accounting, particularly young adults and students who are just starting to think about their future professions. Whether you're in high school, entering college, or even early in your career journey, this book offers valuable insights tailored to those who are new to the field. Here's a closer look at who can benefit from this guide:

1. Students and Young Adults Considering Career Options

Choosing a career path is a big decision, and it's completely natural to feel uncertain about which direction to take. This book aims to clarify what it truly means to work in accounting so that you can make an informed decision. Accounting isn't just about crunching numbers; it's about making a meaningful impact by helping businesses, organizations, and individuals make sound financial decisions. If you're curious but unsure about whether accounting is the right fit, this guide will provide an in-depth look at the profession, the skills it requires, and the potential paths within the field.

2. High School Students Preparing for the Next Step

High school students who are beginning to think seriously about their future may find this guide especially useful. Choosing courses that align with a potential career in accounting can give you a strong foundation and better prepare you for college-level studies in accounting or finance. If you're currently in high school, this book will help you understand how subjects like math, economics, and even computer science play a role in the field of accounting. We'll also cover which extracurricular activities can help you build relevant skills, from managing budgets in a club setting to learning about the financial aspects of running a small business.

3. College Students Exploring Accounting as a Major

For those in college who are weighing the benefits of choosing accounting as a major, this guide serves as a roadmap to understanding the core subjects and concepts in accounting. College can be overwhelming, especially if you're trying to decide on a major that will lead to a fulfilling career. If you're a college student considering an accounting degree or taking introductory accounting courses, this book will demystify what to expect, from core courses to certifications that can boost your career opportunities. You'll gain insights into real-world applications of accounting concepts and hear about various specializations that can make your accounting degree even more valuable.

4. Individuals Interested in a Stable, Rewarding Career

A career in accounting can be rewarding on multiple fronts, from financial stability to opportunities for career advancement. This book is also for young adults who may not yet have a clear career direction but value stability, demand, and respect in their chosen field. If you're interested in a profession that offers diverse career opportunities, has high earning potential, and allows you to play a significant role in the success of businesses, then accounting may be the ideal choice. Through this guide, you'll discover the various ways an accounting career can support your personal and professional goals.

5. Aspiring Entrepreneurs and Business Enthusiasts

Many people interested in entrepreneurship overlook the crucial role accounting plays in running a successful business. If you have an interest in business and think you might want to start your own company someday, understanding the basics of accounting can provide a strong foundation. This guide includes insights into how accounting knowledge benefits business owners, from understanding financial statements to making strategic decisions based on financial data. Learning accounting doesn't necessarily mean you'll become a professional accountant; it can also mean acquiring the skills needed to run a successful, financially sound business.

6. Parents and Mentors of Aspiring Accountants

Parents, mentors, and teachers who are guiding young adults in choosing a career path may also find value in this book. Accounting can be a mysterious field to those unfamiliar with it, often viewed as a niche area only for "math experts." This guide sheds light on the many opportunities within accounting, helping parents and mentors support their children or students in making well-informed decisions. You'll also find sections dedicated to understanding the educational journey of an accountant, including tips on scholarships, internships, and early career opportunities.

7. Anyone Curious About the Versatility of Accounting Skills

Finally, this book is for anyone who sees the value of versatile skills. Accounting knowledge is applicable in various fields, including finance, consulting, law, government, and nonprofit sectors. Whether or not you end up working as an accountant, the skills you gain from studying accounting can enhance your understanding of business operations and improve your financial literacy. This guide will show how the core principles of accounting apply to a variety of professions and how accounting can serve as a springboard to roles outside traditional accounting positions.

What You Can Expect from This Guide

Throughout this book, you'll gain a clear and comprehensive understanding of what the accounting profession entails, along with the education, skills, and experiences that can help you succeed. We'll explore everything from foundational concepts to advanced career pathways, equipping you with the knowledge to make an informed choice about entering the field.

Each chapter includes practical advice, real-life examples, and resources for further exploration. Whether you're on the fence about accounting or already leaning towards it, this book will serve as a valuable tool in your career decision-making process. Our goal is to make accounting accessible, relatable, and—most importantly—exciting as you consider the many opportunities it has to offer.

1.3 How to Use This Guide

Introduction to the Guide's Structure and Purpose

Welcome to So You Want to Be an Accountant? A Youth Career Guide. This book is designed to be your resourceful companion as you explore accounting as a potential career path. Unlike many traditional guides, which might present accounting in a more formal, academic sense, this book is designed to be approachable, informative, and practical. Whether you're curious about accounting, committed to the idea of a career in it, or somewhere in between, you'll find chapters tailored to your unique journey.

As you use this guide, keep in mind that it's structured to be adaptable. You can read it cover-to-cover for a comprehensive overview or jump to specific sections that interest you. The guide is divided into major parts, each focusing on essential aspects of understanding, entering, and growing in the field of accounting. Below, you'll find an outline of how to navigate each part effectively, along with tips on using the guide to maximize its benefits for your personal growth and career goals.

Part 1: Tailoring the Guide to Your Needs

This guide isn't a one-size-fits-all approach to career planning. It's tailored to help each reader develop their understanding and make informed decisions based on their interests, strengths, and individual goals. Here's how to use the guide based on your specific needs and background:

1. Identifying Your Goals and Interests

Before diving into the chapters, take a moment to reflect on your goals and what you're hoping to achieve by reading this book. Are you completely new to accounting and looking to understand if it's the right fit for you? Are you already considering an accounting degree and want more insights into the field? This guide is here to provide tailored information based on your unique starting point.

Use this self-assessment as a personal filter as you read each chapter. For example, if you're more interested in corporate finance, you might find that certain chapters (such as those on financial analysis and managerial accounting) will provide you with especially relevant insights. On the other hand, if public accounting or auditing intrigues you, other sections will be more applicable to your journey.

2. Chapter Summaries and Highlights for Quick Reference

Each chapter begins with a summary of key points, giving you a quick preview of the content. You'll also find key takeaways at the end of each chapter to help reinforce the main ideas. These summaries are ideal for readers who prefer a quick review before or after reading the full chapter, or for those who want a refresher when returning to the book later.

Whether you're a high school student exploring options or a college freshman trying to decide on a major, these summaries allow you to gain a high-level understanding quickly, making it easier to focus on topics that matter most to you.

3. Reflection and Interactive Sections

This guide includes exercises, prompts, and reflective questions throughout. These aren't just extras—they're tools to help you connect what you're learning to your own aspirations and values. Take time with these exercises. Think of them as opportunities to imagine your future, consider what you value most in a career, and how accounting can align with those values. Use a notebook or the margin spaces in the book to jot down thoughts, insights, or questions that arise as you engage with these exercises.

By actively participating in these reflection sections, you're not only building knowledge but also creating a deeper personal connection with the material, which can help clarify your career goals.

Part 2: Exploring the World of Accounting from Different Angles

This guide is structured to offer a well-rounded view of accounting, from entry-level roles to specialized fields. The purpose of these sections is to provide a realistic glimpse into what an accounting career could look like for you.

1. Guiding Young Readers through Career Discovery

Starting with foundational knowledge, the guide introduces readers to a variety of roles within accounting. This range of information helps you make more informed decisions about the areas you might enjoy most. Each section gives you a taste of the day-to-day responsibilities, the skills you'll need, and the challenges you may encounter.

As you read, take notes on what piques your interest. Are you drawn to tax accounting or forensic accounting? Would you prefer working with data in a corporate finance role, or does the idea of public accounting and auditing appeal more to you? Understanding these options early will help you focus your education and training on areas that match your interests.

2. Real-World Scenarios and Case Studies

In addition to descriptions of roles, some chapters include real-world scenarios, illustrating how accountants approach common challenges in their work. These case studies present practical insights into the accounting profession, offering a sense of what it feels like to work in various capacities.

As you read these scenarios, take time to imagine yourself in the accountant's position. Think about how you would handle the tasks described, or what steps you might take in similar situations. These scenarios are designed to give you a chance to envision yourself in the role, making the material more interactive and applicable to your future.

3. Educational Pathways and Certification Options

Accounting has a structured but flexible educational pathway, with many options for specialization. This book will guide you through these pathways, helping you choose the best academic and professional steps for your career goals.

These chapters are essential for anyone considering a formal education in accounting. Here, you'll find a breakdown of relevant degrees, certifications, and licensing options. The sections on certifications—such as the CPA (Certified Public Accountant) and CMA (Certified Management Accountant)—are especially valuable for understanding what credentials are required and why they matter. Use this part of the guide to help you decide which qualifications align with your long-term vision for your career.

Part 3: Practical Tools and Resources for Career Preparation

This part of the guide is focused on equipping you with the tools and skills you'll need as you prepare to enter the workforce.

1. Building Skills Step-by-Step

Success in accounting relies on both technical knowledge and soft skills, and this guide covers both. Technical skills such as financial analysis, regulatory knowledge, and accounting software are crucial, while soft skills like communication, teamwork, and critical thinking set you apart as a professional.

Treat these sections as a step-by-step development plan. Consider creating a checklist for the skills mentioned and gradually work on improving them. You can revisit this part of the guide whenever you're looking to strengthen a specific skill, making it a valuable resource even as you progress beyond entry-level roles.

2. Using Checklists and Actionable Steps

In several chapters, you'll find checklists and actionable steps to help you stay organized and on track as you prepare for internships, interviews, or certifications. These checklists offer concrete tasks, such as how to create a professional resume, prepare for common interview questions, or approach networking in the field.

Use these checklists as ongoing tools. Keep a separate notebook, or even a digital document, where you can track your progress. This way, you can come back to these steps as you work through them, making sure you're steadily moving toward your career goals.

3. Professional Development and Long-Term Growth

The later chapters delve into professional development, offering guidance on how to continue growing and evolving in your career after you've secured your first job. This section is filled with strategies for expanding your network, learning from mentors, and finding specialization opportunities within accounting. As you progress in your career, these chapters can be a source of inspiration and practical advice to help you reach new milestones.

Part 4: Applying the Guide to Real-Life Decisions

Finally, as you approach the end of the guide, you'll find tips and strategies for using this knowledge in real-life decision-making.

1. Taking Ownership of Your Career Journey

One of the book's key messages is that your career in accounting is a journey that you can shape and adapt over time. Encourage readers to revisit the guide whenever they're making a major career decision, such as choosing a specialization, pursuing additional certifications, or exploring leadership roles.

2. Using the Guide as a Long-Term Resource

This guide is not only an introduction to accounting but a reference you can return to throughout your career. As the field of accounting changes with advancements in technology and evolving regulations, you can use the foundational principles in this book to adapt and stay relevant.

Whether you're looking for tips on effective communication, the latest on certifications, or advice on networking, the guide will serve as a resource to support your professional growth for years to come.

CHAPTER I
Understanding the Accounting Profession

1.1 What is Accounting?

Accounting is often referred to as the "language of business" because it is a system of collecting, analyzing, and reporting financial information that is essential for making informed decisions. At its core, accounting revolves around tracking, measuring, and communicating an organization's financial health. But what does that really mean?

To start, accounting helps answer fundamental questions about a business or organization, such as:

- *How much revenue is the business generating?*

- *Are operating costs in line with the budget?*

- *What are the company's assets and liabilities?*

- *Is the business profitable, or is it running at a loss?*

- *How much can the business invest in growth, or what can it afford to pay out in dividends?*

The Purpose and Importance of Accounting

Accounting is integral not just for businesses, but also for individuals, nonprofits, and governments. At the heart of accounting lies the idea of financial accountability, ensuring that organizations use resources responsibly, comply with laws, and make sound financial decisions. Without accounting, it would be difficult for any organization to stay organized, keep track of its financial resources, or operate sustainably.

Key Purposes of Accounting:

1. Decision-Making: Accounting provides vital information that helps managers, investors, and stakeholders make critical financial decisions. For example, a company might decide to launch a new product based on projected revenue or cut back on spending in an area where costs are out of control.

2. Planning and Budgeting: Accounting enables organizations to create budgets, set financial targets, and monitor actual spending versus projected expenses. This is crucial for staying financially healthy and preparing for the future.

3. Regulatory Compliance: Companies must adhere to laws and regulations, such as tax codes and financial reporting standards. Accurate accounting helps ensure that they meet these legal obligations, reducing the risk of penalties or legal issues.

4. Evaluating Performance: Through accounting, organizations can assess performance over time by analyzing trends in revenue, profits, expenses, and growth. This information is invaluable for determining areas of success and identifying areas for improvement.

5. Building Trust with Stakeholders: Transparent accounting practices build trust among investors, creditors, customers, and employees. When stakeholders understand a company's financial status, they're more likely to invest, lend, or engage positively with the organization.

Key Concepts in Accounting

Accounting is governed by several essential concepts and principles that provide a structured framework for how information is recorded and reported. Here are a few key concepts to understand:

1. The Accounting Equation: This equation—Assets = Liabilities + Equity—forms the foundation of double-entry accounting, ensuring that every financial transaction affects at least two accounts and keeps the balance sheet balanced.

2. Double-Entry Accounting: Every transaction affects two accounts in a way that keeps the accounting equation in balance. For example, if a company takes out a loan, it receives *cash (an asset) but also incurs a liability (debt).*

3. Accrual vs. Cash Basis Accounting: In accrual accounting, revenues and expenses are recorded when they're earned or incurred, not necessarily when cash changes hands. Cash basis accounting, on the other hand, only records transactions when cash is actually received or paid out. Most large organizations use accrual accounting, as it provides a more accurate picture of financial health.

4. The Matching Principle: This principle ensures that expenses are recorded in the same period as the revenues they help generate. For example, if a company earns revenue in December, it should also record any expenses associated with that revenue in December, even if they are paid later.

5. The Revenue Recognition Principle: According to this principle, revenue is recognized when it is earned, not necessarily when the cash is received. This helps to provide a more accurate picture of a company's financial performance.

The Role of Accountants

Accountants are responsible for applying these principles in practice to maintain accurate financial records, prepare reports, and analyze financial information. Accountants may work directly for a business, an accounting firm, or even independently as consultants. Their roles vary widely depending on their specialty and industry, but at a high level, accountants typically handle the following tasks:

1. Recording Financial Transactions: Accountants ensure that all business transactions are accurately documented and classified in the appropriate accounts.

2. Preparing Financial Statements: These include the balance sheet, income statement, and cash flow statement, which collectively provide an overview of a company's financial position, performance, and cash flow.

3. Analyzing Financial Data: Accountants interpret financial data to assess business performance and make recommendations for improvement.

4. Ensuring Compliance: Accountants help organizations comply with financial regulations and tax laws, often preparing tax filings and advising on legal compliance.

5. Providing Financial Advice: Accountants often play an advisory role, helping companies make strategic decisions by analyzing costs, identifying risks, and suggesting areas for improvement.

Types of Financial Statements in Accounting

To communicate financial information, accountants create various types of financial statements. Each statement serves a specific purpose and provides a unique perspective on the financial health of an organization.

1. Balance Sheet: The balance sheet gives a snapshot of what a company owns (assets), what it owes (liabilities), and the value of shareholders' equity at a specific point in time.

2. Income Statement: Also known as the profit and loss statement, the income statement shows a company's revenue, expenses, and profits over a period. It helps stakeholders understand how much money the business makes after covering all its costs.

3. Cash Flow Statement: The cash flow statement tracks the cash coming in and out of the business, breaking it down into operating, investing, and financing activities. This statement is crucial for understanding cash liquidity.

4. Statement of Changes in Equity: This statement explains changes in a company's equity over a reporting period, including profits, losses, dividends, and equity injections from shareholders.

The Evolution of Accounting

The roots of accounting can be traced back thousands of years to ancient civilizations, where simple accounting systems were used to keep track of crops, livestock, and trade. Over time, as commerce grew more complex, so did accounting practices.

In the 15th century, Italian mathematician Luca Pacioli laid the foundation for modern accounting with his description of double-entry bookkeeping in Summa de Arithmetica. Since then, accounting has continued to evolve in response to changes in business, technology, and regulation. Today, accountants must adapt to advancements in software, data analytics, and even artificial intelligence, all of which are reshaping how financial data is managed and analyzed.

Accounting Today: Technology and Innovation

The role of technology in accounting cannot be overstated. Accounting software, such as QuickBooks, Xero, and SAP, has simplified many routine tasks, allowing accountants to focus on strategic analysis rather than data entry. Cloud computing has also revolutionized accounting by enabling real-time access to financial data and remote work capabilities.

Recent developments in artificial intelligence (AI) and machine learning are automating repetitive tasks like data entry and reconciliation. Additionally, blockchain technology is making its mark by providing secure, transparent ways to record transactions, which could reduce the risk of fraud and improve the accuracy of financial records.

Why Accounting Matters to Society

Accounting is more than just a business function; it plays a vital role in society. Sound accounting practices contribute to economic stability by fostering transparency, trust, and accountability. Governments rely on accountants to track and manage public funds, and nonprofits depend on accurate accounting to fulfill their missions responsibly.

Moreover, as global issues like environmental impact and social responsibility become increasingly important, accountants are playing a role in measuring and reporting on sustainability initiatives. This branch, known as environmental accounting, focuses on tracking a company's environmental costs and helping organizations make sustainable choices.

This overview gives a foundational understanding of what accounting is and why it matters. As you delve deeper into this guide, you'll explore specific accounting roles and learn more about the skills, education, and career paths available in this ever-evolving field. Accounting offers a stable and impactful career with opportunities to grow, specialize, and make a meaningful contribution to businesses, communities, and society.

1.2 Types of Accounting Roles

1.2.1 Financial Accounting

Financial accounting is one of the most traditional and fundamental areas of the accounting profession. At its core, financial accounting is focused on tracking, recording, and reporting an organization's financial transactions. This role is essential for ensuring that businesses maintain accurate financial records, which is critical for decision-making, securing investments, maintaining legal compliance, and building public trust.

Financial accountants work with a variety of financial statements and reports. They are tasked with compiling data and translating complex transactions into understandable reports that follow established standards, such as Generally Accepted Accounting Principles (GAAP) or International Financial Reporting Standards (IFRS). Let's dive into what financial accounting entails, the types of work it involves, and the impact it has on organizations and stakeholders.

The Purpose of Financial Accounting

Financial accounting is all about providing a clear and standardized view of an organization's financial health. The primary goal is to ensure that financial information is accurate, reliable, and comparable across different organizations. This is crucial for stakeholders such as investors, creditors, regulators, and even employees, as they rely on financial statements to make informed decisions about their engagement with the organization.

In a typical company, financial accounting will address questions like:

- *How profitable is the organization?*

- *What are the sources and amounts of revenue and expenses?*

- *What assets does the company own, and what liabilities does it owe?*

- *What is the net worth or shareholders' equity of the organization?*

Financial accounting, therefore, serves as a "language of business," providing stakeholders with the necessary data to evaluate the financial performance and stability of a business.

Key Responsibilities of a Financial Accountant

Financial accountants perform several essential tasks that keep an organization's financial records in check. Some of the main responsibilities include:

1. Recording Transactions

Financial accountants are responsible for systematically recording transactions using a method known as double-entry bookkeeping. Each transaction is entered into a ledger with two parts: a debit and a credit. This ensures that the accounting equation (Assets = Liabilities + Equity) always remains balanced. For instance, if a company makes a sale on credit, the transaction would be recorded as an increase in both accounts receivable and revenue.

2. Preparing Financial Statements

At the end of each financial period (monthly, quarterly, or annually), financial accountants compile various financial statements that reflect the company's performance. These primary statements include:

- Income Statement: Shows the revenue, expenses, and profit or loss over a period.

- Balance Sheet: Lists assets, liabilities, and shareholders' equity at a specific point in time.

- Cash Flow Statement: Outlines cash inflows and outflows, highlighting how cash is generated and used.

3. Ensuring Compliance

Financial accountants must adhere to established standards, such as GAAP in the United States or IFRS in many other countries. Compliance with these standards ensures that financial reports are consistent, transparent, and comparable across different companies and industries. This is especially important for publicly traded companies that must report financial results to regulatory bodies like the Securities and Exchange Commission (SEC).

4. Analyzing Financial Data

Beyond simply recording data, financial accountants analyze financial information to provide insights. This analysis can highlight trends, identify areas of concern, and offer predictions based on historical data. For example, a financial accountant might notice a steady increase in operating expenses over several quarters, which could prompt management to investigate and address the issue.

5. Supporting External Audits

Financial accountants often work closely with external auditors to validate the accuracy of financial statements. This process involves preparing documentation, clarifying data, and addressing any discrepancies that auditors might find. Successful audits boost stakeholders' confidence in the accuracy and reliability of the organization's financial information.

Financial Accounting vs. Managerial Accounting

While both financial and managerial accounting involve the preparation and analysis of financial information, they serve different purposes and audiences. Financial accounting is primarily focused on creating financial reports for external stakeholders, following strict standards and focusing on the organization's overall performance. Managerial accounting, on the other hand, is aimed at providing internal management with the information needed for operational decision-making, often without adherence to external standards.

For example:

- *Audience:* Financial accounting targets investors, creditors, and regulatory bodies, whereas managerial accounting is used by internal management.

- *Regulations:* Financial accounting must follow GAAP or IFRS, while managerial accounting does not have to follow these standards.

- *Scope:* Financial accounting provides a broad overview of the company's financial status, while managerial accounting often focuses on specific departments or projects.

Understanding these differences can help those entering the accounting profession to decide which path might align better with their interests and career goals.

The Importance of Financial Accounting for Stakeholders

Financial accounting plays a critical role in fostering transparency and accountability within an organization. Each financial statement produced by financial accountants serves specific needs for a variety of stakeholders:

1. Investors: Investors rely on financial statements to assess whether a company is a good investment. The income statement, for example, reveals whether the company is profitable, while the balance sheet provides insights into its financial stability.

2. Creditors: Creditors, such as banks, analyze financial statements to determine whether to extend credit or loans. A healthy balance sheet with manageable liabilities and strong cash flows can indicate that a company is a reliable borrower.

3. Management: While financial accounting primarily serves external stakeholders, it also aids management by providing a high-level overview of the company's performance, allowing them to make informed decisions about resource allocation and growth strategies.

4. Regulatory Bodies: Regulatory agencies like the SEC require publicly traded companies to report their financial results, ensuring that the public has access to reliable information about a company's financial performance. Financial accountants help organizations meet these regulatory requirements.

Career Path in Financial Accounting

Financial accounting offers a variety of career paths, often beginning with entry-level positions such as staff accountant or junior accountant. With experience and additional certifications, professionals can move into roles such as financial analyst, financial reporting manager, or even chief financial officer (CFO). Many financial accountants pursue the Certified Public Accountant (CPA) designation, which is highly regarded and can open doors to more advanced roles in accounting and finance.

Technology and Financial Accounting

In recent years, technology has significantly transformed the field of financial accounting. Financial accountants now use various accounting software platforms, such as

QuickBooks, SAP, or Oracle, to automate many aspects of data entry, transaction tracking, and report generation. The advent of cloud computing allows accountants to access data in real time, making it easier to collaborate and improve efficiency.

Challenges in Financial Accounting

While financial accounting is rewarding, it does come with challenges:

- *Complex Regulations:* Financial accountants must keep up with changing standards, which can vary by country and industry.

- *Ethical Responsibilities*: Accountants are expected to uphold high ethical standards, as inaccuracies or intentional misstatements can have severe consequences for stakeholders.

- *Demanding Deadlines:* Financial reporting is often time-sensitive, especially during year-end or quarter-end periods, which can lead to longer hours and increased stress.

Conclusion: The Value of Financial Accounting

Financial accounting is an essential function that provides clarity, consistency, and accountability to an organization's financial activities. Aspiring accountants interested in this area should be detail-oriented, ethical, and willing to continually learn to stay updated with evolving standards and technology. Whether one is interested in corporate finance, public accounting, or regulatory compliance, a career in financial accounting can offer a challenging yet fulfilling pathway with numerous opportunities for advancement.

Example: Financial Accounting in Action

To help you understand financial accounting more clearly, let's look at a simple example that demonstrates how it works in a real business context. Imagine you are the financial accountant for a small company, ABC Electronics, which sells electronic gadgets.

Step 1: Recording Transactions

Every time a transaction occurs, the financial accountant must record it using double-entry bookkeeping. This means that for every debit (an entry that increases an asset or decreases a liability), there is a corresponding credit (an entry that decreases an asset or increases a liability).

Let's consider the following example

ABC Electronics makes a sale: The company sells 10 smartphones at $500 each, totaling $5,000. The customer will pay on credit, meaning they will pay later, not right away.

- *Debit:* Accounts Receivable (asset) $5,000 (because the company is now owed money by the customer).

- *Credit:* Sales Revenue (income) $5,000 (because the company has earned money from the sale).

Now, the company has an asset (Accounts Receivable) of $5,000, and the revenue has been recorded as well. The transaction is balanced, meaning the company's financial records are accurate.

Step 2: Preparing Financial Statements

At the end of the month, the financial accountant will prepare the income statement, balance sheet, and cash flow statement. These statements give the company and its stakeholders a clear picture of the company's financial performance.

Income Statement Example

The income statement summarizes the company's revenues and expenses over a specific period. For ABC Electronics, let's say the income statement for the month shows:

- *Revenue:* $20,000 (from sales of electronics)

- *Expenses:*

  - Cost of Goods Sold (COGS): $8,000 (the cost to produce or purchase the smartphones)

  - Rent: $1,000

  - Salaries: $4,000

  - Utilities: $500

- *Net Income:* $6,500 (Revenue of $20,000 - Expenses of $13,500)

This tells you that ABC Electronics made a profit of $6,500 in the month after all expenses were paid.

Balance Sheet Example

The balance sheet shows a snapshot of the company's financial position at a specific point in time. At the end of the month, the balance sheet might look like this:

- *Assets:*

  - Accounts Receivable: $5,000 (money owed by customers)

  - Cash: $2,000 (cash the company has on hand)

  - Inventory: $3,000 (unsold smartphones)

- *Liabilities:*

  - Accounts Payable: $2,000 (money the company owes to suppliers for smartphone parts)

  - Bank Loan: $3,000 (loan the company has taken)

- *Owner's Equity:*

  - Retained Earnings: $5,000 (profits that have been reinvested into the company)

The balance sheet shows that the company has $10,000 in assets, $5,000 in liabilities, and $5,000 in owner's equity, which is consistent with the accounting equation:

Assets = Liabilities + Owner's Equity

$10,000 = $5,000 + $5,000

Step 3: Analyzing the Financial Data

After preparing the financial statements, the financial accountant can analyze the data to gain insights. For example:

- *Gross Profit Margin:*

  The gross profit margin tells us how much profit the company made after accounting for the cost of goods sold (COGS).

Gross Profit Margin = (Revenue - COGS) / Revenue

= ($20,000 - $8,000) / $20,000 = $12,000 / $20,000 = 60%

This means that for every dollar of sales, the company made 60 cents in profit after covering the cost of the smartphones. A higher margin suggests the company is good at controlling production costs.

- Net Profit Margin:

The net profit margin tells us how much of each dollar in revenue translates into profit after all expenses are deducted.

Net Profit Margin = Net Income / Revenue

= $6,500 / $20,000 = 32.5%

This means that 32.5% of the company's sales are profit after all expenses, including rent, salaries, and utilities.

These analysis metrics help the company understand its financial health and where improvements might be needed.

Step 4: Supporting External Audits

Let's say ABC Electronics is preparing for an audit by an external auditor, which is common for businesses that need to reassure investors and comply with regulations. The auditor will review the company's financial statements, transactions, and accounting records to ensure everything is accurate and in accordance with GAAP or IFRS.

- The financial accountant must provide documentation for all transactions and answer any questions the auditor may have.

- For example, the auditor may ask for proof of the sale of smartphones. The financial accountant will provide the sales invoices, delivery receipts, and payment confirmations to support the revenue reported.

If everything is in order, the auditor will give an unqualified opinion, meaning the company's financial statements are accurate and reliable.

Conclusion

Through these examples, you can see how financial accounting plays a vital role in ensuring that a company's financial transactions are accurately recorded, analyzed, and reported. The process of recording transactions, preparing financial statements, analyzing data, and supporting audits allows the company to maintain transparency, meet regulatory requirements, and make informed business decisions. Financial accounting is not just about keeping the books in order—it's about providing meaningful information that helps guide a company's growth and success.

If you choose to pursue a career in financial accounting, you will be at the heart of every company's operations, ensuring that its financial health is transparent and trustworthy for all stakeholders.

1.2.2 Managerial Accounting

Managerial accounting, often referred to as management or cost accounting, plays a crucial role in the internal workings of a business. Unlike financial accounting, which focuses on creating financial reports for external stakeholders such as investors, regulators, and creditors, managerial accounting is primarily concerned with providing information for internal decision-making. The aim of managerial accounting is to help managers within an organization make informed business decisions, optimize operations, and drive the overall success of the company.

In this section, we will explore the key responsibilities of managerial accountants, the skills needed for the role, the tools they use, and the career opportunities in this field.

What Does a Managerial Accountant Do?

A managerial accountant's primary responsibility is to support the company's management team in making operational and strategic decisions. While financial accountants focus on recording and reporting historical data, managerial accountants work with real-time data to forecast, plan, and guide decisions about the future. These professionals gather, analyze, and report financial and non-financial information to provide insights into cost management, efficiency improvements, and strategic planning.

The work of a managerial accountant typically revolves around the following core functions:

- *Budgeting and Forecasting:* Managerial accountants assist in developing the company's budget, outlining expected revenues, expenses, and capital requirements. They also forecast financial outcomes based on various assumptions and market conditions, helping management make informed decisions about future operations.

- *Cost Analysis and Control:* One of the key areas of focus for managerial accountants is analyzing and controlling costs. They help the company understand where money is being spent and identify areas where costs can be reduced or efficiencies can be gained. This includes both direct costs, such as raw materials, and indirect costs, like overhead expenses.

- *Cost-Volume-Profit Analysis (CVP):* Managerial accountants conduct CVP analysis to understand how changes in sales volume, costs, and price affect the profitability of a business. This analysis helps managers make decisions about pricing, production levels, and cost structures.

- *Performance Evaluation:* Managerial accountants track and evaluate the performance of different departments, products, or segments within the company. Using various performance metrics like return on investment (ROI), contribution margin, and variance analysis, they provide management with insights into how well the business is performing and where improvements are needed.

- *Internal Controls and Risk Management:* Managerial accountants play a vital role in establishing internal controls to ensure that financial resources are used efficiently and that the company's assets are safeguarded. They are also responsible for identifying and managing financial risks that could impact the business.

- *Decision Support:* Managerial accountants assist in making both short-term and long-term business decisions by analyzing different scenarios, quantifying the financial impact of decisions, and providing advice on the most cost-effective strategies. This can include decisions about product pricing, capital investment, and operational strategies.

Skills Required for Managerial Accounting

To be successful in managerial accounting, individuals need a blend of technical, analytical, and interpersonal skills. Here are some of the key skills that are essential for this role:

- *Analytical Thinking:* Managerial accountants must be able to analyze complex data, recognize trends, and interpret financial information in a way that allows them to draw conclusions and make recommendations. Strong analytical thinking helps them assess the financial health of the company and identify areas for improvement.

- *Knowledge of Accounting Principles:* While managerial accounting focuses on internal decision-making, it still relies on fundamental accounting principles, such as cost accounting, accrual accounting, and financial reporting standards. A solid understanding of these principles is crucial.

- *Attention to Detail:* Accuracy is paramount in accounting. Managerial accountants must ensure that every figure, calculation, and analysis is correct to prevent costly mistakes. Even small errors can have a significant impact on the decision-making process.

- *Communication Skills:* Managerial accountants need to be able to communicate financial information effectively to non-financial managers. They must present data clearly and in a way that is understandable to people without an accounting background. Strong written and verbal communication skills are essential for presenting reports, preparing presentations, and engaging in discussions with senior management.

- *Problem-Solving Skills:* The ability to identify issues and come up with solutions is a key aspect of the managerial accountant's role. Whether it's finding ways to reduce costs, improve efficiency, or evaluate investment opportunities, problem-solving is a core component of the job.

- *Proficiency with Accounting Software and Tools:* Managerial accountants must be proficient in accounting software programs and data analysis tools. These tools help streamline the process of collecting, analyzing, and reporting financial data. Some common tools include Microsoft Excel, QuickBooks, SAP, and Oracle Financials.

- *Time Management and Organization:* Managerial accountants often juggle multiple tasks and deadlines. Good time management skills are essential for balancing different projects and ensuring timely delivery of reports and analyses.

Tools and Techniques Used in Managerial Accounting

Managerial accountants use a variety of tools and techniques to gather, analyze, and report financial information. These tools help them perform their work efficiently and provide valuable insights for decision-making.

- *Activity-Based Costing (ABC):* ABC is a technique used to allocate indirect costs (overhead) to specific products or services based on the activities that drive these costs. It provides a more accurate picture of product costs than traditional costing methods.

- *Standard Costing:* Standard costing is used to compare actual costs to expected or standard costs. It helps identify cost variances, such as the difference between budgeted and actual costs, which can be analyzed to identify areas for improvement.

- *Variance Analysis:* Variance analysis compares the actual performance to the budgeted or standard performance. By analyzing variances in costs and revenues, managerial accountants can determine the causes of discrepancies and suggest corrective actions.

- *Break-even Analysis*: This technique helps businesses determine the point at which they will break even—i.e., when their total revenues equal total costs. This analysis is crucial for pricing decisions and evaluating the profitability of products or services.

- *Budgeting Tools:* Budgeting software and tools help create, manage, and track company budgets. These tools allow managerial accountants to set financial goals, forecast future revenues and expenses, and monitor the company's financial performance against those goals.

Career Opportunities in Managerial Accounting

Managerial accounting offers a wide range of career opportunities, as companies across all industries need skilled professionals to help them make informed financial decisions. Some common career paths within managerial accounting include:

- *Cost Accountant:* A cost accountant specializes in analyzing and controlling costs within an organization. They calculate the costs of production, track expenses, and recommend cost-saving measures. They often work closely with the operations team to ensure that the company's production processes are cost-efficient.

- *Management Accountant:* Management accountants work closely with senior managers to provide them with financial information that helps in decision-making. They may prepare reports on financial performance, analyze investment opportunities, and assist with budgeting and forecasting.

- *Financial Analyst:* Financial analysts in managerial accounting assess the financial health of the business and its investment opportunities. They often analyze financial data to support strategic decisions, such as mergers, acquisitions, and capital expenditures.

- *Internal Auditor:* Internal auditors assess the effectiveness of an organization's internal controls, risk management processes, and compliance with laws and regulations. They identify areas of financial risk and suggest improvements to safeguard the company's assets.

- *Financial Planning and Analysis (FP&A) Specialist:* FP&A specialists focus on forecasting and budgeting for the company's financial performance. They help management plan for future growth by providing data on expected revenues, expenses, and capital needs.

- *Chief Financial Officer (CFO):* The CFO is responsible for overseeing all financial activities within an organization. With a background in managerial accounting, CFOs are well-equipped to guide companies through complex financial decisions and ensure long-term profitability.

Is Managerial Accounting Right for You?

If you enjoy working with numbers, analyzing data, and providing solutions to business problems, then a career in managerial accounting could be a perfect fit. Managerial accounting offers the opportunity to work closely with management teams, influence business decisions, and make a direct impact on a company's performance.

This career path offers great prospects for growth, with managerial accountants in high demand across industries. Whether you are working for a large corporation, a small business, or even a nonprofit organization, the skills and expertise of a managerial accountant are valued in virtually every sector.

Conclusion

Managerial accounting is an essential part of business operations, providing critical data and insights that help organizations make sound financial decisions. With its focus on internal financial management, cost control, and strategic planning, this field offers diverse career opportunities and the chance to make a tangible impact on a company's success. If you are someone who enjoys problem-solving, data analysis, and working closely with decision-makers, managerial accounting could be the ideal career path for you.

Here's a concrete, easy-to-understand example to illustrate managerial accounting:

Example: Managerial Accounting in Action

Imagine you are a managerial accountant working for a company that manufactures and sells custom-made bicycles. The company has been struggling with its production costs, and management has asked you to help identify ways to reduce expenses and improve profitability.

Step 1: Cost Analysis

Your first task is to analyze the company's production costs. The company has both direct costs (like materials and labor) and indirect costs (like overhead costs such as electricity, rent, and management salaries). You decide to break down these costs using a method called Activity-Based Costing (ABC).

- *Direct Costs:*

  - Materials: $100 per bicycle (frame, wheels, tires, etc.)

  - Labor: $50 per bicycle (pay for the workers assembling the bicycles)

- *Indirect Costs* (based on activities that drive costs):

  - Rent for the factory: $5,000 per month

  - Utilities (electricity and water): $2,000 per month

  - Salaries of the production supervisors: $3,000 per month

To allocate indirect costs, you use ABC to link them to specific activities. For example, you know the factory produces 1,000 bicycles per month, so the indirect costs are divided as follows:

- Rent per bicycle: $5,000 ÷ 1,000 = $5 per bicycle

- Utilities per bicycle: $2,000 ÷ 1,000 = $2 per bicycle

- Supervisors' salaries per bicycle: $3,000 ÷ 1,000 = $3 per bicycle

Now, your total cost per bicycle is:

- Direct costs: $100 (materials) + $50 (labor) = $150

- Indirect costs: $5 (rent) + $2 (utilities) + $3 (supervisor salaries) = $10

Total cost per bicycle = $150 + $10 = $160

Step 2: Identifying Cost Savings

After analyzing the costs, you present your findings to the management team. You point out that while materials and labor costs are relatively fixed, there may be opportunities to reduce indirect costs. Specifically, you notice that the company has been overpaying for utilities due to inefficient machinery and could reduce costs by $500 per month. You also suggest renegotiating the rent for the factory, which could save another $1,000 per month.

- New utilities cost: $2,000 - $500 = $1,500 per month

- New rent cost: $5,000 - $1,000 = $4,000 per month

Now, recalculate the indirect costs per bicycle with these savings:

- New utilities per bicycle: $1,500 ÷ 1,000 = $1.50

- New rent per bicycle: $4,000 ÷ 1,000 = $4

Your revised total cost per bicycle is:

- Direct costs: $150

- Revised indirect costs: $4 (rent) + $1.50 (utilities) + $3 (supervisors' salaries) = $8.50

Revised total cost per bicycle = $150 + $8.50 = $158.50

Step 3: Decision-Making and Profitability

You present your findings to management and recommend the following:

- *Lowering the production costs per bicycle by $1.50* will increase profitability.

- With the reduced costs, the company can now adjust pricing strategy. For instance, if the company was selling bicycles for $200 each, the new profit margin is:

  - Old profit margin = $200 - $160 = $40 per bicycle

  - New profit margin = $200 - $158.50 = $41.50 per bicycle

This small reduction in costs improves the company's profit margin by $1.50 per unit.

Additionally, since the company is producing 1,000 bicycles per month, this means a total savings of:

- $1.50 per bicycle x 1,000 bicycles = $1,500 in monthly savings.

These savings can be reinvested into other areas of the business, such as expanding marketing efforts, improving product quality, or even increasing worker wages to boost morale and productivity.

Step 4: Forecasting Future Costs and Improvements

As a managerial accountant, your role doesn't stop with identifying cost savings. You also forecast future costs and potential scenarios to help guide management decisions. For example, you project that as the company scales up production to 1,500 bicycles per month, the company will need to increase its overhead, such as rent and utilities.

However, you also advise management to continue monitoring efficiency, as increased production could lead to better economies of scale, helping to offset some of these higher costs.

Key Takeaways

- *Cost Analysis:* Managerial accountants break down costs into direct and indirect categories to understand where money is being spent.

- *Cost Reduction:* Through tools like ABC, managerial accountants can identify inefficiencies and suggest ways to save money, such as reducing overhead costs or renegotiating supplier contracts.

- *Improved Decision-Making:* With accurate cost data, managerial accountants help management make decisions that can improve profitability, whether by adjusting pricing or changing operational strategies.

- *Long-Term Impact:* Managerial accountants also help with forecasting future costs and planning for growth, ensuring the business can maintain profitability as it expands.

This example shows how managerial accounting not only helps to understand where a company's money is going but also actively contributes to improving its financial performance and decision-making processes.

By using this approach, managerial accountants help businesses like the bicycle company achieve greater efficiency, control costs, and ultimately increase profitability, all of which are crucial for long-term success.

1.2.3 Auditing and Assurance

Auditing and assurance are essential areas within the accounting profession, playing a critical role in maintaining trust and transparency within the financial reporting system. These fields focus on evaluating financial statements, internal controls, and compliance with laws and regulations, which are vital for businesses, investors, and stakeholders. In this section, we will explore the nature of auditing and assurance services, the different types of audits, the skills required for professionals in this field, and how auditing and assurance contribute to the success of businesses and the global economy.

What is Auditing and Assurance?

At its core, auditing is the process of independently reviewing and examining a company's financial statements to ensure their accuracy and adherence to accounting standards. Auditors are responsible for evaluating whether the financial records accurately reflect a company's financial position and performance. Auditing is often carried out by external auditors, who are independent of the organization they are auditing. This independent review serves to provide assurance to investors, regulators, and other stakeholders that the company is being managed in a transparent and legally compliant manner.

Assurance services, on the other hand, go beyond traditional financial audits. They involve reviewing a company's processes, operations, and controls to provide an objective evaluation and assurance that business practices and financial statements are accurate, reliable, and free from fraud or error. Assurance services can also extend to non-financial information, such as sustainability reports, environmental impact disclosures, and more.

While both auditing and assurance aim to build confidence and trust, assurance services are broader and can be tailored to meet the specific needs of an organization, ensuring credibility in a wide range of reporting areas.

Types of Audits

Auditors perform several types of audits, depending on the purpose of the review, the size of the organization, and the regulations governing their work. The most common types of audits are:

1. External Audit

An external audit is an independent examination of a company's financial statements, usually conducted by an external auditor or a public accounting firm. The goal is to assess whether the financial statements are free of material misstatement, whether due to fraud or error. External auditors provide an audit opinion, which is included in the audit report. This opinion can be:

- Unqualified (Clean) Opinion: The financial statements are accurate and comply with the applicable accounting standards.

- Qualified Opinion: The financial statements are generally accurate, but there are some exceptions or limitations in the audit.

- Adverse Opinion: The financial statements are materially misstated and do not comply with accounting standards.

- Disclaimer of Opinion: The auditor was unable to obtain sufficient evidence to form an opinion.

External audits are typically required for publicly traded companies, large private companies, and nonprofit organizations, as they provide a level of transparency and assurance to investors, creditors, and regulatory bodies.

2. Internal Audit

Unlike external audits, internal audits are conducted by employees of the organization, usually within the internal audit department. Internal auditors assess the company's internal controls, risk management processes, and operational efficiency. Their role is to identify any weaknesses in the company's internal processes, ensure compliance with regulations, and recommend improvements. Internal audits are crucial for maintaining the integrity of financial operations and preventing fraud.

Internal auditors often work closely with senior management to provide recommendations on improving efficiency, effectiveness, and compliance. Their findings are typically used by the company to strengthen its internal controls and protect against financial mismanagement.

3. Forensic Audit

A forensic audit is a specialized type of audit used to investigate fraud, corruption, or financial misconduct within an organization. Forensic auditors often work with law enforcement agencies or attorneys to uncover fraudulent activities or to provide evidence in legal disputes. These audits may involve examining financial records, interviews with employees, and scrutinizing accounting procedures to detect illegal or unethical behavior.

Forensic auditors need a deep understanding of both accounting and law, as their findings may be used in court to prosecute criminals or settle legal disputes. They may also be called upon to assess whether the company's internal controls were adequate to prevent financial misconduct.

4. Government Audit

A government audit is conducted by government agencies to evaluate the use of public funds, ensure compliance with legal requirements, and assess the effectiveness of government programs. Auditors in this field work for federal, state, or local governments, reviewing government expenditures, contracts, and services to ensure taxpayer money is being spent efficiently and in accordance with regulations.

Government audits also play a key role in detecting and preventing fraud or mismanagement in public sector organizations. Auditors may evaluate the performance of government agencies, assess compliance with laws and regulations, and recommend improvements to ensure accountability in the public sector.

The Role of Assurance Services

While auditing focuses primarily on financial accuracy, assurance services provide broader evaluations that help enhance the reliability and credibility of a company's reporting and operations. Assurance services are typically provided by public accounting firms, and they can cover a range of areas, including:

1. Financial Assurance

Financial assurance services involve reviewing financial statements and providing an independent opinion on their accuracy and adherence to relevant accounting standards.

This is similar to external auditing, but assurance services can also cover a variety of non-audited financial information, such as budgets, forecasts, and management reports.

2. Non-Financial Assurance

Non-financial assurance services extend beyond financial information to include assessments of environmental, social, and governance (ESG) reports, corporate social responsibility (CSR) practices, and sustainability disclosures. As organizations are under increasing pressure to provide transparent and reliable reporting on their environmental and social impact, assurance professionals evaluate the credibility of these reports and verify that the data provided is accurate and supported by evidence.

3. Compliance Assurance

Compliance assurance focuses on assessing whether an organization is meeting the regulatory requirements specific to its industry or region. This can involve evaluating adherence to financial regulations, labor laws, environmental standards, and other legal obligations. Assurance services in compliance help mitigate risks associated with non-compliance, such as legal penalties or reputational damage.

Skills and Qualifications for Auditors and Assurance Professionals

To succeed in the field of auditing and assurance, professionals need a blend of technical accounting knowledge, analytical skills, and the ability to communicate effectively with clients and stakeholders. Key skills and qualifications include:

1. Education and Certifications

To become an auditor, a bachelor's degree in accounting or a related field is required. Many auditors also pursue professional certifications, such as the Certified Public Accountant (CPA), which is a common credential for external auditors in the United States. Other certifications that may be pursued include the Certified Internal Auditor (CIA), Certified Information Systems Auditor (CISA), and Certified Fraud Examiner (CFE).

2. Analytical and Problem-Solving Skills

Auditors must possess strong analytical abilities to evaluate financial data, identify discrepancies, and assess the accuracy of financial statements. They need to be able to think critically and investigate irregularities to uncover fraud or misstatements.

3. Communication Skills

Auditors and assurance professionals must be able to explain complex financial information in a clear and understandable way. Effective communication with clients, management, and stakeholders is crucial, as auditors often provide recommendations based on their findings.

4. Attention to Detail

Auditing requires meticulous attention to detail, as auditors must review large volumes of financial data and identify inconsistencies or errors. Small mistakes can have significant consequences, making precision a critical skill.

The Importance of Auditing and Assurance

Auditing and assurance services are integral to maintaining trust in the financial markets. By providing independent evaluations of financial information, auditors and assurance professionals help prevent fraud, ensure regulatory compliance, and enhance the credibility of financial reporting. This ultimately protects investors, improves corporate governance, and contributes to the stability of the global economy.

As businesses become more complex and the regulatory environment continues to evolve, the demand for skilled auditors and assurance professionals is expected to grow. For young people considering a career in accounting, auditing and assurance offer exciting opportunities to work in a dynamic field that plays a crucial role in shaping the future of business and finance.

Example 1: Understanding External Audits

Imagine you own a small business that sells handmade furniture online. Every year, you need to submit your financial statements to a bank because you're applying for a business loan. However, the bank doesn't just take your word for it that your numbers are correct. To ensure that your financial statements are accurate and reliable, the bank requires you to hire an external auditor.

What does the external auditor do?

The external auditor is like a detective. They come to your business and review your financial documents, such as income statements, balance sheets, and receipts. The auditor checks that your sales numbers match your bank deposits and that your expenses are properly accounted for. They also make sure you've followed the proper accounting rules and standards.

Once they've finished their review, the auditor will write an audit report that includes their opinion on the accuracy of your financial statements. If everything looks good, they'll give you an unqualified opinion (a "clean" opinion), which means your financial statements are free from errors or fraud. This audit report becomes part of your loan application, and the bank uses it to decide whether or not to approve your loan.

Example 2: Internal Audit in Action

Let's say you work for a large company that manufactures electronic gadgets. As the company grows, there are more employees, more transactions, and more risks involved. To ensure that the company's operations are running smoothly and efficiently, the company hires an internal auditor.

What does the internal auditor do?

Unlike external auditors, who are independent, internal auditors are employees of the company. Their job is to evaluate how the company's processes and controls are working. For example, the internal auditor might look at the company's inventory system. They check whether the company's inventory records are accurate and if the proper procedures are followed to avoid theft or waste.

The internal auditor may find that there is a problem—perhaps the company's employees are not following the correct procedure for recording inventory, which leads to discrepancies in the records. The internal auditor will write a report with their findings and recommend improvements, such as better training for employees or tighter controls on inventory.

Why does this matter?

Internal auditors help identify weaknesses in the company's operations before they turn into big problems. Their recommendations can save the company money and improve efficiency.

Example 3: Forensic Audit to Detect Fraud

Imagine a situation in which a company's management begins to suspect that one of their employees is embezzling funds. The company hires a forensic auditor to investigate.

What does the forensic auditor do?

A forensic auditor specializes in investigating financial fraud. They dive deep into the company's financial records, looking for signs of suspicious transactions or irregularities. In this case, the forensic auditor examines the company's bank statements, expense reports, and receipts. They notice that several payments to vendors seem unusually high and are not supported by legitimate invoices.

The forensic auditor then tracks the payments and finds that the employee involved was directing the payments to their own personal bank account. The forensic auditor's report provides solid evidence of embezzlement and can be used in court to prosecute the employee.

Why is this important?

Forensic auditors play a key role in uncovering fraud and other financial crimes. Their expertise helps businesses and law enforcement address financial misconduct and hold wrongdoers accountable.

Example 4: Assurance Services for Non-Financial Information

Let's say you're the CEO of a company that produces eco-friendly products. Your company is very focused on sustainability, and you want to show your customers and investors that you're committed to reducing your environmental impact. To do this, you publish an annual sustainability report that outlines your company's environmental goals, achievements, and carbon footprint reduction strategies.

What does an assurance professional do?

To add credibility to your report, you hire a firm to provide assurance services. The assurance professionals review the information in your sustainability report to ensure that it is accurate, consistent, and reliable. They may verify data such as how much energy your company used or the amount of carbon dioxide your company reduced during the year.

Once the assurance professionals are satisfied with the data, they will issue an assurance statement, which adds credibility to your report. This statement assures stakeholders—

such as investors, customers, and regulatory bodies—that the information you provided is trustworthy.

Why does this matter?

In today's business environment, many companies are expected to report on their environmental and social impact. Assurance services ensure that this non-financial information is as accurate and reliable as financial data. For businesses, this can lead to better relationships with customers and investors who value transparency and sustainability.

Example 5: Government Audit

Imagine you're a local government official in charge of managing funds for public projects, such as building new roads and parks. Every year, the government undergoes a government audit to ensure that taxpayer money is being used properly.

What does the government audit do?

Government auditors review how public funds are spent, ensuring that the money is used for the intended purpose. They check whether your spending on the new roads aligns with the budget and whether the proper procedures were followed when awarding contracts to construction companies.

If the auditors find that the funds were misused or misallocated, they will issue a report highlighting the issues and suggesting improvements. The goal of the government audit is to ensure that taxpayer money is being spent efficiently and in accordance with the law.

Why is this important?

Government audits help maintain accountability and transparency in the use of public funds. Without these audits, there could be misuse of public money, which could undermine public trust in government institutions.

These examples simplify the different types of audits and assurance services, making them easier to understand for young readers or anyone unfamiliar with the field of auditing. Each example highlights the role of auditors in ensuring accuracy, transparency, and accountability in various contexts, from small businesses to large government operations.

1.2.4 Tax Accounting

Introduction to Tax Accounting

Tax accounting focuses on preparing and managing tax returns and ensuring compliance with tax regulations. This branch of accounting plays a vital role in both personal and business financial planning, as it impacts how individuals and organizations manage their finances, save money, and navigate complex tax laws. For young people interested in a career that blends financial expertise with legal knowledge, tax accounting offers a dynamic path with a variety of career options.

The Role of Tax Accountants

Tax accountants primarily help individuals, businesses, and organizations understand and comply with tax obligations. Their responsibilities include preparing tax returns, advising on tax planning strategies, analyzing tax issues, and ensuring clients adhere to the latest tax laws and regulations. Unlike general accountants, tax accountants work with specific codes and statutes related to taxes and must stay up-to-date with changes in tax law.

Tax accountants are highly analytical, detail-oriented, and skilled in problem-solving. They help clients optimize their tax outcomes, often identifying deductions, credits, and other strategies to minimize tax liabilities. As experts in navigating the tax code, tax accountants are valued for their ability to manage complex tax situations while adhering to ethical and legal standards.

Types of Tax Accountants

Tax accountants work in a variety of settings and specialize in different areas based on client needs and their own expertise. Common types include:

1. Personal Tax Accountants: These accountants help individuals with personal tax returns, ensuring compliance and maximizing deductions. They may assist with complex situations, such as capital gains on investments or estate taxes.

2. Corporate Tax Accountants: These professionals handle taxes for businesses, focusing on minimizing tax liabilities, planning for future tax scenarios, and ensuring compliance with corporate tax laws.

3. *Public Sector Tax Accountants:* These accountants work for government agencies, where they may review tax records, audit businesses, and ensure compliance with tax regulations on a larger scale.

4. *International Tax Accountants:* Working with multinational companies or clients with international finances, these accountants manage tax obligations across multiple countries, addressing issues like transfer pricing and tax treaties.

Key Skills and Knowledge for Tax Accounting

To excel in tax accounting, certain skills and knowledge areas are essential:

1. *In-depth Knowledge of Tax Codes and Laws:* Tax accountants must have a comprehensive understanding of federal, state, and local tax laws. This knowledge is constantly evolving, so tax accountants must keep up with updates in tax legislation.

2. *Analytical and Problem-Solving Skills:* Tax issues can be complex and require careful analysis to find the most beneficial solutions for clients.

3. *Attention to Detail:* Accuracy is crucial in tax accounting, as mistakes can lead to costly penalties for clients.

4. *Technological Proficiency:* Tax accountants use specialized software for tax preparation, data analysis, and reporting. Proficiency in these tools is increasingly important as tax processes become more digitized.

5. *Communication Skills:* Tax accountants must be able to explain complex tax concepts in simple terms and communicate effectively with clients who may not be familiar with financial jargon.

Career Path and Education for Tax Accountants

Most tax accountants start by obtaining a bachelor's degree in accounting, finance, or a related field. Many also pursue certification as a Certified Public Accountant (CPA), which requires passing a rigorous exam. In addition, some tax accountants may choose to obtain a Master of Science in Taxation or other advanced degrees to deepen their knowledge.

Ongoing education is crucial in tax accounting, as the field requires a continuous understanding of changes in tax codes. Professional organizations, such as the American Institute of CPAs (AICPA), offer resources and certifications like the Certified Tax Specialist (CTS) designation to enhance credibility and expertise in the field.

The Tax Accounting Process

The tax accounting process involves several key steps that ensure compliance and accuracy in tax reporting:

1. Gathering Financial Information: Tax accountants begin by collecting financial data, including income, expenses, and receipts relevant to the client's tax situation. This step is critical for both individuals and businesses to capture an accurate financial picture.

2. Applying Tax Regulations: Once financial data is collected, tax accountants apply current tax laws to identify potential deductions, credits, and other benefits. This step requires expertise in the tax code and an understanding of how it applies to the client's unique situation.

3. Preparing and Filing Tax Returns: Tax accountants use specialized software to prepare and file tax returns. They check and double-check calculations to ensure compliance and accuracy before submitting returns.

4. Providing Tax Advice: Beyond compliance, tax accountants also advise clients on tax planning. This includes making recommendations on financial decisions that could reduce future tax liabilities, such as timing of income, investment strategies, and retirement planning.

5. Representing Clients in Audits: In cases where clients are audited by the IRS or another tax authority, tax accountants may represent them, answering questions and providing documentation to support the tax return's accuracy.

Challenges and Opportunities in Tax Accounting

Tax accounting offers rewarding opportunities but also presents unique challenges. The complexity and evolving nature of tax laws mean that tax accountants must be lifelong learners. Many find satisfaction in helping clients navigate tax issues and achieve financial security, but the work can be stressful, especially during tax season when workloads increase significantly.

For those interested in a stable career with a diverse client base, tax accounting can be a great fit. The demand for tax accountants is steady, as taxes are a universal requirement and tax laws frequently change. Additionally, tax accounting offers opportunities for specialization and advancement, allowing professionals to build a niche in areas such as international tax, estate planning, or corporate tax strategies.

Emerging Trends in Tax Accounting

The field of tax accounting is evolving, influenced by technology, regulatory changes, and the globalization of business. Here are some trends that are reshaping the profession:

1. Technology and Automation: Tax software and artificial intelligence (AI) are transforming tax accounting, automating routine tasks like data entry and calculations. Tax accountants are increasingly required to be technologically proficient and to understand how to leverage software tools to enhance efficiency.

2. Increased Focus on Compliance and Reporting Standards: With governments around the world adopting stricter regulations, tax accountants are expected to ensure their clients are fully compliant with these requirements, especially for multinational corporations.

3. Specialization in Niche Areas: As tax laws become more complex, some tax accountants are choosing to specialize in areas such as international tax or estate planning. This allows them to offer more tailored advice and potentially command higher fees for specialized expertise.

4. Rise of Remote Tax Services: With advancements in digital technology, many tax accountants can now work remotely, providing tax consulting services online. This shift has opened up opportunities to serve clients across different regions and broadened the reach of tax accounting services.

5. Sustainability and ESG (Environmental, Social, Governance) Reporting: As companies increasingly report on ESG factors, tax accountants may be called upon to provide tax-related data and analysis that support sustainable business practices.

Conclusion

Tax accounting is a specialized field within accounting that offers diverse opportunities for those interested in a career that combines finance, law, and problem-solving. Whether working with individuals to file tax returns or advising corporations on strategic tax planning, tax accountants play a crucial role in helping clients navigate complex tax landscapes. For young people considering a career in accounting, tax accounting presents a path with solid job prospects, continual learning, and the chance to make a tangible difference in clients' financial lives.

By developing expertise in tax codes, honing analytical skills, and staying informed about industry trends, aspiring tax accountants can look forward to a rewarding and impactful career.

Example 1: Personal Tax Accounting

Suppose Maria is an individual taxpayer who has a regular job, earns a salary, and makes some investment income from stocks. Maria hires a tax accountant to help prepare her annual tax return. The tax accountant will gather her financial records, including her income statements from her job and her investment statements, and will look for any deductions and credits that can lower her tax bill.

For instance, Maria made a charitable donation of $1,000 to a local nonprofit. Her tax accountant includes this donation as a deductible item, which reduces her taxable income. This means Maria will pay taxes on a lower income amount, potentially lowering her overall tax bill.

Explanation: In this example, the tax accountant helps Maria navigate tax deductions and credits, ensuring she's only paying the necessary amount in taxes while remaining compliant with tax laws.

Example 2: Corporate Tax Accounting

Imagine a small business called "GreenThumb Landscaping" that provides gardening and landscaping services. The owner, Tom, hires a corporate tax accountant to ensure his business complies with tax regulations and takes advantage of any tax breaks available. Throughout the year, Tom buys new equipment, such as lawnmowers and gardening tools, which are considered business expenses.

The tax accountant categorizes these purchases as capital expenditures, which are deductible expenses for tax purposes. Instead of deducting the entire amount in one year, the accountant uses depreciation, allowing Tom to spread out the deductions over several years. This helps lower his taxable income for the current year and reduces his tax burden.

Explanation: The tax accountant's knowledge of capital expenditure rules and depreciation helps Tom maximize his tax benefits by spreading out deductions, keeping more cash in his business for other investments.

Example 3: International Tax Accounting

A global corporation, "TechGlobal Inc.," has operations in both the United States and Europe. They earn revenue in multiple countries and face different tax rates in each location. TechGlobal hires an international tax accountant to navigate these complexities.

For example, TechGlobal earns $500,000 in profit from its European branch. The international tax accountant examines tax treaties between the U.S. and Europe to prevent double taxation, where the company would otherwise be taxed on the same income in both regions. The accountant may find applicable tax credits that allow TechGlobal to reduce its tax bill in the U.S., thus ensuring they don't overpay.

Explanation: The international tax accountant's role here is to prevent TechGlobal from being taxed twice on the same income, using tax treaties and credits to keep the company's tax burden manageable.

Example 4: Tax Accounting for Estate Planning

Sarah is a high-net-worth individual who wants to ensure that her children inherit her assets with minimal tax impact. She consults a tax accountant specializing in estate planning to discuss strategies for passing on her wealth. The accountant advises Sarah to set up a trust as a legal entity to hold her assets. By transferring her assets to a trust, Sarah can reduce estate taxes on these assets when they are inherited by her children.

The tax accountant also suggests using annual gift exclusions to transfer a portion of her wealth to her children each year. This strategy allows Sarah to give each child $15,000 per year (as per IRS limits) without triggering gift taxes.

Explanation: In this example, the tax accountant uses knowledge of trust structures and gift tax exclusions to create a tax-efficient plan for Sarah's estate, helping her preserve more wealth for her children.

Example 5: Handling an IRS Audit

A small business owner named Jenny receives a notification from the IRS that her business is being audited. She had significant deductions related to travel and meals and is worried about whether these deductions were claimed correctly. Jenny's tax accountant assists her by gathering documentation for each deduction, including receipts and records of business trips.

During the audit, the accountant helps Jenny explain how each expense was necessary for her business operations. For example, the travel expenses were for conferences to meet potential clients, and meal expenses were for client meetings.

Explanation: In this case, the tax accountant's knowledge and support during the audit process ensure that Jenny has all the necessary records to justify her deductions, reducing her risk of penalties and additional taxes.

Example 6: Tax Planning for a Growing Business

ABC Retail is a growing online business looking to expand its operations. Their tax accountant suggests several tax planning strategies to support this growth. For instance, the accountant advises ABC Retail to consider Section 179 Deduction, which allows them to fully deduct the cost of equipment purchases, such as new computers or warehouse shelving, in the year they are purchased instead of depreciating these assets over multiple years.

This large upfront deduction helps ABC Retail reduce their taxable income, allowing them to reinvest their savings into the business.

Explanation: By taking advantage of Section 179, the tax accountant helps ABC Retail lower their current tax burden, providing them with additional funds for reinvestment, which is particularly beneficial for small businesses focused on growth.

These examples illustrate various ways tax accountants apply their knowledge to real-life scenarios, helping individuals and businesses minimize their tax obligations while ensuring compliance with complex tax regulations.

1.3 Common Myths about Accounting

The field of accounting is often misunderstood, largely due to long-standing myths and stereotypes. These misconceptions can deter young people from exploring a rewarding and dynamic career path. In this section, we will debunk some of the most common myths about accounting, helping you gain a clearer picture of what this profession truly entails.

Myth 1: Accounting Is Just About Math

One of the biggest myths is that accountants spend their days crunching numbers and doing little else. While math is indeed a component, accounting is much more about understanding financial principles, analyzing data, and communicating insights. Basic math skills are necessary, but advanced mathematics is rarely required. Instead, accountants rely on analytical skills, critical thinking, and problem-solving abilities to interpret financial information and make sound recommendations.

Today, technology has further minimized the need for manual number-crunching. Accounting software, calculators, and spreadsheets handle the heavy lifting, allowing accountants to focus on data analysis and decision-making. In fact, accountants spend more time interpreting data than calculating it, making this field ideal for those who enjoy solving problems and uncovering patterns in financial data.

Myth 2: Accounting Is Boring

This myth stems from the stereotype of accountants as introverted individuals working in solitude. While there are quieter tasks, the profession can be highly engaging, challenging, and rewarding. Accountants often collaborate with teams, interact with clients, and advise businesses on important financial decisions. Each day can bring new tasks, whether it's preparing reports, conducting audits, or analyzing a client's finances.

Accounting offers a range of opportunities, from consulting and financial planning to working on mergers and acquisitions. These roles can require travel, collaboration, and quick thinking. For example, forensic accountants investigate fraud, while management accountants help businesses shape strategies. Rather than being dull, accounting can be dynamic, with variety and meaningful responsibilities.

Myth 3: Accountants Only Work with Taxes

Another common misconception is that all accountants work in tax preparation. While tax accounting is a significant branch, it's only one part of the field. Accounting offers a diverse set of specializations, including auditing, financial accounting, forensic accounting, and cost accounting. Each specialization has unique responsibilities and skill sets, and accountants often switch between fields as their careers progress.

Additionally, many accountants work in advisory roles, assisting companies with budgeting, financial planning, and strategic decision-making. Others may work in nonprofit organizations or government roles, where their focus is on compliance, internal controls, or grants. The possibilities in accounting extend far beyond taxes, making it a versatile career.

Myth 4: Accountants Don't Need People Skills

Since accounting involves working with numbers, many assume it's a solitary job that doesn't require much interaction with others. In reality, accountants need strong interpersonal skills, as they frequently work with clients, present financial findings, and provide advice. Effective communication is essential for explaining complex financial data to individuals without a finance background.

For accountants in managerial or consulting roles, building trust with clients or team members is crucial. Accountants also work closely with other departments, such as sales, human resources, and management, requiring a high level of collaboration and teamwork. Far from being isolated, accounting is a profession that values strong people skills.

Myth 5: Accounting Is Only for "Numbers People"

Many people believe that only those who love numbers will succeed in accounting. While comfort with numbers is helpful, success in accounting is more about attention to detail, analytical thinking, and strategic decision-making. Accountants are tasked with identifying patterns, spotting inaccuracies, and providing meaningful insights.

Accountants work as advisors, guiding their clients or companies to make sound financial decisions. Those with creative and critical thinking skills can excel in this field, as they offer unique perspectives on financial challenges. For those who enjoy logic, analysis, and helping others make informed decisions, accounting can be an ideal fit.

Myth 6: Accounting Is a Dead-End Job with No Room for Growth

Some view accounting as a static career, with little room for advancement. However, the reality is quite the opposite. Accounting is a field with a clear career path and ample opportunities for growth. Entry-level positions can lead to managerial roles, such as senior accountant or accounting manager, and many accountants move on to executive positions like chief financial officer (CFO) or partner in an accounting firm.

Certifications, such as Certified Public Accountant (CPA) or Certified Management Accountant (CMA), can open doors to specialized and higher-paying roles. The demand for accountants with expertise in forensic accounting, IT auditing, and sustainability is growing, offering new and exciting career pathways. With dedication and continuous learning, accountants can achieve significant career advancement.

Myth 7: Accountants Are Only Needed in Large Firms

This myth implies that only large corporations or firms employ accountants, but in reality, accountants are essential in almost every type of organization, from small businesses to government agencies and nonprofits. Small business owners rely on accountants to manage their books, ensure tax compliance, and provide financial advice. Government agencies employ accountants to ensure transparency and compliance with regulations, and nonprofits need accountants to manage funds and maintain financial records.

Freelance accountants and consultants are also in demand, as they can provide specialized financial expertise to multiple clients. Accountants are needed in various sectors, which gives flexibility and job security to those in the profession.

Myth 8: Accounting Is All About Following Rules

While accounting does involve compliance with regulations and standards, it is also a field that requires creativity and problem-solving. Accountants develop strategies to improve financial performance, assess risks, and plan for future growth. In management accounting, for instance, accountants create budgets and forecasts, using their judgment to guide a company's financial decisions.

Innovation is also becoming more prominent in accounting, especially with the rise of data analytics, artificial intelligence, and blockchain. Accountants are often at the forefront of technological advancements, integrating new tools to provide better insights and streamline processes.

Myth 9: All Accountants Are the Same

The image of an accountant as a person in a suit behind a desk does not capture the diversity of roles within accounting. Accounting includes a broad array of specialties and work environments. Public accountants work for firms that provide auditing, tax, and consulting services to clients, while management accountants work within organizations to support internal decision-making.

Forensic accountants investigate financial fraud, while environmental accountants work on sustainability initiatives. This diversity of roles allows individuals to find their niche within accounting, whether they prefer a client-facing role, an investigative role, or a corporate support role.

Myth 10: Accountants Are Always the "Bad Guys" Who Find Faults

People often think of accountants as strict rule-enforcers who only focus on finding mistakes. While auditors and compliance professionals ensure accuracy and adherence to standards, the majority of accountants work to support their clients or organizations. They offer insights to help businesses grow, assist in planning for taxes, and help manage financial risks.

Accountants are also seen as trusted advisors, especially for small business owners who rely on them for guidance. Rather than playing the role of "bad guys," accountants work as valuable partners who help ensure financial health and stability.

Conclusion

These myths about accounting paint an inaccurate picture of the profession and can discourage potential talent from considering it as a career. Accounting is a dynamic, multifaceted field that offers significant opportunities for growth, creativity, and personal fulfillment. By breaking these stereotypes, young individuals can see accounting for what it truly is—a valuable, rewarding profession with a wide range of possibilities.

CHAPTER II
Skills and Qualities for Success

2.1 Essential Technical Skills

In accounting, technical skills provide the backbone of a professional's ability to accurately manage and interpret financial data. These essential skills enable accountants to analyze business health, provide valuable insights, and guide sound financial decisions. Mastering technical skills is a critical step for anyone looking to thrive in an accounting career. Some of the most fundamental technical skills include financial analysis, software proficiency, and knowledge of regulatory standards. This section explores each of these essential skills and explains why they are vital in accounting.

2.1.1 Financial Analysis

Financial analysis is a core competency for accountants, enabling them to assess the financial well-being of organizations, evaluate performance, and make strategic recommendations. Financial analysis skills empower accountants to sift through large volumes of data, identify key trends, and provide insights that inform business decisions. In this section, we'll explore the foundational aspects of financial analysis, including ratio analysis, trend analysis, benchmarking, and interpreting financial statements.

Understanding Financial Statements

To perform effective financial analysis, accountants must be well-versed in reading and interpreting financial statements. These include:

- *Income Statement:* Shows the company's revenue, expenses, and net profit over a period. By examining the income statement, accountants can understand profitability and revenue trends, helping to pinpoint areas where the company can control costs or improve margins.

- *Balance Sheet:* Reflects the company's assets, liabilities, and shareholder equity at a specific point in time. This snapshot provides insight into the company's financial stability, liquidity, and how effectively it's using resources.

- *Cash Flow Statement:* Tracks the inflow and outflow of cash, revealing the company's liquidity and cash generation. Understanding cash flow is crucial for assessing a company's ability to sustain its operations and fund future growth.

- *Statement of Changes in Equity:* Shows changes in equity over a reporting period, helping to understand contributions, retained earnings, and dividend policies.

A thorough understanding of these statements is foundational to performing deeper financial analysis and drawing meaningful insights about an organization's financial health.

Key Financial Ratios

Financial ratios are tools that help accountants evaluate various aspects of a company's performance. Ratios offer valuable insights by putting raw numbers into context. Below are some of the primary categories of financial ratios:

- Profitability Ratios: Measure a company's ability to generate income relative to revenue, assets, or equity.

  - Gross Profit Margin: Calculated as (Gross Profit / Revenue) x 100, this ratio indicates the profitability of core business activities.

  - Net Profit Margin: Shows how much profit a company makes after all expenses, offering insight into efficiency.

  - Return on Assets (ROA) and Return on Equity (ROE): Indicate how effectively management is using assets and equity to generate profits.

- Liquidity Ratios: Assess a company's ability to cover its short-term obligations.

  - Current Ratio: Calculated as (Current Assets / Current Liabilities), it shows whether a company has enough resources to meet its short-term debts.

  - Quick Ratio: Also known as the acid-test ratio, it measures a company's capacity to meet obligations without relying on inventory sales.

- Efficiency Ratios: Evaluate how effectively a company uses its assets.

  - Inventory Turnover: Indicates how quickly inventory is sold, calculated by dividing cost of goods sold by average inventory.

  - Receivables Turnover: Reflects the efficiency of collecting payments from customers.

- Solvency Ratios: Measure long-term financial stability and the company's ability to meet long-term obligations.

  - Debt-to-Equity Ratio: This ratio compares total liabilities to shareholders' equity, indicating how much leverage a company is using.

  - Interest Coverage Ratio: Calculated as (EBIT / Interest Expense), this ratio indicates the company's ability to pay interest on its debt.

Trend Analysis

In financial analysis, spotting trends over time is critical. Trend analysis involves examining financial statements from multiple periods to detect patterns. For example:

- Revenue Trends: Assessing whether revenue is increasing, stable, or declining over time provides insights into business growth and market positioning.

- Expense Trends: Identifying rising expenses or areas where costs can be controlled can help improve profitability.

- Asset and Liability Trends: Analyzing changes in assets and liabilities helps assess if the company is building or consuming resources wisely.

Accountants often use graphs and charts to visualize trends, making it easier for stakeholders to understand performance over time.

Benchmarking

Benchmarking compares a company's performance with industry standards or competitors. Accountants use benchmarking to:

- Identify Performance Gaps: Spot areas where the company falls short of competitors or industry averages, providing a roadmap for improvement.

- Set Realistic Goals: By understanding how peers perform, companies can set achievable and aspirational targets.

- Drive Competitive Advantage: Benchmarking reveals opportunities to improve processes or adopt best practices from industry leaders.

Types of benchmarks may include industry averages, performance standards, or comparisons to best-in-class organizations.

Scenario and Sensitivity Analysis

Financial analysts often use scenario analysis to predict how changes in certain variables will affect outcomes. For example:

- Scenario Analysis: Examines multiple "what-if" scenarios, such as changes in market conditions, to evaluate potential impacts on financial performance.

- Sensitivity Analysis: Tests how sensitive financial outcomes are to changes in specific variables, such as interest rates or sales volume.

These techniques allow accountants to model financial performance under various conditions, helping stakeholders make informed decisions based on potential risks and opportunities.

Budgeting and Forecasting

Budgeting and forecasting are essential tools in financial analysis, enabling organizations to set financial goals, monitor progress, and make adjustments as needed. Accountants who excel in budgeting and forecasting can:

- Set Realistic Financial Goals: By analyzing historical data, accountants can help set achievable revenue, expense, and profit targets.

- Monitor Financial Performance: Comparing actual results to budgeted figures helps identify variances and areas that require attention.

- Plan for the Future: Forecasting involves projecting future financial performance based on historical data, industry trends, and economic indicators.

Interpreting Financial Data for Stakeholders

Accountants play a key role in communicating financial information to non-financial stakeholders. This often involves:

- Simplifying Complex Data: Translating numbers into clear, concise insights that are accessible to decision-makers.

- Highlighting Key Insights: Focusing on the most significant findings, such as profitability, liquidity, or expense issues.

- Making Actionable Recommendations: Offering suggestions based on analysis, such as reducing certain expenses or investing in specific areas.

Developing strong financial analysis skills requires practice, continuous learning, and a commitment to staying current with industry trends and tools. As a young accountant, mastering financial analysis will enhance your ability to support strategic decision-making and contribute meaningfully to an organization's success.

Here are concrete examples to illustrate the financial analysis skills covered above:

Understanding Financial Statements: Practical Example

Let's say you're analyzing the financial health of a company called "TechEdge Inc."

1. Income Statement: You notice TechEdge Inc. has a gross profit margin of 60%, meaning it retains 60% of each dollar of sales as profit after deducting the cost of goods sold. However, their net profit margin is only 10%, indicating high operating and non-operating expenses. By pinpointing these expenses, you could recommend cost-cutting measures in non-essential areas, improving profitability.

2. Balance Sheet: You find that TechEdge Inc. has a debt-to-equity ratio of 1.5, meaning they're financing 1.5 times their equity with debt. This ratio may indicate higher risk if interest rates rise, so you could suggest the company explore refinancing options to reduce interest expense and improve financial stability.

3. Cash Flow Statement: By examining TechEdge's cash flow statement, you notice that, despite strong revenue, cash flow from operations has been declining due to increasing inventory. You might recommend inventory optimization strategies to improve liquidity, which could be essential for meeting short-term obligations.

Key Financial Ratios: Practical Example

Imagine analyzing "GreenGro Inc.," an organic food supplier.

1. Profitability Ratios: GreenGro's gross profit margin is 50%, which is in line with industry standards. However, the net profit margin is only 5%, lower than the industry average of 8%. Upon closer examination, you identify high shipping costs as the primary expense. By recommending partnerships with more cost-efficient logistics providers, you aim to raise the net profit margin.

2. Liquidity Ratios: GreenGro's current ratio is 1.2, meaning its current assets exceed current liabilities by 20%, giving it a slight cushion. However, its quick ratio is 0.8, showing it relies on inventory sales to meet obligations. To strengthen liquidity, you might advise reducing inventory levels or securing a short-term line of credit.

3. Efficiency Ratios: The inventory turnover ratio is 3, meaning GreenGro restocks three times per year. If industry norms are closer to 5, this suggests excess inventory. You could recommend using demand forecasting tools to better manage inventory, increasing cash flow and reducing storage costs.

Trend Analysis: Practical Example

For the past three years, you've been tracking sales and expenses for "EcoCloth Co.," a sustainable clothing brand.

1. Revenue Trends: You notice that EcoCloth's annual revenue growth rate has slowed from 15% to 5%. Analyzing market conditions reveals increased competition. Based on these findings, you might propose a targeted marketing campaign emphasizing EcoCloth's unique eco-friendly approach to attract environmentally conscious consumers.

2. Expense Trends: EcoCloth's production costs have been gradually increasing, squeezing margins. Upon investigation, you discover that raw material costs are rising. You recommend locking in prices through long-term contracts with suppliers, stabilizing costs and improving predictability.

Benchmarking: Practical Example

Assume you're evaluating "HealthNut Ltd.," a startup in the health and wellness industry.

1. Industry Comparison: HealthNut's profitability ratios are below the industry average. Its gross margin is 30%, compared to an industry standard of 40%. Through benchmarking, you find that competitors source cheaper ingredients from local suppliers. You suggest similar sourcing adjustments to improve HealthNut's gross margin.

2. Efficiency Comparison: HealthNut's inventory turnover ratio is 2, while the industry average is 5. By suggesting inventory management techniques used by competitors, such as just-in-time inventory, you aim to improve HealthNut's efficiency and reduce holding costs.

Scenario and Sensitivity Analysis: Practical Example

Imagine you're working with "SolarTech Solutions," a renewable energy company. You run scenario and sensitivity analyses based on future energy market conditions:

1. Scenario Analysis: In one scenario, energy costs increase by 20% due to regulatory changes. This increase would significantly impact SolarTech's production expenses. Based on this analysis, you might recommend investing in alternative suppliers or renewable energy credits to offset rising costs.

2. Sensitivity Analysis: You conduct a sensitivity analysis on SolarTech's revenue to see how changes in sales volume impact profitability. You find that a 5% drop in sales would lead to a 10% drop in profit due to fixed costs. To mitigate this risk, you suggest reducing fixed expenses or diversifying SolarTech's product line.

Budgeting and Forecasting: Practical Example

You're tasked with creating a budget for "NextGen Fitness," a chain of gyms.

1. Setting Revenue Targets: Based on historical data, you set a monthly revenue target of $200,000. By incorporating expected seasonal trends, you adjust the target for peak seasons (like New Year's) and slower months (summer).

2. Monitoring Variances: Midway through the quarter, you notice that actual revenue is consistently 10% below budgeted targets. After analyzing market conditions, you discover increased competition from budget-friendly gyms. You propose promotional discounts or partnerships with local businesses to attract new members.

3. Planning for Future Growth: In forecasting, you project that NextGen Fitness could expand by opening three additional locations over the next two years. You calculate expected costs and potential returns, making a case for strategic growth based on financial feasibility.

Interpreting Financial Data for Stakeholders: Practical Example

Suppose you're presenting findings on "GreenWave Energy" to senior executives.

1. Simplifying Data: Instead of showing raw numbers, you use visuals (charts, graphs) to highlight key metrics, such as revenue growth and expense trends over the past year. This visual approach helps non-financial stakeholders grasp financial performance quickly.

2. Highlighting Key Insights: You focus on GreenWave's strong cash flow position but caution about its high debt-to-equity ratio. You explain how refinancing could lower interest payments, allowing the company to reinvest savings into innovation.

3. Making Recommendations: Based on your analysis, you suggest strategies like reallocating resources toward high-growth areas (such as renewable energy projects) and exploring cost-saving opportunities in less profitable departments. These recommendations align with the company's long-term goals and improve decision-making.

These examples bring financial analysis to life, illustrating how each skill is applied in real-world scenarios and guiding you to make data-driven recommendations.

2.1.2 Software and Tools

Introduction to Accounting Software and Technology

In today's accounting world, technology has become an essential part of the profession. Accountants need to be proficient in various software tools that simplify data entry, ensure compliance, and facilitate financial analysis. Whether you work in corporate finance, auditing, or tax accounting, using the right software effectively is a critical skill.

Key Types of Accounting Software and Tools

1. General Ledger Software

The general ledger is the foundation of accounting, as it records all transactions. Accountants often use general ledger software to ensure accurate financial reporting and keep a detailed record of business transactions. Examples include:

- QuickBooks: Primarily used by small to medium businesses, QuickBooks is user-friendly and handles tasks such as invoicing, tracking expenses, and generating financial statements.

- Sage 50cloud: Known for its scalability, Sage 50cloud is a comprehensive accounting solution widely used by medium to large businesses.

- Microsoft Dynamics: Offers advanced features for managing finances, operations, and customer relations, often used in larger enterprises.

2. Spreadsheet Software

Excel is one of the most widely used tools in accounting. Spreadsheet software provides flexibility and customizability, allowing accountants to create formulas, pivot tables, and various financial models. Key skills include:

- Formula Creation: Learning Excel's formulas is essential, as they automate calculations.

- Data Analysis and Visualization: Pivot tables, charts, and conditional formatting help make financial data more understandable.

- Macros: These automate repetitive tasks, which is beneficial for data-heavy processes.

3. Enterprise Resource Planning (ERP) Systems

ERPs integrate all departments within a business, streamlining data across functions such as finance, inventory, HR, and sales. For accountants, ERP systems provide a holistic view of financial health. Popular ERP systems include:

- SAP: Known for its extensive capabilities in financial management, asset management, and risk compliance.

- Oracle NetSuite: Cloud-based and popular with growing businesses, it includes accounting modules for invoicing, payroll, and cash flow management.

- Infor: Specialized for industries such as healthcare and manufacturing, providing financial and operational visibility.

4. Audit Software

Auditors use specialized software to analyze large data sets for anomalies and streamline the auditing process. Common audit tools include:

- ACL Analytics: Assists auditors by providing data analytics and auditing capabilities, useful for detecting fraud or errors.

- CaseWare IDEA: A tool for analyzing data and ensuring compliance, IDEA is especially useful in handling large, complex data sets.

- TeamMate: Designed for internal audit management, helping organize audit workflows, track findings, and generate reports.

5. Tax Software

Tax accounting requires precise calculations and an understanding of current tax laws. Tax software helps accountants file accurate returns and comply with regulations. Examples include:

- TurboTax and ProSeries: Commonly used by smaller firms or individuals, TurboTax streamlines the tax preparation process.

- Lacerte: This is designed for professional accountants, especially those handling high volumes of returns.

- Thomson Reuters ONESOURCE: Known for its robust features for tax compliance and reporting, it is often used by large multinational corporations.

6. Data Analytics Tools

The accounting field increasingly relies on data analytics for insight. Skills in analytics software allow accountants to interpret trends, forecast revenue, and make strategic decisions. Notable tools include:

- Tableau: Enables visual analytics, allowing accountants to create interactive dashboards.

- Power BI: Microsoft's business analytics tool provides rich data visualization and integration with other Microsoft tools.

- Alteryx: Offers a platform for blending and analyzing data, which is valuable for data-intensive accounting tasks.

7. Financial Modeling Software

In fields such as investment banking and corporate finance, financial modeling is a key skill. Financial modeling software helps build forecasts and scenario analyses. Examples include:

- Anaplan: Offers cloud-based modeling and planning for finance teams, useful for budget management and forecasting.

- Adaptive Insights: Integrates financial planning and analysis, allowing users to forecast and conduct "what-if" scenarios.

- Quantrix: Primarily used for advanced modeling, providing flexibility in creating complex financial scenarios.

Importance of Data Security and Compliance Tools

As financial data is highly sensitive, maintaining data security is critical in accounting. Many accounting firms and departments use cybersecurity tools and compliance software to protect information. Examples of security tools include:

- Encryption Software: Tools like BitLocker and Veracrypt help encrypt sensitive financial data.

- Firewall and Antivirus Programs: Norton, McAfee, and other firewall solutions are essential for protecting against cyber threats.

Building Proficiency with Accounting Software

1. Learning Resources

Many software companies provide online training, certifications, and tutorials. For instance, Microsoft and Tableau offer certifications that demonstrate proficiency, which can enhance your resume.

2. Practical Application and Internships

The best way to learn accounting software is through hands-on experience. Internships provide opportunities to work with real data and solve practical problems. Look for internships that expose you to multiple tools, as this will help you build adaptability.

3. Keeping Up with Technology Trends

Technology in accounting is constantly evolving. To stay current, follow industry news, attend technology-focused conferences, and complete continuing education courses.

Conclusion

Mastering accounting software and tools is crucial for any aspiring accountant. While the learning curve may seem steep, proficiency in these tools opens up a world of opportunities. With consistent practice, training, and a willingness to learn, you can develop the technical skills necessary for a successful career in accounting.

Certainly! Here's a detailed example to illustrate the use of some of these accounting tools in real-world scenarios:

Example 1: Using Excel for Financial Analysis

Imagine you're an entry-level accountant at a small company, and your manager asks you to prepare a monthly financial report that highlights revenue, expenses, and net profit. The goal is to provide a snapshot of the company's financial performance and trends.

1. Building the Financial Report

Using Excel, you enter data for each month's revenue and expenses. With Excel's formula features, you set up basic calculations:

- SUM Function: To calculate total revenue and total expenses.

- Net Profit Calculation: You create a formula to calculate net profit by subtracting total expenses from total revenue.

2. Data Visualization with Charts

After completing the report, you add a bar chart and a line graph to visually represent revenue and expenses over time. This helps your manager quickly see trends, such as an increase in expenses or a steady growth in revenue.

3. Automating with Pivot Tables

Your manager also wants to view the financial data by category. Using a pivot table, you organize expenses by category (e.g., rent, utilities, payroll) and create a summary without manually sorting the data. This pivot table is easily updated each month, saving you time in future reporting.

4. Setting Up Macros for Repetitive Tasks

To streamline the process, you record a macro that formats and sets up the financial report each month. This macro allows you to automate repetitive steps—like adding headers, applying filters, and formatting cells—saving you valuable time.

Example 2: Managing Invoices and Expenses with QuickBooks

Let's say you're tasked with managing accounts payable for a small business. Each month, the company receives various invoices for services like IT support, office supplies, and utility bills. Here's how QuickBooks helps:

1. Entering and Tracking Invoices

You enter each invoice into QuickBooks, associating it with the appropriate expense category. QuickBooks automatically calculates the due dates and alerts you when a payment is approaching. This system helps ensure you never miss a payment deadline.

2. Generating Financial Reports

At the end of each quarter, your manager requests a detailed report of expenses by category. Using QuickBooks' built-in reporting tools, you generate an Expense Summary Report that shows total spending per category. This report helps your manager see where the budget is being spent and identify potential areas for cost savings.

3. Reconciling Bank Statements

QuickBooks allows you to reconcile transactions with the company's bank statement. You verify that all payments, receipts, and expenses match the records in QuickBooks. This process helps catch any errors, such as duplicate entries or incorrect amounts, ensuring the company's financial records are accurate.

Example 3: Leveraging SAP for Comprehensive Financial Management

In a larger company setting, you're part of the accounting team using SAP to manage financial data across departments. Your role is focused on budgeting and financial planning for multiple business units.

1. Creating a Centralized Budget in SAP

Each department submits its projected budget, which you consolidate in SAP. You enter data for each unit, including anticipated revenue, expected costs, and special project budgets. SAP's comprehensive database structure allows you to view and adjust budgets in real-time, considering any recent updates or management decisions.

2. Automating Budget Variance Analysis

SAP has built-in tools for variance analysis, comparing actual spending against the budget. With this feature, you automatically track if departments are over or under budget, enabling you to provide timely feedback to managers. SAP generates visual reports that highlight budget variances, allowing management to make informed decisions on cost control.

3. Tracking Inter-Departmental Transactions

In SAP, you also record inter-departmental transactions, such as a marketing department buying services from the IT department. SAP's integrated modules ensure that such internal transactions are tracked and accounted for, maintaining transparency and consistency in financial reporting.

Example 4: Conducting an Audit with ACL Analytics

Suppose you're a junior auditor at a mid-sized accounting firm. Your current assignment is to audit a client's financial records to detect any anomalies in their payroll system.

1. Importing Data into ACL

First, you import the client's payroll data into ACL. The software allows you to handle large data sets efficiently, even those with millions of transactions. ACL automatically standardizes the data format, making it easier to analyze.

2. Using Data Analytics to Detect Anomalies

With ACL's analysis tools, you set up queries to identify unusual transactions. For instance, you create a filter to find payroll entries with unusually high overtime hours, signaling potential fraud or data entry errors.

3. Generating an Audit Report

Once you've completed the analysis, ACL helps you generate a detailed audit report that includes charts and summaries of any suspicious findings. This report provides the client with a clear view of potential risks and recommendations for improving their payroll processes.

Example 5: Creating Financial Forecasts with Anaplan

Imagine you're an analyst in the finance department of a rapidly growing startup. The company's CEO requests a financial forecast to project revenue and expenses for the next three years.

1. Building a Financial Model in Anaplan

Anaplan allows you to create a detailed financial model. You enter revenue drivers such as projected sales growth, pricing, and anticipated new customers. On the expense side, you include variables like payroll costs, overhead, and marketing expenses.

2. Running "What-If" Scenarios

Using Anaplan's "what-if" feature, you create multiple scenarios. For example, you model the impact on profitability if the company achieves a 15% increase in customer acquisition versus a 10% increase. These scenarios help the CEO make informed strategic decisions based on possible outcomes.

3. Collaboration and Real-Time Updates

Anaplan's cloud-based nature allows team members to collaborate on the forecast in real time. When the marketing department revises their budget, the changes are immediately reflected in the model, giving you the most up-to-date data for accurate forecasting.

Conclusion

Through these examples, you can see how software and tools play a crucial role in accounting. Proficiency in tools like Excel, QuickBooks, SAP, ACL, and Anaplan allows accountants to deliver detailed, accurate, and actionable financial insights. Learning these tools is an investment that pays off with the ability to handle complex data, streamline workflows, and make impactful contributions to any organization.

2.1.3 Regulatory Knowledge

Regulatory knowledge is an essential part of an accountant's skillset, enabling professionals to navigate the complex landscape of rules, regulations, and standards that govern financial reporting, auditing, and tax compliance. Understanding these regulations is vital for ensuring that businesses operate ethically and legally while providing transparent and reliable financial information to stakeholders. In this section, we'll explore the importance of regulatory knowledge for accountants, key regulatory frameworks, and how accountants stay updated in a constantly evolving regulatory environment.

The Importance of Regulatory Knowledge for Accountants

Accounting is fundamentally rooted in compliance and adherence to established standards, as financial data must be accurate, consistent, and comparable. Regulatory knowledge ensures that accountants can prepare and interpret financial statements that meet the required standards, allowing businesses to maintain credibility and integrity in their financial practices. A solid understanding of regulations helps accountants to:

1. *Ensure Compliance:* By adhering to local and international laws and regulations, accountants minimize the risk of penalties, fines, or legal action against their organizations.

2. *Provide Transparency:* Regulators require companies to follow certain rules to ensure accurate and fair financial reporting. This helps stakeholders, including investors, creditors, and tax authorities, make well-informed decisions.

3. *Build Trust with Stakeholders:* When companies demonstrate strong compliance, it enhances their reputation and builds trust with investors, customers, and the public.

4. *Minimize Financial Risk:* Regulatory compliance often requires accountants to identify potential risks, assess their impact, and implement strategies to minimize them.

Key Regulatory Frameworks

Several key frameworks and standards shape the regulatory landscape for accountants. Understanding these is crucial for anyone entering the field:

1. Generally Accepted Accounting Principles (GAAP)

GAAP is a collection of standards, principles, and procedures that accountants in the United States must follow when compiling financial statements. These principles cover everything from how to recognize revenue and expenses to the way financial statements are presented. Some important aspects of GAAP include:

- Revenue Recognition Principle: Revenue should be recognized when it is earned, not necessarily when payment is received.

- Matching Principle: Expenses should be matched with the revenues they help generate, ensuring an accurate portrayal of a company's profitability.

- Historical Cost Principle: Assets should generally be recorded based on their original cost, not their current market value.

Mastering GAAP is essential for anyone aiming to work in U.S.-based accounting roles, as it provides a foundation for accurate and consistent financial reporting.

2. International Financial Reporting Standards (IFRS)

Outside of the United States, many countries adhere to IFRS, a set of global accounting standards developed by the International Accounting Standards Board (IASB). IFRS promotes transparency and comparability across international boundaries. Some significant IFRS principles include:

- Fair Value Measurement: IFRS often requires or permits assets and liabilities to be measured at fair value, rather than historical cost.

- Principle-Based Approach: Unlike GAAP's more rule-based structure, IFRS is principle-based, giving accountants flexibility to apply judgment in complex situations.

Accountants who aim to work for multinational corporations or in regions outside the U.S. need to develop a deep understanding of IFRS, as it is used in over 140 countries worldwide.

3. The Sarbanes-Oxley Act (SOX)

The Sarbanes-Oxley Act of 2002 is a key regulatory framework in the United States focused on increasing corporate transparency and preventing fraud. SOX affects how companies maintain records, conduct audits, and report financial information. Important elements of SOX include:

- Internal Controls: SOX requires companies to implement internal controls to ensure accurate financial reporting. Accountants often work closely with these systems to evaluate and document their effectiveness.

- CEO and CFO Certifications: Under SOX, top executives must certify the accuracy of financial statements, making them personally liable for any inaccuracies or misstatements.

Understanding SOX compliance is critical for accountants in public companies, as it shapes the structure and accuracy of financial records.

4. Tax Regulations and Compliance

Accountants working in tax-related fields must stay updated on tax codes, rates, and deductions, which vary widely by country and state. Key areas of tax knowledge include:

- Federal, State, and Local Tax Codes: In the U.S., for example, accountants need to be aware of federal tax codes governed by the IRS, as well as state and local tax requirements.

- Tax Deductions and Credits: Accountants help businesses and individuals legally reduce their taxable income through deductions and credits.

- Tax Filing Deadlines and Requirements: Accountants need to understand tax deadlines, filing requirements, and potential penalties for late or incorrect submissions.

Keeping up-to-date with tax regulations helps accountants to provide valuable tax planning and compliance services, ultimately saving clients time and money.

5. Anti-Money Laundering (AML) and Know Your Customer (KYC) Regulations

AML and KYC regulations play a significant role in preventing financial crime. Accountants, particularly those in financial services, often need to understand these regulations to:

- Identify Suspicious Activity: By understanding what constitutes suspicious activity, accountants can help detect and prevent money laundering.

- Verify Customer Identity: KYC regulations require organizations to verify the identity of their clients and assess potential risks of illegal intentions.

Staying Updated in a Dynamic Regulatory Landscape

Because regulations change frequently in response to economic shifts, technological advances, and global events, maintaining up-to-date regulatory knowledge is a challenge but essential for accountants. Here are some strategies:

1. Continuing Education and Certifications: Accountants often participate in ongoing professional education to stay current on regulatory changes. Many organizations offer courses on regulatory updates, and certifications such as CPA and CMA require periodic continuing education.

2. Professional Organizations and Associations: Joining organizations such as the American Institute of Certified Public Accountants (AICPA) or the Association of Chartered Certified Accountants (ACCA) provides access to resources, conferences, and webinars that focus on regulatory changes.

3. Industry Publications and Journals: Regularly reading publications such as The CPA Journal or Journal of Accountancy keeps accountants informed of regulatory shifts and emerging issues.

4. Networking and Peer Learning: Engaging with peers in the accounting community, whether through professional forums or social media, can be an effective way to learn about recent changes and share best practices.

How Regulatory Knowledge Enhances Career Prospects

Possessing strong regulatory knowledge is a highly valued skill that can set young accountants apart in a competitive job market. Regulatory expertise enables accountants to take on roles such as:

- Compliance Officer: These professionals focus on ensuring that companies adhere to legal and regulatory standards.

- Tax Advisor: Specializing in tax regulations allows accountants to help clients minimize tax liabilities and ensure compliance.

- Internal Auditor: Regulatory knowledge is essential for internal auditors, who examine and improve a company's internal controls, ensuring regulatory compliance.

For aspiring accountants, building a foundation in regulatory knowledge opens doors to these specialized roles, all of which contribute to maintaining the integrity and stability of financial systems. As they gain experience, accountants may also influence regulatory practices through consultation or policy advising, enhancing their impact within the field.

Conclusion

Regulatory knowledge is more than just understanding rules—it is about fostering ethical practices, providing reliable financial information, and supporting transparency in business. For young accountants, building a strong foundation in this area early in their careers is essential. With the right tools and resources, they can navigate the complexities of compliance and be a driving force for integrity and trust in the financial world.

2.2 Key Soft Skills

2.2.1 Communication

In accounting, technical skills like understanding financial statements or tax regulations are essential. However, soft skills, particularly communication, play a critical role in shaping an accountant's effectiveness and career success. Communication in accounting is multi-faceted: it involves conveying complex financial information clearly to clients or stakeholders, collaborating with colleagues, and documenting findings concisely and accurately. In this section, we'll explore why communication is so crucial for accountants, the different types of communication accountants use, and practical strategies to hone this skill.

Why Communication Matters in Accounting

Accountants often serve as the bridge between financial data and decision-makers who rely on this information to guide their actions. If an accountant cannot communicate findings effectively, even the most accurate and insightful analysis may go unappreciated or misinterpreted. Effective communication can:

- *Clarify Financial Concepts*: Accounting professionals often need to explain complex financial concepts to non-accountants, such as managers or clients, who may have limited financial knowledge. A clear explanation can facilitate better decision-making.

- *Build Trust:* Good communication helps establish trust with clients and colleagues. Clear, honest, and timely communication shows professionalism and transparency, which are vital in maintaining strong relationships.

- *Enhance Collaboration:* Accountants often work in teams or with other departments like marketing, operations, and legal. Strong communication fosters collaboration, enabling teams to work more effectively towards shared goals.

- *Prevent Misunderstandings*: Miscommunication in financial matters can lead to significant misunderstandings, mistakes, or even legal issues. Precise communication minimizes errors and ensures that everyone is aligned on expectations and requirements.

Types of Communication in Accounting

Accountants use various types of communication, each requiring specific approaches and techniques. Here are the key types of communication you'll use in accounting:

1. Verbal Communication: Verbal communication includes everything from one-on-one discussions with colleagues to presentations for board members. Mastering verbal communication is essential for delivering clear messages, answering questions, and responding to feedback.

2. Written Communication: Accountants frequently write reports, emails, and financial summaries. Written communication must be concise, accurate, and well-organized, as these documents often serve as records and references for future decision-making.

3. Nonverbal Communication: Nonverbal communication includes body language, eye contact, and tone of voice, which can strongly impact how your message is received. In professional settings, maintaining a confident posture, making eye contact, and using an appropriate tone are key to conveying competence and reliability.

4. Listening Skills: Good communication is as much about listening as it is about speaking. Active listening enables you to understand your clients' needs, respond to questions appropriately, and interpret feedback accurately.

Developing Effective Verbal Communication Skills

Verbal communication in accounting involves more than just talking; it's about conveying information clearly and confidently. Here are some strategies to improve verbal communication:

- *Practice Simplifying Complex Ideas:* Accountants often need to explain technical information to people with no accounting background. Practice breaking down complex ideas into simple terms without losing accuracy. Use analogies or examples to make the information more relatable.

- *Be Clear and Concise:* In accounting, being concise is essential. Avoid jargon or overly complex language when simpler words will do. The goal is to make sure your audience understands the key points without getting lost in unnecessary details.

- *Adapt to Your Audience*: Tailor your communication style to fit your audience's level of understanding. For example, when speaking with other accountants, technical terms may be appropriate, but for clients or non-financial colleagues, use accessible language.

- *Engage in Active Listening:* Listening carefully to others is key in conversations, especially when discussing financial matters. Active listening involves giving your full attention, asking clarifying questions, and paraphrasing to confirm understanding.

Enhancing Written Communication Skills

Accountants often rely heavily on written communication to convey financial information. Reports, memos, and emails are part of daily work, and written records can have lasting implications. Here are some tips to improve written communication skills:

- *Focus on Clarity and Accuracy:* Avoid ambiguous language and ensure that each sentence is as clear as possible. In finance, small misinterpretations can have major consequences, so take time to double-check that your message is precise.

- *Structure Your Documents Effectively:* Organize your documents logically, with clear headings, bullet points, and short paragraphs where appropriate. A well-structured document helps readers quickly find the information they need.

- *Use Plain Language:* Avoid overly technical jargon, particularly when writing for clients or non-accountants. If you must use technical terms, include a brief explanation.

- *Proofread for Errors:* Accuracy is paramount in accounting, so proofread carefully. A document with errors may be perceived as careless, which can undermine credibility.

Mastering Nonverbal Communication

Nonverbal cues can strongly impact how others interpret your message and perceive you as a professional. Here's how to make your nonverbal communication work in your favor:

- *Maintain Confident Posture:* Standing or sitting up straight with an open posture conveys confidence and attentiveness. Avoid crossing your arms, as it can appear defensive or closed off.

- *Use Appropriate Eye Contact:* Eye contact shows that you're engaged and paying attention. In conversations, make regular eye contact to demonstrate interest and confidence, but avoid prolonged staring, which can be uncomfortable.

- *Be Mindful of Tone and Facial Expressions:* Your tone of voice and facial expressions can add warmth and clarity to your message. Smiling occasionally and speaking in a friendly tone can help establish rapport, particularly with clients.

Strengthening Listening Skills

Listening is an often-overlooked part of communication, but it's crucial for accountants who need to understand client needs, internal directives, or collaborative goals. Here's how to improve listening skills:

- *Practice Active Listening*: Show engagement by nodding or using small verbal acknowledgments like "I see" or "I understand." Avoid interrupting and wait for pauses to ask clarifying questions.

- *Take Notes if Necessary:* In complex conversations, jotting down key points can help ensure that you don't miss essential details. It also shows that you're taking the discussion seriously.

- *Paraphrase for Confirmation:* After the other person speaks, paraphrase their main points to confirm understanding. For example, say, "So if I understand correctly, you're looking for..." This helps avoid misunderstandings.

Tips for Developing Effective Communication in Accounting

Improving communication skills is an ongoing process. Here are some practical ways to develop your communication abilities:

- *Seek Feedback:* Ask for feedback on your communication style from colleagues or mentors. Constructive feedback can provide insights into areas where you can improve.

- *Engage in Public Speaking:* If you struggle with verbal communication, public speaking practice can build confidence. Try joining a club like Toastmasters or taking on small speaking opportunities at work.

- *Work on Writing Regularly:* Practice your writing by crafting clear and concise emails or creating summaries of reports. The more you write, the more comfortable you'll become with structuring your thoughts on paper.

- *Observe Skilled Communicators*: Pay attention to how effective communicators in your field express themselves, handle questions, and respond to feedback. Learning from their approach can inspire improvements in your own style.

- *Take Courses on Communication*: Many organizations offer workshops or online courses on business communication, which can enhance both your verbal and written skills.

In Summary

Communication is one of the most valuable soft skills an accountant can possess. It strengthens client relationships, enhances teamwork, and ensures that your insights and recommendations are clearly understood. By developing verbal, written, nonverbal, and listening skills, you'll become a more effective and respected professional, capable of making a real impact in any accounting role.

Here is a detailed example to illustrate the importance of communication skills for an accountant, which is integrated into the content from the previous section.

Example: Effective Communication in Action

Imagine you're an accountant at a growing company, and you're tasked with preparing the quarterly financial report. The report is critical for the management team to make key decisions about the company's future, such as whether they can expand operations or need to cut costs. Once the financials are ready, you need to present them to the executive team, which includes the CEO, CFO, marketing director, and operations manager.

Step 1: Verbal Communication during the Presentation

When presenting the report, you start by explaining the key numbers — revenue, expenses, and profits — to the team. However, many of the executives, especially those in marketing and operations, don't have a deep understanding of accounting. Instead of diving directly into technical jargon such as EBITDA (Earnings Before Interest, Taxes, Depreciation, and Amortization), you break it down into simple language.

- *Clear Explanation:* "EBITDA is essentially the company's earnings from its core operations before we account for things like taxes and interest payments. This is important because it gives us a clear picture of how much the company is actually making from its business activities."

- *Using Relatable Examples:* To explain the decrease in net profit, you use a real-world analogy that everyone can understand. "Imagine your personal bank account. If you've spent more than you earn, even though you may have received a bonus, you won't have any savings. In the same way, although our company has high revenue, our costs have outgrown our earnings, impacting profitability."

By presenting the information in clear terms and using examples, you ensure that the executives not only understand the data but can also discuss it meaningfully.

Step 2: Written Communication in the Financial Report

After the presentation, you need to submit the written financial report to the executive team. The report must be precise and well-structured so that the executives can reference it later. Here's how you approach it:

- *Clear Structure:* You organize the report into sections: Executive Summary, Revenue and Expense Overview, Profit and Loss Analysis, and Recommendations. Each section is broken down into bullet points for clarity, making it easy to navigate.

- *Concise Language:* In the section discussing expenses, you write: "Expenses increased by 15% this quarter, primarily due to increased raw material costs and higher distribution fees. These increases have outpaced revenue growth, impacting profitability. A detailed breakdown of expenses is provided on page 4."

By structuring the report clearly and using concise language, you ensure that the executives can quickly find the information they need without being overwhelmed by unnecessary details.

Step 3: Nonverbal Communication During the Meeting

During the presentation, nonverbal communication plays a crucial role. You maintain an open posture, make eye contact with the audience, and nod when someone asks a question. When the marketing director asks about the impact of increasing social media marketing expenses, you lean forward slightly, indicating interest and engagement, while responding calmly and confidently.

- *Engaged Body Language*: Throughout the meeting, you maintain good posture, avoid crossing your arms, and make eye contact with each team member as you speak. This conveys confidence and openness, ensuring that your audience remains engaged and receptive.

- *Tone of Voice:* When answering a question, you adjust your tone to be reassuring. "Yes, I understand that marketing expenses are increasing, but we've also seen a corresponding increase in leads, which is a positive sign for future sales." Your tone reassures the team that, while expenses are rising, there is a strategic purpose behind the spending.

Step 4: Listening and Responding

One of the key moments during the meeting comes when the operations manager asks for more detailed information on how expenses will affect the upcoming quarter's budget.

You actively listen, nodding along to show you understand, and paraphrase their question to ensure clarity.

- *Active Listening:* "So, if I understand correctly, you're asking how the increased expenses will affect our budget for the next quarter?" This confirms that you've understood the manager's concern.

- *Clarification and Confirmation:* You then respond, "We're forecasting a 5% reduction in discretionary spending to compensate for the rising operational costs. However, we can adjust based on the final budget numbers once we review them with the finance team." Your clear, concise answer directly addresses the manager's concern, while also offering a solution.

Conclusion: The Impact of Communication

This example illustrates how effective communication can make a significant difference in an accountant's work. In the scenario above, your ability to clearly explain financial terms, structure a report for easy understanding, use nonverbal cues to build trust, and listen actively to your colleagues created an atmosphere of collaboration. As a result, the executive team not only understood the financial situation but also felt confident in the actions needed to address any concerns.

In contrast, if you had used too much jargon, been unclear in your explanations, or failed to engage with the team, it would have been much harder for them to make informed decisions. In accounting, communication is just as critical as technical knowledge — it bridges the gap between numbers and meaningful action.

By refining your communication skills, you'll ensure that your insights are not only heard but also acted upon, driving success in your accounting career.

2.2.2 Critical Thinking

Critical thinking is one of the most valued soft skills for an accountant. As the world of accounting evolves, accountants are required not only to possess technical proficiency but also to demonstrate an ability to think critically. The ability to analyze and evaluate complex financial information, draw logical conclusions, and provide actionable insights is what distinguishes a successful accountant from a good one. Critical thinking enables accountants to handle ambiguity, solve problems creatively, and make sound decisions based on evidence.

In this section, we will explore the significance of critical thinking in accounting, the steps involved in critical thinking, and how young aspiring accountants can cultivate and sharpen this vital skill.

The Role of Critical Thinking in Accounting

At its core, critical thinking involves the ability to think clearly and rationally, understanding the logical connection between ideas. For accountants, this means not only performing basic calculations or completing data entries but also evaluating the meaning and relevance of financial data in broader contexts. It requires accountants to assess the implications of decisions, identify trends, and recognize potential risks.

Accounting is much more than a straightforward task of balancing books. It requires accountants to ask questions, challenge assumptions, and analyze data from different perspectives. A critical thinker in the accounting field is constantly asking:

- *What does this data really mean?*

- *What assumptions are we making about these numbers?*

- *What implications do these trends have for business strategy or financial planning?*

For instance, when reviewing a financial report, a critical thinker would not just look at whether the numbers add up. They would evaluate whether the financial statements align with the company's overall performance, assess any discrepancies or anomalies, and investigate the underlying causes. This deeper analysis helps identify potential problems before they escalate and suggests areas for improvement.

Critical thinking allows accountants to provide value-added services that go beyond simple data entry. It empowers accountants to act as business advisors, offering insights into financial health, advising on strategy, and identifying potential opportunities for growth or cost-saving.

The Steps Involved in Critical Thinking

While critical thinking is often seen as an innate skill, it is, in fact, a process that can be developed and refined. The following are key steps involved in critical thinking that aspiring accountants can follow to improve their problem-solving abilities:

1. Identifying the Problem

The first step in critical thinking is recognizing that a problem or challenge exists. This involves noticing discrepancies, inconsistencies, or areas where the information does not align with expectations. For accountants, this could mean identifying unusual fluctuations in financial data or noticing errors in financial reporting.

For example, if a financial report shows an unexpected dip in revenue, the accountant's first step is to recognize this anomaly and investigate further to understand why it has occurred. Identifying the problem early on allows for timely intervention and prevents bigger issues from arising down the line.

2. Gathering Information

Once the problem has been identified, the next step is to gather relevant data. Accountants should seek out all available information, including financial reports, supporting documentation, and any additional insights from colleagues or clients.

Effective critical thinking requires not only gathering data but also ensuring that the information is accurate, relevant, and complete. A critical thinker will ask questions like:

- *What data do I need to solve this problem?*

- *Where can I find this information?*

- *Is there any data that might be missing or unreliable?*

For instance, if a company is facing cash flow issues, an accountant would need to look at various sources such as accounts payable, receivable, revenue trends, and operational costs. They would also look for external factors like market trends or economic conditions that might influence the company's cash flow situation.

3. Analyzing the Information

With all the necessary data in hand, the next step is to analyze it. This is where critical thinking truly comes into play. An accountant must evaluate the information, looking for patterns, relationships, or anomalies.

For example, when reviewing financial data, an accountant might ask:

- What does this data tell me about the company's financial health?

- Are there any trends that stand out?

- What can I infer from the financial statements?

During this stage, the accountant must also ensure that they are not making assumptions based on incomplete or biased data. Critical thinkers know that it's essential to question their own assumptions and keep an open mind, always looking for alternative explanations or interpretations.

4. Drawing Conclusions

Based on the analysis, the next step is to draw conclusions. In accounting, this might mean identifying potential risks, opportunities for improvement, or discrepancies that need to be addressed. Critical thinking helps accountants avoid drawing hasty or incorrect conclusions by requiring them to evaluate the evidence carefully.

For example, after analyzing a company's budget, an accountant may conclude that certain expenses are disproportionate to the company's revenue generation. This insight could then prompt further investigation into the cause of the expense or lead to recommendations for cost-saving measures.

5. Making Decisions and Taking Action

Critical thinking is not just about gathering and analyzing information but also about making informed decisions and taking action. Once conclusions have been drawn, the next step is to develop an actionable plan based on the findings.

For accountants, this could involve making recommendations for improving financial processes, suggesting strategic initiatives, or advising on corrective measures. It may also involve working with other departments or leadership to implement these changes and ensure that the necessary steps are taken to improve the company's financial position.

How to Cultivate Critical Thinking

Now that we've explored the role and steps of critical thinking, the next question is: how can young aspiring accountants develop this skill?

Critical thinking is a skill that can be nurtured through practice and intentional learning. Here are several strategies to help you develop critical thinking in accounting:

1. Practice Questioning Assumptions

One of the most effective ways to develop critical thinking is by regularly questioning assumptions. In accounting, this means not taking things at face value and always asking why something is the way it is.

For instance, if you are reviewing a set of financial statements, ask yourself:

- Why are these numbers reported this way?

- What assumptions were made in preparing these statements?

- Could there be another interpretation of the data?

By questioning assumptions, you will gain a deeper understanding of the data and avoid the pitfall of relying on surface-level analysis.

2. Engage in Regular Problem-Solving Exercises

To enhance your critical thinking skills, it's important to engage in exercises that challenge your ability to analyze and solve problems. Participate in case studies, simulations, or real-world accounting problems that require you to apply your knowledge and think critically.

For example, try working through financial analysis exercises, budgeting scenarios, or audits. These exercises will help you hone your ability to analyze complex data and make informed decisions.

3. Develop a Habit of Reflective Thinking

Reflective thinking involves taking the time to look back on your decisions and processes. After completing an accounting task or project, take a moment to reflect on how you approached the problem. Consider whether your conclusions were correct and whether there were any missed opportunities or insights.

By regularly reflecting on your decisions, you will learn from both your successes and mistakes and become better equipped to handle future challenges.

4. Seek Feedback and Collaborate

Critical thinking is enhanced by collaboration. Working with colleagues, mentors, or clients can provide different perspectives on a problem and help you see things you may have missed. Actively seek feedback on your work, ask questions, and be open to other viewpoints.

Collaborating with others will not only help you expand your knowledge but will also encourage you to think more critically by exposing you to new ideas and approaches.

Conclusion

Critical thinking is an indispensable skill for aspiring accountants. It empowers them to analyze complex financial data, evaluate different perspectives, and make informed decisions that drive business success. As the accounting profession continues to evolve, the ability to think critically will set you apart as a trusted advisor and leader in the field.

By practicing the steps of critical thinking, questioning assumptions, engaging in problem-solving exercises, and seeking feedback, you can cultivate this essential skill and position yourself for success in your accounting career.

Certainly! Here's a more detailed, practical example to illustrate the concepts of critical thinking in accounting.

Example 1: Analyzing Financial Statements for Discrepancies

Imagine you're an accountant working for a mid-sized retail company. Your task is to review the company's quarterly financial statements to ensure everything is in order. While going through the report, you notice an unusual spike in the cost of goods sold (COGS), despite the fact that sales have remained relatively steady. A basic review of the numbers would simply show the increase, but a critical thinker goes deeper.

Step 1: Identifying the Problem

At first glance, the increase in COGS stands out as a potential issue, as it doesn't align with the steady sales. A critical thinker immediately sees this as a red flag that warrants further investigation. Instead of accepting the numbers at face value, you identify the need to explore why the costs have increased disproportionally.

Step 2: Gathering Information

To address this issue, you begin gathering more detailed information. You review the company's purchasing records to check if the cost of raw materials or products has increased. You also examine the company's vendor contracts to see if there have been any price hikes from suppliers. Additionally, you check the sales figures of the specific products that make up a large portion of the COGS to see if any sales patterns could explain the higher cost.

Step 3: Analyzing the Information

After gathering the information, you analyze it thoroughly. You notice that while the prices of some raw materials have increased slightly, there is no significant price change that could explain the large spike in COGS. Further investigation reveals that a specific supplier made an error in billing and overcharged the company for several large orders, which contributed to the spike. A critical thinker, at this point, would recognize that the data needs to be cross-referenced and examined from various angles before making any conclusions.

Step 4: Drawing Conclusions

Based on your analysis, you conclude that the spike in COGS was not due to market conditions or operational changes but rather an error from the supplier. The next step is clear: you'll need to contact the supplier to resolve the billing issue, correct the financial statements, and adjust the budget forecast to account for the error.

Step 5: Making Decisions and Taking Action

Your next move would be to document the issue, communicate with the supplier to rectify the overcharges, and update the financial records. You may also need to advise the management team on how to prevent similar issues in the future, perhaps by implementing more stringent checks in the procurement process.

This example illustrates how critical thinking plays a key role in identifying, analyzing, and solving problems in accounting. The accountant doesn't just accept the numbers— they dig deeper to uncover the root cause, draw evidence-based conclusions, and take proactive measures to solve the issue.

Example 2: Assessing a Company's Investment in New Technology

Now, let's say you're working in a corporate accounting department, and your company is considering investing in a new technology system to improve efficiency. The proposal has been presented, but you are tasked with assessing its financial impact.

Step 1: Identifying the Problem

The company's leadership wants to know if the investment will provide a return on investment (ROI) within a reasonable time frame. A critical thinker would understand that simply calculating the ROI based on the initial cost savings isn't enough. Instead, they would also consider other factors, such as long-term costs, the potential for increased productivity, and any risks that could arise from implementing the technology.

Step 2: Gathering Information

You begin gathering data related to the cost of the technology system, including upfront installation fees, ongoing maintenance costs, training expenses for employees, and any other associated costs. Additionally, you gather data on expected efficiency gains, such as reduced labor costs, fewer errors, or faster processing times. You also look at similar companies that have implemented this technology to assess the real-world impact on productivity and profitability.

Step 3: Analyzing the Information

With all this data in hand, a critical thinker would begin to break it down. For example, you analyze the financial impact by creating a financial model that projects costs and benefits over the next few years. You may find that while the upfront investment is high, the long-term benefits—such as increased productivity and reduced errors—could lead to significant cost savings.

However, a deeper analysis could reveal that the technology might require a longer period to integrate fully into the company's existing systems, meaning the immediate financial benefits may not be as large as anticipated in the short term. Additionally, there may be risks related to system downtime during the transition or challenges in employee adaptation.

Step 4: Drawing Conclusions

After carefully analyzing all the information, you conclude that the technology investment is a sound decision in the long term but may require some adjustments to the implementation timeline to ensure smoother integration. You also determine that the company should budget for potential unforeseen expenses in the first year due to the learning curve and system adjustments.

Step 5: Making Decisions and Taking Action

As a critical thinker, you prepare a report for the leadership team, presenting a balanced view of the investment. You recommend proceeding with the purchase but suggest a phased rollout and additional employee training to mitigate any risks. You also advise on setting up a monitoring system to track the ROI over time to ensure the investment delivers the expected results.

In this case, critical thinking helped you assess not just the immediate financial figures but the broader picture, factoring in both risks and long-term benefits. You made a well-rounded decision based on evidence, rather than simply taking the proposal at face value.

Example 3: Identifying Fraudulent Activity in Financial Reporting

Let's consider an example of an accountant working in internal auditing. You are reviewing the company's financial reports when you notice several inconsistencies in the reported revenue, such as sudden, unexplained spikes in the final quarter of the year.

Step 1: Identifying the Problem

Your initial reaction is to identify the inconsistency and flag it for further investigation. A critical thinker in this situation would be particularly diligent, considering the possibility of fraudulent activity or errors in the reporting process.

Step 2: Gathering Information

To investigate the irregularities, you gather data on the company's revenue sources, including customer contracts, sales invoices, and payment records. You also review the timing of the transactions, looking for any that might seem out of place.

Step 3: Analyzing the Information

A critical thinker would not just look at the numbers but also consider the context in which they were reported. You find that the suspicious spikes in revenue are associated with large, one-time transactions that were recorded at the end of the fiscal year. These transactions, while legitimate, were recognized in a way that artificially inflated revenue for the quarter.

Step 4: Drawing Conclusions

Based on your analysis, you conclude that the accounting practice, while not fraudulent, violated standard revenue recognition practices. This was done to meet revenue targets or manipulate financial results for that particular period.

Step 5: Making Decisions and Taking Action

You report the issue to senior management and suggest a revision of the financial reports. You recommend implementing stricter guidelines for revenue recognition to prevent this from happening in the future and to ensure the company remains compliant with accounting standards.

This example demonstrates how critical thinking can help identify not just errors but potential ethical issues or violations. Through careful investigation, you're able to draw conclusions and make recommendations that protect the integrity of the financial reporting process.

These examples highlight how critical thinking is applied in various real-world accounting situations. By analyzing problems from multiple angles, questioning assumptions, and considering both immediate and long-term impacts, accountants can make informed, thoughtful decisions that drive business success and ensure financial integrity.

2.2.3 Attention to Detail

Introduction

In the accounting profession, attention to detail is more than a desirable trait—it's an absolute necessity. Accountants handle complex financial data and must ensure accuracy at every level. Even a small mistake, such as a misplaced decimal or an overlooked transaction, can have significant repercussions, leading to financial discrepancies, compliance issues, or even regulatory penalties. Accountants act as the final checkpoint for financial integrity, making attention to detail essential not just for individual success but for the entire organization's stability and credibility.

This section explores why attention to detail is crucial in accounting, how it supports various aspects of the profession, and actionable strategies for developing and refining this skill.

The Importance of Attention to Detail in Accounting

Attention to detail is essential in accounting for several key reasons:

1. Accuracy in Financial Reporting

 - One of the primary responsibilities of an accountant is to produce financial statements and reports with complete accuracy. These documents inform decision-making for stakeholders, so accuracy is paramount.

 - Errors in financial reporting can lead to misunderstandings of a company's financial health, influencing everything from investment decisions to company reputation. When preparing financial reports, accountants need to meticulously check calculations, cross-reference figures, and ensure that every entry aligns with accounting standards.

2. Compliance with Regulations and Standards

 - Accountants work within a framework of rules and regulations, such as the Generally Accepted Accounting Principles (GAAP) or International Financial Reporting Standards (IFRS). Detailed attention to these guidelines is essential, as non-compliance can result in fines, legal consequences, or loss of business credibility.

 - For example, if an accountant incorrectly categorizes expenses or fails to follow specific guidelines for revenue recognition, the company may face regulatory scrutiny or penalties. By paying close attention to regulatory details, accountants ensure compliance and uphold the company's financial reputation.

3. Effective Budgeting and Forecasting

 - When creating budgets or forecasts, accountants rely on accurate data to guide business planning. Attention to detail helps prevent inaccurate estimates that could impact resource allocation and strategic planning.

 - For example, if an accountant overlooks a cost or miscalculates a trend, it could lead to underfunding critical projects or overestimating available resources. In this way, attention to detail is not just about accuracy; it's about supporting wise and well-informed decisions for the company's future.

Key Aspects of Developing Attention to Detail

To excel in attention to detail, accountants must develop habits and mindsets that support meticulous work. Here are some key areas to focus on:

1. Double-Checking Work

- Creating a habit of double-checking is invaluable for accountants. After completing a task, accountants should review their work to catch any errors before final submission.

- Techniques like using checklists or breaking down tasks into smaller steps help in cross-verifying information. Many professionals also benefit from peer review systems, where a colleague reviews their work to provide an additional layer of scrutiny.

2. Focusing on Data Entry and Analysis

- Accountants deal with vast amounts of data, and even a single mistake in data entry can lead to errors across entire reports. By establishing a method of double-checking entries and periodically verifying totals, accountants can ensure data reliability.

- A practical tip is to break down data entry tasks and take short breaks to avoid fatigue, which can often lead to oversight. Verifying entries against source documents, such as bank statements or invoices, is also an effective way to catch errors early.

3. Learning to Catch Patterns and Inconsistencies

- An essential part of attention to detail is noticing patterns or inconsistencies that may indicate errors or areas that need further investigation. For example, if a particular account shows an unusual increase in expenses, it might be worth revisiting the transactions to confirm accuracy.

- Seasoned accountants develop an intuitive sense for when something doesn't "look right." This ability comes from experience and involves developing a familiarity with financial patterns. Accounting software can assist here by highlighting unusual entries, but a trained eye is still crucial.

4. Using Digital Tools to Enhance Accuracy

- Many accounting software programs, such as QuickBooks, SAP, and others, offer error-checking features that alert users to potential issues in their entries. Accountants should learn to use these tools effectively but also remember that technology is a supplement, not a substitute, for their own attention to detail.

- While digital tools can enhance accuracy, accountants must still apply judgment and cross-verify outputs, especially when working with complex or customized data sets.

Practical Strategies for Enhancing Attention to Detail

Improving attention to detail requires a combination of practice, habits, and environmental adjustments. Here are some practical strategies:

1. Daily Practice of Accuracy-Enhancing Habits

- Adopting a mindset of "measure twice, cut once" is useful in accounting. This principle encourages double-checking every calculation, entry, and report.

- Exercises such as proofreading, crosswords, or even logic puzzles can improve concentration and focus over time. The more an accountant practices these skills, the more they will integrate attention to detail into their daily workflow.

2. Time Management and Task Organization

- Effective time management supports attention to detail by reducing the urge to rush through tasks. Accountants who organize their tasks and set aside adequate time for each one tend to work more accurately.

- Breaking tasks into smaller steps, with time allocated for reviewing each part, is a helpful strategy. For example, rather than rushing through an entire financial statement, an accountant could focus on specific sections, double-check them, and then compile the report as a whole.

3. Active Listening and Note-Taking

- Accountants often work on projects based on instructions from supervisors or clients. Active listening during these interactions ensures they understand all details and can clarify anything that seems unclear.

- Taking thorough notes during meetings also reduces the risk of forgetting crucial details and allows for better documentation, which accountants can refer to when needed.

Common Pitfalls and How to Avoid Them

Even the most detail-oriented accountants can encounter challenges. Here are common pitfalls and how to overcome them:

1. Overlooking Minor Details

- In accounting, even the smallest details matter. Something as minor as a decimal point or a misclassified expense can alter the accuracy of a report. One way to prevent this is by developing checklists that include common errors to look out for, such as double-checking all numbers for correct decimal placement or ensuring that entries match documentation.

- Accountants should also learn to prioritize critical details in their reviews. For instance, while all figures are important, items such as revenue recognition and major expenses should be given extra scrutiny.

2. Balancing Speed with Accuracy

- The fast-paced nature of some accounting roles can lead to a tendency to rush, especially during busy periods like tax season or year-end reporting. However, rushing increases the likelihood of errors.

- Emphasizing accuracy over speed, especially during review stages, is essential. Accountants can improve their workflow efficiency by automating routine calculations and setting up templates, which reduces the need to start from scratch on repetitive tasks.

Conclusion

Attention to detail is a foundational skill for anyone aspiring to succeed in accounting. It's a skill that requires ongoing practice, constant vigilance, and a commitment to accuracy. Accountants who master this skill can protect their organization's financial integrity, avoid costly errors, and establish themselves as reliable professionals in the field.

Ultimately, attention to detail is about more than catching mistakes—it's about delivering quality work that others can trust. Whether through careful review practices, the use of digital tools, or simply by cultivating good habits, attention to detail sets successful accountants apart and positions them for long-term career growth.

2.3 Developing a Growth Mindset

In today's fast-paced and ever-evolving work environment, the ability to learn, adapt, and grow is as important as technical knowledge. This is especially true in fields like accounting, where technology and regulations frequently shift, and adaptability is key. Developing a growth mindset can help you build resilience, pursue continuous improvement, and ultimately enhance your career in accounting. But what exactly is a growth mindset, and how can it impact your journey?

Understanding a Growth Mindset

The concept of a growth mindset was introduced by psychologist Carol Dweck and centers around the belief that skills and abilities can be developed through effort, learning, and persistence. People with a growth mindset embrace challenges, learn from feedback, and view setbacks as opportunities to improve. In contrast, a fixed mindset is the belief that abilities are static and unchangeable. Those with a fixed mindset may avoid challenges, feel discouraged by failure, and give up easily when faced with difficulties.

As a young professional entering accounting, adopting a growth mindset is invaluable. The field requires ongoing learning—whether it's mastering new accounting software, keeping up with changes in tax law, or developing leadership skills. Viewing each challenge as a stepping stone for growth will empower you to continually push beyond your current limits and keep up with industry demands.

The Importance of a Growth Mindset in Accounting

Accountants face a variety of unique challenges, from understanding complex regulations to ensuring accuracy in financial reporting. Adopting a growth mindset enables you to:

1. Embrace Continuous Learning: Accounting standards and tax regulations frequently change, and new technology reshapes the way accountants work. A growth mindset encourages you to stay curious and continuously seek knowledge, positioning yourself as a lifelong learner.

2. Adapt to Technology: As technology advances, more tasks are being automated. Accountants now have to understand and use software for data analysis, financial modeling, and auditing. A growth mindset helps you adapt to these tools without fear, turning technology into an advantage rather than a barrier.

3. Turn Mistakes into Learning Opportunities: In accounting, accuracy is critical, but mistakes happen, especially when you're new. Instead of being discouraged, a growth mindset allows you to view mistakes as a learning process, identifying where things went wrong and improving in the future.

4. Enhance Problem-Solving Abilities: Accountants frequently solve problems for clients, such as optimizing tax strategies or analyzing financial data to support decision-making. Embracing challenges with a growth-oriented approach will make you a more creative, adaptable, and effective problem-solver.

5. Thrive Under Pressure: Accounting can be demanding, with tight deadlines, complex tasks, and sometimes high stakes. A growth mindset promotes resilience, enabling you to see stressful situations as opportunities to develop stress-management and time-management skills.

Strategies to Cultivate a Growth Mindset

To foster a growth mindset, here are several strategies you can incorporate into your daily life and career:

1. Embrace Challenges

In your accounting journey, you'll encounter tasks that seem daunting at first—whether it's learning advanced Excel functions, preparing tax filings, or understanding regulatory compliance. Instead of avoiding these challenges, view them as opportunities to expand your skillset. For instance, if you find certain concepts in financial reporting difficult, approach them as puzzles to solve. Seek resources, ask for help, and remember that the more you practice, the easier it will become.

2. Reframe Failure as Feedback

Failure is a common fear, especially in a profession where precision is key. However, every setback is a valuable teacher. Suppose you make an error in financial analysis or overlook a detail in an audit. Reflect on the experience: What caused the error? How can you prevent it in the future? This reflective process can help you improve and prevent similar mistakes.

3. Set Incremental Goals

Setting achievable, incremental goals is a great way to see consistent progress. For example, if you're learning a new accounting software or studying for a certification, set daily or weekly goals. Breaking down big tasks into smaller, manageable goals not only makes the process less overwhelming but also gives you a sense of achievement with each milestone reached.

4. Seek Constructive Feedback

Feedback is essential for growth, yet it can be hard to accept, especially if it's critical. To truly benefit from feedback, approach it with an open mind and an eagerness to learn. If a supervisor points out areas for improvement, see this as a way to enhance your skills. Ask for clarification, take notes, and follow up on their suggestions. Over time, this feedback loop will lead to significant improvement.

5. Surround Yourself with a Growth-Minded Community

The people around you can have a significant impact on your mindset. Seek out mentors, colleagues, and peers who are passionate about learning and willing to embrace challenges. Whether it's a study group for CPA exams or a team in the workplace, being in a supportive environment fosters a culture of growth. Discuss challenges, share resources, and learn from each other's experiences.

6. Commit to Lifelong Learning

Accounting isn't a field where learning ends after graduation. Pursue additional certifications, attend workshops, or enroll in online courses related to new accounting software, tax regulations, or financial analysis techniques. Regularly dedicating time to learning new skills will not only make you a better accountant but also keep your career future-proof in a constantly evolving industry.

Practicing a Growth Mindset in Everyday Accounting Work

Building a growth mindset is an ongoing process, one that requires daily effort and reflection. Here's how you can apply it to your everyday tasks:

- *Reflect on Your Progress:* Set aside time each week to reflect on your growth. What new skills did you acquire? What challenges did you face, and how did you overcome them? This practice of self-reflection reinforces your growth and helps you stay motivated.

- *Challenge Yourself with New Tasks:* Volunteer for projects that might be out of your comfort zone. If you've never worked on a tax audit, for example, ask if you can shadow or assist someone with experience. Expanding your experience beyond your immediate responsibilities can accelerate your learning.

- *Celebrate Small Wins:* Recognize and celebrate even minor progress. If you complete a challenging task or master a new concept, take a moment to acknowledge your effort. Small successes build confidence and make bigger challenges feel more achievable.

Stories of Growth in Accounting

To illustrate the power of a growth mindset, here are some real-life scenarios from successful accountants who have embraced this approach:

1. Sarah's Story: Starting out, Sarah found tax accounting overwhelming and made a mistake in a client's tax form. Instead of being discouraged, she reviewed her errors and sought guidance from her manager. By doing so, she not only learned from her mistakes but also built a stronger foundation in tax regulations.

2. Michael's Journey: Michael, a young staff accountant, felt intimidated by new accounting software. He proactively took online courses and experimented with features outside of work. His effort paid off when he became the go-to person for software support, enhancing his confidence and value within the team.

The Long-Term Impact of a Growth Mindset on Your Career

Developing a growth mindset is not just about overcoming short-term challenges—it shapes your entire career. Accountants with a growth mindset are more likely to:

- *Progress Faster in Their Careers:* Growth-minded individuals are often seen as proactive and adaptable, which can lead to quicker promotions and more opportunities.

- *Remain Resilient Amid Industry Changes:* As automation, artificial intelligence, and blockchain transform accounting, those with a growth mindset will stay relevant by adapting to these advancements.

- *Achieve Personal Fulfillment:* A growth mindset allows you to view your career as a journey. Rather than just focusing on immediate successes, you find fulfillment in the process of learning and growing over time.

Conclusion

A growth mindset will be your greatest ally in navigating a successful accounting career. It empowers you to tackle challenges, adapt to industry changes, and embrace lifelong learning. As you embark on your journey, remember that growth doesn't happen overnight—it's a continuous process that will shape both your personal and professional life. Embrace it, nurture it, and watch as it opens doors to a fulfilling and resilient career in accounting.

CHAPTER III
Education and Certification Paths

3.1 High School Preparation

3.1.1 Recommended Courses

Introduction

High school is an excellent time to lay the groundwork for a future in accounting. The courses you choose now will shape your skills in mathematics, critical thinking, communication, and financial awareness. A solid foundation in specific subjects will not only prepare you for college-level accounting courses but also help you develop essential qualities for the profession. In this section, we'll explore key high school subjects that are especially beneficial for aspiring accountants.

Core Courses for Aspiring Accountants

1. Mathematics

 - Importance in Accounting: Mathematics is central to accounting, as the profession revolves around numbers, calculations, and financial analysis. A strong grasp of mathematics is essential for understanding financial statements, solving complex problems, and making data-driven decisions.

 - Courses to Consider: Algebra, Geometry, and Statistics are especially relevant. Advanced classes like Pre-Calculus and Calculus can provide an extra edge, as they cover more complex concepts that you may encounter in business mathematics or financial modeling.

- Skills Developed: Studying math helps develop logical reasoning, problem-solving skills, and analytical thinking—all critical traits for an accountant.

2. Economics

- Importance in Accounting: Economics gives students insight into how markets work, the impact of government policies, and the basics of supply and demand. Accountants need to understand these economic principles to analyze how they affect businesses and to advise clients accordingly.

- Courses to Consider: Look for courses like Microeconomics and Macroeconomics if they're available. These will provide a solid foundation in understanding the broader economic factors that influence business decisions.

- Skills Developed: Economics courses teach students to evaluate data, understand market trends, and think strategically—all of which are essential for financial analysis and decision-making in accounting.

3. Business Studies (if available)

- Importance in Accounting: High school business courses introduce students to the basic concepts of finance, marketing, and management, giving a well-rounded understanding of how businesses operate. This is invaluable for anyone considering a career in accounting.

- Courses to Consider: Some schools offer introductory courses in Business or Finance, which can be extremely beneficial for understanding fundamental business concepts.

- Skills Developed: Business courses improve skills in financial literacy, decision-making, and strategic thinking, which will help you grasp the essentials of accounting.

4. Computer Science and Information Technology

- Importance in Accounting: Technology plays a massive role in modern accounting. Familiarity with basic software applications and coding can be a huge asset, especially as accountants are often tasked with using accounting software and managing digital data.

- Courses to Consider: If possible, take courses in basic computer applications (like Microsoft Excel), which are essential in accounting. A course in programming or data management is also useful for those interested in specialized fields like data analytics or forensic accounting.

- Skills Developed: Computer science courses improve problem-solving abilities, data literacy, and software skills, all of which are increasingly valuable in accounting as technology becomes more integral to the profession.

5. English and Communication

- Importance in Accounting: Accountants must communicate effectively with clients, colleagues, and stakeholders. This involves writing clear reports, presenting findings, and explaining complex information in a way that others can understand.

- Courses to Consider: English Literature, Composition, or Speech and Debate can be incredibly helpful. Emphasize classes that require writing, research, and critical analysis, as these skills will help in drafting reports and conducting research.

- Skills Developed: Communication courses build written and verbal skills, teaching students to present ideas logically and clearly—qualities crucial for a successful career in accounting.

Elective Courses Beneficial for Accounting

1. Financial Literacy

- Importance in Accounting: Financial literacy courses introduce students to personal finance, budgeting, and basic financial principles. These are foundational skills that every accountant needs.

- Courses to Consider: Courses labeled as "Personal Finance" or "Financial Literacy" are often designed to help students understand budgeting, saving, and managing money.

- Skills Developed: These courses foster budgeting skills, financial awareness, and decision-making abilities, which are essential for handling both personal and business finances.

2. Psychology and Sociology

- Importance in Accounting: Psychology and sociology offer insights into human behavior, decision-making, and social dynamics. Understanding these aspects can be valuable for accountants, especially in roles that involve auditing, consulting, or client interaction.

- Courses to Consider: Basic courses in Psychology or Sociology can help students develop a broader understanding of human behavior, which is beneficial in understanding consumer behavior and decision-making.

- Skills Developed: These courses enhance interpersonal skills, empathy, and an understanding of group dynamics—qualities useful in teamwork and client-facing roles.

3. Advanced Placement (AP) or International Baccalaureate (IB) Courses

- Importance in Accounting: AP and IB courses provide college-level content and challenge students to think critically, manage complex tasks, and engage deeply with their studies.

- Courses to Consider: If available, AP Economics, AP Statistics, AP Calculus, and AP English are highly recommended. These courses are rigorous and can prepare students for the academic demands of college accounting programs.

- Skills Developed: AP and IB courses cultivate high-level thinking, academic discipline, and a strong work ethic, which are invaluable for anyone pursuing accounting.

Extracurricular Activities to Support Accounting Skills

While not courses, extracurricular activities can complement your academic studies and build additional skills relevant to accounting. Here are some suggested activities:

- Math Club or Economics Club: Involvement in a Math or Economics club reinforces quantitative and analytical skills.

- Business or Entrepreneurship Programs: These programs provide hands-on experience in business concepts, often allowing you to apply accounting principles.

- Volunteer Positions with Financial Tasks: Volunteering in roles that involve budgeting or managing finances can provide practical experience and a taste of real-world accounting tasks.

Conclusion

Preparing for an accounting career starts with a strategic selection of high school courses. By focusing on subjects like mathematics, economics, business, computer science, and communication, students will gain a strong academic foundation that aligns with the demands of accounting. These recommended courses and elective options help develop the analytical, problem-solving, and communication skills that accountants use daily. Additionally, participating in relevant extracurricular activities can further enhance the knowledge and abilities needed for a future in this field. As you plan your course selections, remember that each of these subjects will help you approach accounting with a well-rounded perspective and a readiness to succeed.

3.1.2 Extracurricular Activities

As you embark on the journey to becoming an accountant, it's essential to understand that extracurricular activities are more than just a way to fill your free time—they are a valuable part of your overall educational experience. While your high school classes lay the foundation for your academic knowledge, extracurricular activities provide you with the opportunity to develop the skills that will set you apart in the professional world.

For aspiring accountants, extracurricular activities can help sharpen key soft skills like leadership, communication, and teamwork, while also providing you with hands-on experience in real-world financial situations. In fact, many employers look at a candidate's involvement in extracurriculars to gauge their commitment, organizational abilities, and personal interests. So, how can you leverage extracurricular activities to prepare for a career in accounting? Let's dive into some of the most beneficial activities for young people aiming for a career in accounting.

Why Extracurricular Activities Matter for Aspiring Accountants

Extracurricular activities contribute to your personal and professional growth in ways that classroom learning cannot always achieve. They complement the technical knowledge you gain through your studies by developing your soft skills—such as time management, problem-solving, and the ability to work collaboratively with others. These are qualities that are highly valued in accounting professionals, who often work with diverse teams, manage multiple tasks simultaneously, and communicate complex financial data to clients and colleagues.

Engaging in extracurriculars also helps you develop a sense of responsibility and discipline, as you are required to balance academic work with other commitments. In doing so, you learn how to prioritize tasks, manage deadlines, and stay organized— critical skills for any accountant. Beyond the technical side of accounting, these activities help you become a well-rounded individual, better prepared for the diverse challenges of the profession.

Top Extracurricular Activities for Aspiring Accountants

Several types of extracurricular activities are particularly beneficial for those interested in accounting. Let's take a closer look at some of them:

1. Business and Finance Clubs

Business-related clubs, such as Future Business Leaders of America (FBLA) or DECA, provide students with a direct link to the world of finance and accounting. These clubs often organize competitions that require participants to develop business plans, manage budgets, or present financial proposals. By taking part in such competitions, students gain valuable experience in solving real-world financial problems, often using accounting principles.

Joining a business club can also expose you to networking opportunities with peers, mentors, and professionals in the field, which could help you down the road when seeking internships or employment. Furthermore, many of these organizations offer opportunities to learn about corporate accounting, financial analysis, and other related topics—critical for any aspiring accountant.

2. Math and Economics Clubs

A strong foundation in math is essential for accounting. Participating in math or economics clubs allows you to enhance your analytical skills, which are crucial for problem-solving in accounting. These clubs often involve activities that require mathematical reasoning, such as creating financial models, solving complex algebraic problems, or analyzing economic data.

Additionally, participating in these clubs can help you strengthen your understanding of macroeconomics and microeconomics, which will be beneficial when dealing with financial statements, forecasts, and economic trends in your accounting career. Your involvement in such clubs may also lead to opportunities to compete in math or economics competitions, helping to further develop your technical skills and your ability to work under pressure.

3. Student Government and Leadership Roles

While accounting is often thought of as a technical profession, strong leadership and organizational skills are just as important. Student government provides an excellent platform for you to develop these qualities. Whether you are managing budgets, organizing events, or representing the student body, you'll learn firsthand the importance of financial management, decision-making, and accountability.

Taking on leadership roles in student government or any other school organization allows you to manage and allocate resources, set priorities, and collaborate with others to achieve goals—all of which are crucial skills in the accounting profession. In fact, many accountants eventually go on to hold leadership positions in their firms, so gaining leadership experience early on can set you on the right path.

4. Volunteering and Community Service

Volunteering is another excellent way to gain practical experience, develop personal skills, and give back to your community. Many volunteer organizations, particularly nonprofits, require assistance with financial planning, budgeting, or fundraising. Volunteering in such settings offers you the chance to gain hands-on experience in managing money, tracking expenses, and understanding how organizations operate within financial constraints.

Beyond financial skills, volunteering also helps you develop a sense of social responsibility, which is important for any professional in today's business world. Ethical considerations play a significant role in accounting, and by volunteering, you can gain insight into how businesses, government agencies, and nonprofits prioritize transparency, responsibility, and accountability in their financial practices.

5. Internships or Part-Time Jobs Related to Finance

Internships and part-time jobs provide the most direct way to gain real-world experience in accounting. Many businesses, from local firms to large corporations, offer opportunities for high school students to work in administrative roles that involve basic accounting tasks such as bookkeeping, invoicing, or assisting with tax preparation. These jobs can give you a taste of the responsibilities you'll face as a full-time accountant and help you build a professional network.

Even if you're not able to find an accounting-specific internship, any job that involves managing money or working with customers can help you develop transferable skills. For example, working as a cashier or a bank teller can help you learn how to handle financial transactions, understand cash flow, and practice accuracy and attention to detail—skills that are crucial in the accounting profession.

6. School Newspaper or Yearbook Committees

While it may not seem like an obvious choice for aspiring accountants, participating in school newspaper or yearbook committees can teach you valuable organizational and financial skills. These projects often have budgets to manage, advertising sales to coordinate, and costs to balance. By contributing to the financial side of these publications, you will gain experience in tracking expenses, balancing budgets, and working with sponsors—all of which are key components of accounting work.

In addition, being part of a creative team helps you hone your teamwork and communication skills, which are just as important as technical skills when it comes to working in accounting. Accountants often need to present their findings clearly and collaborate with various departments, and these experiences can prepare you for that.

How to Choose the Right Extracurriculars for Your Goals

When selecting extracurricular activities, it's important to consider both your personal interests and your career goals. If you enjoy math and finance, a business or economics club might be the best fit for you. If you're drawn to leadership and management, student government could be a great way to develop those skills. The key is to find activities that challenge you, align with your interests, and allow you to build skills that will benefit your future career in accounting.

At the same time, it's important not to overcommit yourself. Balancing extracurriculars with your academic work is essential, so be sure to choose activities that you're passionate about and can realistically commit to. Quality is more important than quantity, and employers will appreciate the depth of your involvement in a few key activities rather than superficial participation in many.

Making the Most of Your Extracurricular Experience

Once you've selected your extracurricular activities, it's essential to make the most of them. Take on leadership roles whenever possible. Being a president, treasurer, or committee head can demonstrate your ability to manage projects and lead teams—skills that are highly valued in the accounting profession.

Networking is also key. Attend meetings, seek advice from mentors, and engage with others who share your interests. You never know when a connection made in a school club or community service activity might lead to an internship, job shadowing, or even a full-time job in the future.

Finally, make sure to document your extracurricular achievements. Keep track of your roles, responsibilities, and any accomplishments or recognition you receive. When it comes time to apply for college or internships, having a well-organized list of your extracurricular activities will help set you apart from other candidates.

Extracurricular activities are an integral part of your high school preparation for a career in accounting. They help you develop both technical and soft skills, giving you a competitive edge as you move forward in your academic and professional journey. Whether you're managing budgets for a school event, volunteering for a nonprofit, or leading a business club, these activities will shape the qualities that make you a strong candidate for any accounting role.

3.2 College and University Degrees

3.2.1 Bachelor's in Accounting

When it comes to pursuing a career in accounting, obtaining a solid educational foundation is essential. One of the most common and direct paths for aspiring accountants is earning a Bachelor's degree in Accounting. This degree provides students with the necessary technical knowledge, practical skills, and professional expertise to thrive in various accounting roles.

The Importance of a Bachelor's Degree in Accounting

A Bachelor's degree in Accounting is often the starting point for individuals pursuing a career in the accounting field. It offers students a deep dive into the principles of accounting, financial management, taxation, and auditing. In addition to the academic rigor, the degree program typically includes opportunities for hands-on experience through internships, projects, and case studies, which are invaluable for gaining real-world exposure.

This degree equips students with the ability to analyze financial statements, perform audits, and manage financial records in compliance with legal and regulatory frameworks. Furthermore, it helps develop strong problem-solving and critical-thinking skills—essential qualities for accountants. Many employers in the accounting industry consider a Bachelor's in Accounting a fundamental requirement for entry-level positions, especially in public accounting firms, corporate accounting departments, and government organizations.

Core Courses in a Bachelor's in Accounting Program

A Bachelor's degree in Accounting usually spans four years of study and is structured around both general education courses and accounting-specific courses. The general education courses typically include English, mathematics, economics, and basic business principles, while the accounting-specific courses delve into more specialized topics. Below are some core courses that are commonly offered in a Bachelor's in Accounting program:

1. Introduction to Accounting

This introductory course covers the fundamental concepts of accounting, including the basic principles, procedures, and techniques used to record, classify, and summarize financial transactions. Students learn the essentials of preparing and interpreting financial statements.

2. Financial Accounting

This course teaches students how to prepare and analyze financial statements, such as the income statement, balance sheet, and cash flow statement. Financial accounting focuses on ensuring that financial reports adhere to Generally Accepted Accounting Principles (GAAP) or International Financial Reporting Standards (IFRS).

3. Managerial Accounting

Unlike financial accounting, which focuses on external reporting, managerial accounting is concerned with providing information for internal decision-making. Students learn how to analyze costs, budget effectively, and assess financial performance to guide management decisions.

4. Intermediate Accounting

Intermediate accounting courses offer a deeper exploration of accounting principles and practices. Students focus on more complex topics, such as the recognition of revenue, lease accounting, and accounting for pensions. The course also provides a comprehensive understanding of accounting regulations and standards.

5. Cost Accounting

In this course, students learn about the methods used to track, allocate, and manage the costs of goods and services. Cost accounting helps businesses determine how much it costs to produce a product or deliver a service, which is critical for pricing strategies and budgeting.

6. Auditing

The auditing course introduces students to the process of evaluating financial statements to ensure their accuracy and compliance with accounting standards. Students also learn about the role of external auditors in reviewing financial records and ensuring transparency and trustworthiness.

7. Tax Accounting

This course focuses on the preparation and planning of taxes for individuals and businesses. Students explore tax laws, regulations, and procedures for preparing tax returns, along with strategies for minimizing tax liabilities and ensuring compliance with tax authorities.

8. Accounting Information Systems

In today's digital age, knowledge of accounting information systems is essential. This course teaches students how to use software and technological tools to record, process, and analyze financial data efficiently and securely. Students learn about the integration of accounting processes with technology and how to protect financial information.

9. Ethics in Accounting

Ethics play a crucial role in accounting, and this course helps students understand the ethical considerations that accountants face in their professional work. Topics include integrity, objectivity, confidentiality, and compliance with regulatory standards. Students learn about the ethical challenges accountants may encounter and how to navigate them.

The Benefits of Earning a Bachelor's in Accounting

1. Access to Career Opportunities

With a Bachelor's in Accounting, graduates can apply for a wide variety of entry-level accounting positions. Many employers require a degree in accounting as a basic qualification for roles such as junior accountant, tax preparer, auditor, or financial analyst. Having a recognized degree from a reputable university also gives students a competitive edge in the job market.

2. Foundation for Advanced Certifications

A Bachelor's in Accounting lays the groundwork for earning advanced certifications that are essential for career progression. For instance, students who complete their Bachelor's degree can pursue certifications like Certified Public Accountant (CPA) or Certified Management Accountant (CMA), which enhance career prospects and earning potential.

3. Skills Development

A key advantage of the Bachelor's in Accounting program is the development of critical technical and soft skills. In addition to learning accounting techniques, students sharpen their analytical thinking, attention to detail, communication, and problem-solving skills—

qualities that are essential in the accounting field. These skills are highly transferable and sought after in various industries.

4. Preparation for Graduate Studies

For those who wish to continue their education, a Bachelor's in Accounting can serve as the foundation for pursuing graduate studies, such as a Master's in Accounting, Finance, or Business Administration. Graduate studies open up opportunities for specialized roles and leadership positions in the accounting field.

5. Job Security and Stability

Accounting is often regarded as a stable and recession-resistant profession. Graduates with a Bachelor's in Accounting are well-positioned for job security, as businesses and governments always need skilled accountants to handle their financial records, taxes, and compliance. Furthermore, accounting professionals are in demand globally, offering flexibility to work in various geographic locations.

Choosing the Right College or University for a Bachelor's in Accounting

When selecting a college or university for a Bachelor's in Accounting, several factors should be considered:

1. Accreditation

Ensure that the institution offering the program is accredited by a recognized accrediting body. Accreditation guarantees that the degree program meets established standards of quality and rigor. In the United States, the Association to Advance Collegiate Schools of Business (AACSB) accreditation is highly regarded for accounting programs.

2. Reputation and Faculty Expertise

Research the reputation of the university's accounting department and the qualifications of its faculty members. A strong reputation can enhance the value of your degree and provide better networking and internship opportunities.

3. Internship Opportunities

Look for programs that offer internships or cooperative education (co-op) opportunities. Internships allow students to gain practical experience, apply what they've learned in the classroom, and build a professional network.

4. Support Services

Consider institutions that offer academic advising, career counseling, and mentorship programs. These services help students stay on track and provide guidance as they prepare for a career in accounting.

5. Cost and Financial Aid

Evaluate the cost of tuition and available financial aid options, including scholarships, grants, and student loans. While the cost of obtaining a degree is an important consideration, many accounting students find that the potential earnings from an accounting career make the investment worthwhile in the long run.

The Job Market for Accounting Graduates

The job market for accounting graduates is generally strong, with the demand for skilled professionals continuing to grow across various sectors. Accounting graduates can find work in a variety of industries, including public accounting, corporate accounting, government, nonprofit organizations, and financial services. The U.S. Bureau of Labor Statistics (BLS) reports that the median annual wage for accountants and auditors is competitive, and the profession is expected to grow in the coming years.

The flexibility of an accounting degree is one of its greatest advantages. Graduates can choose to work in large corporations, small businesses, public accounting firms, or even start their own accounting practices. Furthermore, accountants have the opportunity to specialize in areas such as tax accounting, forensic accounting, auditing, or management accounting, allowing for continued growth and advancement in their careers.

Conclusion

A Bachelor's in Accounting serves as an essential stepping stone for those pursuing a career in the accounting field. It provides students with a strong technical foundation, essential skills, and opportunities for professional growth. Whether you are interested in working for a large accounting firm, a corporation, or a government agency, this degree equips you with the tools necessary to succeed. By investing in your education and completing a Bachelor's in Accounting, you are setting the stage for a rewarding and secure career in one of the most vital industries in the business world.

3.2.2 Alternative Degrees and Double Majors

When it comes to pursuing a career in accounting, a traditional accounting degree is undoubtedly the most common route. However, the world of business and finance is rapidly evolving, and the increasing complexity of global markets, technology, and regulations is creating new opportunities for accounting professionals with diverse academic backgrounds. Alternative degrees and double majors are becoming increasingly popular among students looking to differentiate themselves in the competitive accounting field.

In this section, we will explore some of the alternative degrees that can serve as strong foundations for a career in accounting, as well as the advantages and challenges of pursuing a double major. Both of these options provide unique ways to enhance your skill set, broaden your career prospects, and open doors to specialized accounting roles that may not be accessible with a single, traditional degree.

1. Alternative Degrees for Aspiring Accountants

While a Bachelor's degree in Accounting is the most direct path into the profession, there are other degrees that can also provide a solid foundation for a career in accounting. These degrees offer skills and knowledge that are highly valued in the accounting industry and can be particularly beneficial if you are interested in pursuing specific niches, such as forensic accounting, financial analysis, or management accounting. Let's look at a few alternative degrees that can help you launch a successful career in accounting.

a) Business Administration (BBA or MBA)

A Bachelor of Business Administration (BBA) or a Master of Business Administration (MBA) with a concentration in accounting can be an excellent alternative for students interested in combining accounting with broader business skills. A BBA in Business Administration typically covers key areas of business such as management, marketing, operations, economics, and finance, alongside accounting courses. This well-rounded education allows graduates to approach accounting from a strategic business perspective, which is especially valuable for those aspiring to become financial managers, CFOs, or entrepreneurs.

An MBA with an accounting focus can be particularly useful for individuals who want to pursue advanced roles in accounting, management, or consulting. The MBA program typically provides leadership training, deep dives into financial strategy, and an opportunity to specialize in a particular area of accounting, such as tax or financial reporting. This is an ideal route for those who are not only looking to become skilled accountants but also want to rise to the top levels of business management.

b) Finance Degrees

For those interested in working in investment banking, financial planning, or corporate finance, a degree in Finance can also serve as an excellent foundation for a career in accounting. A finance degree typically covers a wide range of topics, including financial markets, investments, corporate finance, and risk management. These subjects align closely with accounting, as both disciplines deal with managing and analyzing financial data, albeit from different perspectives.

While accounting focuses on financial reporting, tax compliance, and auditing, finance emphasizes maximizing value and profitability. If you combine a finance degree with accounting knowledge, you can specialize in areas like financial analysis, financial management, or even forensic accounting, which investigates financial discrepancies and fraud. For students looking to enter financial roles that require both strategic financial thinking and accounting expertise, a finance degree is an excellent option.

c) Economics Degrees

Economics is another alternative degree that can lead to a career in accounting. Economics focuses on the study of markets, resource allocation, and decision-making, all of which are essential to understanding how financial systems work. An economics degree provides students with an in-depth understanding of macroeconomic and microeconomic trends, market behaviors, and government policies. These skills can be highly valuable in accounting, particularly in roles that require understanding broader economic factors, such as public accounting, government finance, or international business.

Students with an economics degree often work in fields like economic consulting, government finance, policy analysis, or banking, but the skills they acquire can be applied directly to accounting practices. For instance, economic forecasting and understanding the impact of macroeconomic events can help accountants offer strategic advice on financial planning, budgeting, and risk management.

d) Information Systems or IT Degrees

In today's digital age, technology is an integral part of almost every industry, including accounting. Accounting firms and businesses are increasingly relying on data analytics, blockchain, cloud computing, and other technological tools to streamline their operations.

A degree in Information Systems or IT, with a focus on business systems or data analytics, can provide a strong complement to a career in accounting.

Accountants with an IT background are well-positioned to take advantage of emerging technologies such as artificial intelligence (AI), machine learning, and data visualization tools that are transforming how financial data is processed and analyzed. Those who study information systems will be prepared to take on roles that bridge the gap between accounting and technology, including positions like IT auditor, business systems analyst, or technology consultant for accounting firms. This combination of accounting knowledge and technical expertise is increasingly in demand as businesses seek professionals who can navigate both the financial and technological aspects of accounting.

2. Benefits and Drawbacks of Alternative Degrees

Choosing an alternative degree can provide several benefits, but it's important to weigh these advantages against the challenges. Let's look at some of the pros and cons of pursuing an alternative degree for a career in accounting.

Benefits:

- Broader Skill Set: Alternative degrees, such as Business Administration, Finance, or Information Systems, allow students to develop a broader skill set that can make them more versatile in the job market. A well-rounded education can provide a competitive edge when applying for jobs in accounting or related fields.

- Specialization Opportunities: Degrees like Finance or Economics allow students to specialize in specific niches that intersect with accounting. For instance, a finance degree may be more suitable for roles in financial analysis or investment banking, while an economics degree can be useful for public accounting or policy-related positions.

- Increased Job Market Appeal: Many businesses are looking for accountants who have both technical financial skills and business or strategic acumen. Alternative degrees can make you more appealing to employers who value a combination of accounting knowledge and broader business expertise.

Drawbacks:

- Additional Time and Cost: Alternative degrees may require additional time and coursework, which can increase both the time it takes to graduate and the cost of your education. While the potential salary increase may offset these costs in the long term, it's important to carefully consider the financial investment.

- Lack of Direct Focus on Accounting: Some alternative degrees may not provide as deep a focus on accounting principles as a traditional accounting degree. If your primary goal is to become an accountant, you may need to take additional coursework or pursue certifications to gain the specialized knowledge required by the profession.

3. Double Majors: A Strategy for Specialization

A double major, where you pursue two distinct fields of study simultaneously, is another option for those looking to combine their accounting education with another area of interest. Many students choose to double major in fields that complement accounting, such as Finance, Economics, Business Administration, or Information Systems. This approach can provide an even more comprehensive skill set, allowing you to stand out in the job market.

Advantages of Double Majors:

- Increased Marketability: Graduates with double majors have a unique blend of skills that can appeal to employers in a variety of industries. For example, combining Accounting with Finance or Economics can open doors to more specialized roles in investment banking, financial analysis, or corporate strategy.

- Expanded Career Options: A double major allows you to explore career paths in both fields. With an accounting and finance double major, for instance, you could pursue roles in corporate finance, financial management, or financial accounting. This provides more flexibility and options when it comes to job opportunities.

- Enhanced Problem-Solving Abilities: Having expertise in two areas enables you to approach problems from multiple angles. For instance, understanding both accounting and business strategy can help you identify financial opportunities or risks that others might overlook.

Challenges of Double Majors:

- Increased Workload: Double majoring requires careful time management and an increased workload. You will need to balance the demands of two fields of study, which may limit your time for extracurricular activities or internships.

- Potential for Burnout: The pressure of maintaining high academic performance across two disciplines can be overwhelming, especially during final exams or group projects. It's important to ensure that you are ready for the commitment and responsibility that comes with pursuing two majors.

Conclusion

Choosing an alternative degree or pursuing a double major is an excellent strategy for students who want to enhance their accounting education and open the door to a wider range of career opportunities. Whether you choose a degree in Business Administration, Finance, Economics, or Information Systems, or opt for a double major, the goal is to build a skill set that is both deep in accounting and broad enough to give you a competitive edge in the job market. As the accounting profession continues to evolve, those who can combine technical expertise with business acumen and technological know-how will be well-positioned for success in the future.

3.3 Certifications and Licenses

When pursuing a career in accounting, certifications and licenses play a crucial role in distinguishing you from other candidates, opening doors to higher-level opportunities, and ensuring that you are equipped with the knowledge and skills required in the field. In this section, we will focus on one of the most prestigious certifications in the accounting world: the Certified Public Accountant (CPA) credential.

3.3.1 Certified Public Accountant (CPA)

What is the CPA Certification?

The Certified Public Accountant (CPA) designation is the most widely recognized accounting certification in the United States and many other countries around the world. It is a mark of excellence in the accounting profession, indicating that an individual has met specific educational, professional, and ethical standards. Becoming a CPA demonstrates your expertise in accounting principles, financial reporting, taxation, auditing, and business law.

In most cases, the CPA designation is required for individuals who wish to work as auditors or in other high-level accounting positions. It is also critical for those seeking to open their own accounting practice or provide independent auditing services to clients.

To become a CPA, you must complete a series of requirements set by your state or country, including passing the CPA exam, obtaining relevant work experience, and meeting ongoing continuing education requirements. These requirements ensure that CPAs maintain their knowledge of the latest developments in accounting standards, laws, and technology.

The Path to Becoming a CPA

The process of becoming a CPA can be lengthy and challenging, but it is a rewarding journey that will significantly enhance your career prospects. Below is an overview of the steps required to obtain the CPA certification.

1. Educational Requirements

The first step toward becoming a CPA is meeting the educational requirements. Most states in the U.S. require aspiring CPAs to have a minimum of a Bachelor's degree in accounting or a closely related field. While the degree itself is important, most states also require candidates to have a specific number of college credit hours, typically 150 hours, which is more than a standard four-year degree provides.

To meet this requirement, students often take additional coursework in subjects like business law, ethics, taxation, financial accounting, and auditing. Many students choose to pursue a Master's degree in accounting or business administration to fulfill the 150-hour requirement while gaining advanced knowledge in the field.

Having a degree is not only essential for meeting the academic requirements but also for building a solid foundation in accounting principles that will prepare you for the CPA exam.

2. The CPA Exam

The CPA exam is one of the most challenging professional exams you will ever face. The exam is designed to assess your knowledge and ability to apply accounting principles and concepts in practical, real-world scenarios. The exam is broken down into four sections, and you must pass each section to earn your certification.

The four sections of the CPA exam are:

1. Auditing and Attestation (AUD): This section focuses on auditing procedures, internal controls, and the ethical responsibilities of CPAs. It tests your ability to perform audits and provide attest services to clients.

2. Financial Accounting and Reporting (FAR): This section tests your knowledge of accounting principles and financial reporting requirements, including the preparation of financial statements in accordance with U.S. GAAP (Generally Accepted Accounting Principles).

3. Regulation (REG): This section focuses on tax laws, business law, and professional ethics. You will need to demonstrate your understanding of tax regulations and the legal issues that affect businesses and individuals.

4. Business Environment and Concepts (BEC): This section covers business operations, corporate governance, economics, and financial management. You will be tested on your ability to apply business concepts in various accounting settings.

To pass the CPA exam, you must score at least 75 points on each section, and you can take the sections in any order. The exam is computer-based and consists of multiple-choice questions, task-based simulations, and written communication tasks.

The CPA exam is notoriously difficult, so preparation is essential. Many candidates spend months studying for each section, and many opt for review courses that provide structured study materials and practice exams. It's important to stay focused and dedicated during the preparation phase, as passing the exam is one of the most challenging hurdles in the process of becoming a CPA.

3. Work Experience

In addition to completing the educational requirements and passing the CPA exam, most states also require candidates to gain practical work experience in the accounting field. The exact work experience requirements vary by state but typically require candidates to work for at least one to two years under the supervision of a licensed CPA.

During this time, you will gain hands-on experience in accounting tasks such as preparing financial statements, conducting audits, preparing tax returns, and advising clients on accounting matters. This experience not only helps you develop your skills but also ensures that you are fully prepared for the responsibilities that come with being a licensed CPA.

4. The Ethics Exam

Some states also require candidates to pass an ethics exam, which tests your understanding of the ethical responsibilities of a CPA. This exam typically covers topics like professional conduct, conflicts of interest, confidentiality, and the duty to maintain objectivity in your work. The ethics exam is usually a separate test that candidates take after passing the main CPA exam.

Maintaining Your CPA License

Once you have earned your CPA certification, it is important to maintain it through continuous education and professional development. In the U.S., CPAs must complete a minimum number of continuing professional education (CPE) hours each year to stay up to date with changes in accounting standards, tax laws, and technology.

The number of required CPE hours can vary by state, but most states require 40-80 hours of CPE annually. CPAs are also expected to adhere to a strict code of professional ethics and may face disciplinary actions if they fail to meet the required standards.

In addition to completing CPE requirements, CPAs may choose to specialize in a particular area of accounting, such as taxation, forensic accounting, or information systems auditing, to enhance their career prospects. Specialization often requires additional certifications and advanced education.

Benefits of Becoming a CPA

The benefits of becoming a CPA are numerous and far-reaching. Below are some of the most significant advantages that come with earning the CPA designation:

1. Job Security and High Demand

The demand for qualified accountants is consistently high, and CPAs are often in demand for specialized roles such as auditing, tax preparation, and financial management. The U.S. Bureau of Labor Statistics projects that the demand for accountants and auditors will grow at a rate of 6% from 2018 to 2028, faster than the average for all occupations.

As a CPA, you are more likely to secure higher-paying jobs and have greater job security, as the certification is often required for advanced roles in accounting and finance. Many employers specifically seek out CPAs because they possess the necessary expertise and credibility to handle complex accounting tasks.

2. Career Advancement and Earning Potential

CPAs tend to earn higher salaries than their non-certified counterparts. According to the AICPA (American Institute of Certified Public Accountants), CPAs earn an average of 10-15% more than non-CPAs in similar positions. The certification opens the door to higher-paying roles and greater career advancement opportunities, including leadership positions such as Controller, CFO, or Partner in an Accounting Firm.

In addition to higher salaries, CPAs also have access to more diverse career paths, whether in corporate accounting, government, nonprofit organizations, or private practice.

3. Professional Recognition and Credibility

The CPA designation is a globally recognized symbol of professional excellence. It demonstrates your commitment to the highest standards of accounting practice and ethical conduct. As a CPA, you gain the trust and respect of clients, employers, and peers, which can be essential for advancing your career and building a strong professional network.

4. Ability to Start Your Own Accounting Practice

One of the key advantages of being a CPA is the ability to open your own accounting firm. Many CPAs choose to work independently, providing services such as tax preparation, auditing, financial planning, and business consulting. Having the CPA designation allows you to offer services to the public and provides the legal and ethical authority to conduct audits and issue financial statements, which is essential for building a successful practice.

Conclusion

The Certified Public Accountant (CPA) certification is one of the most valuable and respected credentials in the accounting profession. While the path to becoming a CPA can be long and challenging, the benefits of earning the certification are well worth the effort. As a CPA, you will gain access to better job opportunities, higher salaries, and the ability to work in a wide range of industries and specialized roles.

Becoming a CPA is a commitment to professionalism, ethical conduct, and continuous learning. For those passionate about accounting and looking to make a long-lasting impact in the business world, the CPA certification is an essential step toward a successful and fulfilling career.

3.3.2 Certified Management Accountant (CMA)

The Certified Management Accountant (CMA) designation is one of the most respected certifications for professionals in the field of management accounting. A CMA is a financial expert who not only has the technical know-how of accounting principles but also possesses the business acumen to help drive company performance and profitability. This section will explore what it takes to earn the CMA certification, why it's important for your accounting career, and how it sets you apart from others in the accounting and finance field.

What is a CMA?

The CMA is a professional certification offered by the Institute of Management Accountants (IMA), an organization based in the United States but recognized globally. Unlike the Certified Public Accountant (CPA) designation, which focuses heavily on auditing and tax accounting, the CMA focuses more on the strategic side of accounting. It emphasizes financial management, decision-making, and business analysis. A CMA is trained to act as a business partner, providing insight and recommendations that guide an organization's long-term strategy.

Management accountants play a crucial role in businesses across industries. They are involved in budgeting, forecasting, cost management, financial analysis, and performance evaluation. As companies seek to optimize their operations and improve profitability, CMAs are relied upon to provide the data and insights that will shape the decisions at the executive level.

Why Pursue the CMA Certification?

For young aspiring accountants, earning a CMA can significantly enhance your career prospects. Here are a few reasons why the CMA is an attractive certification:

1. Career Advancement: The CMA can open doors to senior-level roles, including positions such as finance manager, controller, and chief financial officer (CFO). It's highly regarded in industries that require detailed financial insight, such as manufacturing, healthcare, technology, and finance.

2. Global Recognition: The CMA is a globally recognized certification, which means it can give you opportunities to work in diverse geographic markets. Whether you want to work in multinational corporations or gain exposure to different economies, the CMA can provide a broad and flexible career path.

3. Increased Earning Potential: According to various surveys, CMAs tend to earn higher salaries compared to their non-certified counterparts. This is because the certification not only reflects a higher level of expertise but also demonstrates a commitment to professional growth and a willingness to go above and beyond.

4. Enhanced Skill Set: Earning the CMA involves mastering advanced accounting concepts, financial analysis, strategic planning, and cost management. These skills are highly valued by employers looking for individuals who can manage complex financial data and use it to drive business decisions.

5. Credibility and Trust: The CMA credential is recognized as a mark of excellence and professionalism. Having the certification gives you an edge in the highly competitive accounting field and establishes credibility with employers, colleagues, and clients alike.

Requirements for CMA Certification

To become a CMA, there are specific requirements that must be met. Unlike the CPA, which generally requires a specific number of accounting and business credits in university, the CMA has a more flexible pathway for candidates. The following are the requirements for earning the CMA:

1. Educational Background: You must have a bachelor's degree in any field from an accredited institution. While an accounting or finance degree is ideal, it's not a strict requirement. The degree can be in any discipline, as long as you have a basic understanding of financial and business principles.

2. Work Experience: Before you can receive the CMA certification, you need at least two years of professional experience in management accounting or financial management. This experience can be gained before or after you pass the CMA exam, but it must be completed within seven years of passing the exam.

3. Passing the CMA Exam: The CMA exam consists of two parts:

  - *Part 1:* Financial Planning, Performance, and Analytics: This part covers financial reporting, planning, performance management, and financial analysis. Topics include financial statements, budgeting, forecasting, and variance analysis.

  - *Part 2:* Strategic Financial Management: This section covers corporate finance, decision analysis, risk management, investment decisions, and professional ethics. It focuses on helping organizations make informed financial decisions.

Both parts of the exam are comprehensive and require extensive preparation. Each part of the exam consists of multiple-choice questions and essay questions, requiring both theoretical knowledge and practical application of accounting principles. To pass each part, you must achieve a score of 360 or higher on a scale of 500.

4. Continuing Education: After earning the CMA, you are required to complete continuing professional education (CPE) credits to maintain your certification. This ensures that you stay updated with the latest trends, standards, and best practices in the industry. The IMA mandates a minimum of 30 hours of CPE per year, with at least 2 hours dedicated to ethics.

The CMA Exam Process

The process of becoming a CMA is systematic and well-structured. Let's break it down:

1. Register for the CMA Exam: To begin the certification process, you need to become a member of the IMA. As part of your membership, you can register for the CMA exam. Membership also provides access to a wide range of resources, including study materials, practice exams, and networking opportunities.

2. Prepare for the Exam: While there is no set curriculum for the CMA exam, the IMA provides study resources to help you prepare. Many candidates opt to take prep courses or purchase study guides to ensure they understand the content thoroughly. These resources are especially useful for tackling the complex financial concepts and analytical skills required in both exam parts.

3. Take the Exam: The CMA exam is offered at Pearson VUE test centers worldwide, and you can schedule the exam at a time that suits you. The exam is computer-based, and you must complete it within a four-hour window for each part. The exams are available year-round, which provides flexibility in scheduling.

4. Receive Your Results: Results for the CMA exam are typically available within six weeks of the exam date. You will receive a score report that details your performance in both the multiple-choice and essay sections of the exam. If you pass both parts, you will receive your CMA designation.

5. Earn the CMA Credential: Once you have passed both parts of the exam and met the experience requirements, you will officially earn the CMA certification. This can be a major milestone in your career, marking you as a highly skilled and respected management accountant.

CMAs in the Workforce: Job Opportunities and Career Growth

With a CMA certification, you open up numerous job opportunities in both the private and public sectors. Some of the roles that CMAs often occupy include:

- *Cost Accountant:* Specializing in cost analysis, CMAs in this role help businesses understand how to reduce costs and increase profitability. They assess the costs of production and recommend strategies for more efficient operations.

- *Financial Analyst:* CMAs working as financial analysts use their expertise in budgeting and financial forecasting to advise businesses on their financial strategy. They analyze trends and provide reports that help guide decision-making.

- *Corporate Treasurer:* In this role, CMAs help manage a company's finances, including overseeing investment decisions, managing cash flow, and ensuring compliance with financial regulations.

- *Chief Financial Officer (CFO):* A CMA can rise to an executive level role, such as CFO, where they are responsible for the financial health of the entire organization. CMAs in these positions oversee budgeting, financial planning, reporting, and strategic financial decisions.

Conclusion

Becoming a Certified Management Accountant (CMA) is a valuable career move for any aspiring accountant who wants to specialize in management accounting. The CMA offers an opportunity to develop a broad set of skills in financial analysis, strategy, and management that are in high demand across industries. Although it requires hard work, preparation, and dedication, the rewards of becoming a CMA—both professionally and financially—are well worth the effort.

By earning the CMA, you demonstrate your commitment to your profession and your ability to provide strategic financial insights that can help businesses thrive. As the business world continues to evolve and grow more complex, the role of the CMA will remain crucial, providing a stable and rewarding career path for years to come.

3.3.3 Other Specialized Certifications

While the Certified Public Accountant (CPA) and Certified Management Accountant (CMA) are two of the most well-known and widely pursued certifications in the accounting field, there are numerous other specialized certifications that can further enhance an accountant's career prospects. These certifications cater to specific areas within accounting, offering professionals the opportunity to gain expertise in niche fields. Pursuing these certifications can not only increase one's knowledge base but also open doors to specialized roles that are highly valued in the market.

Here, we explore some of the prominent specialized certifications that accounting professionals may pursue:

1. Certified Internal Auditor (CIA)

The Certified Internal Auditor (CIA) certification is ideal for those interested in pursuing careers in internal auditing. Internal auditors evaluate and improve the effectiveness of internal controls, risk management, and governance processes within organizations. This certification, offered by the Institute of Internal Auditors (IIA), is globally recognized and is particularly valuable for individuals working in or aspiring to work in internal auditing roles.

To obtain the CIA certification, candidates must pass a series of exams that assess their knowledge in areas such as risk management, governance processes, and audit techniques. Candidates must also meet experience requirements, typically involving at least two years of professional internal auditing experience. This certification is highly regarded by employers and demonstrates an individual's ability to identify and address potential risks within an organization.

2. Certified Fraud Examiner (CFE)

The Certified Fraud Examiner (CFE) certification is awarded by the Association of Certified Fraud Examiners (ACFE) to professionals who specialize in detecting and preventing fraud. This certification is especially beneficial for accountants who are interested in forensic accounting or fraud examination.

A CFE is responsible for investigating financial fraud, analyzing fraud risks, and ensuring that organizations implement effective anti-fraud measures. The certification process requires candidates to demonstrate knowledge in areas such as fraud prevention, investigation techniques, legal considerations, and ethical practices. Obtaining a CFE certification can be a game-changer for accounting professionals who want to specialize in combating fraud, whether in the private or public sector.

Moreover, the CFE credential is highly respected within law enforcement, government agencies, and corporate fraud investigation departments, making it a valuable asset for accountants who want to work in these areas.

3. Chartered Accountant (CA)

The Chartered Accountant (CA) designation is internationally recognized and awarded to accountants in many countries, including the UK, Canada, India, and Australia. The CA designation is equivalent to the CPA in the United States but often carries a more international focus. It is awarded by various professional bodies depending on the country, such as the Institute of Chartered Accountants in England and Wales (ICAEW) or the Institute of Chartered Accountants of India (ICAI).

The CA qualification involves a combination of academic education, professional training, and passing a series of exams. The exams test knowledge in areas such as financial reporting, taxation, auditing, and business strategy. To achieve the CA designation, candidates must also complete a period of practical work experience.

Chartered Accountants typically work in auditing, taxation, consulting, and financial management roles. They may work in accounting firms, corporations, or government agencies. The CA certification is especially beneficial for professionals looking to work in international markets or for global companies.

4. Certified Information Systems Auditor (CISA)

The Certified Information Systems Auditor (CISA) certification is a specialized credential for accounting professionals who wish to focus on information systems auditing. This certification is offered by ISACA (Information Systems Audit and Control Association) and is particularly relevant in today's increasingly digital and data-driven business environment.

CISA-certified professionals specialize in assessing and auditing information systems to ensure that they are secure, efficient, and meet the organization's objectives. This certification is valuable for those interested in combining accounting with IT auditing, risk management, and cybersecurity.

To become a CISA, candidates must pass an exam that covers topics like information systems auditing, IT governance, risk management, and protection of information assets. CISA professionals are in demand due to the growing importance of cybersecurity, data privacy, and digital transformation in organizations.

5. Chartered Global Management Accountant (CGMA)

The Chartered Global Management Accountant (CGMA) certification is a globally recognized credential for professionals working in management accounting. The CGMA designation is jointly awarded by the American Institute of CPAs (AICPA) and the Chartered Institute of Management Accountants (CIMA). It focuses on the skills needed for leadership roles in management accounting, including strategic thinking, financial analysis, and decision-making.

Professionals with the CGMA credential are typically responsible for providing financial insight to guide business strategy. They help organizations make informed decisions, optimize performance, and drive long-term financial success. To earn the CGMA, candidates must demonstrate expertise in areas such as financial strategy, risk management, and business performance management.

The CGMA certification is ideal for accountants who aspire to take on senior management roles or want to transition into a more strategic, leadership-focused career path. This certification can also help individuals working in financial planning and analysis (FP&A) roles, where strategic thinking is key.

6. Enrolled Agent (EA)

The Enrolled Agent (EA) certification is specifically designed for accountants who wish to specialize in taxation. EAs are tax professionals who are licensed by the IRS (Internal Revenue Service) to represent taxpayers before the agency. They have specialized knowledge in tax law and can assist individuals and businesses with tax preparation, filing, and audits.

The process to become an EA involves passing the Special Enrollment Examination (SEE) or having prior experience working for the IRS. Once certified, EAs can represent clients in all matters before the IRS, including audits, collections, and appeals. This certification is highly regarded in the field of tax accounting and can lead to a rewarding career helping individuals and businesses navigate complex tax issues.

7. Certified Government Financial Manager (CGFM)

The Certified Government Financial Manager (CGFM) certification is ideal for accountants who want to work in government accounting roles. This certification is offered by the

Association of Government Accountants (AGA) and is designed for professionals who manage financial operations in local, state, or federal government agencies.

The CGFM certification focuses on accounting practices, budgeting, auditing, and financial management specific to the public sector. To earn the CGFM, candidates must pass exams covering topics such as governmental accounting principles, public financial management, and ethics in government. The certification is highly beneficial for accountants looking to work in public finance, government budgeting, or public sector auditing.

8. Financial Risk Manager (FRM)

The Financial Risk Manager (FRM) certification is designed for accounting professionals who wish to specialize in risk management within the financial sector. Offered by the Global Association of Risk Professionals (GARP), the FRM certification focuses on identifying and managing financial risks, including market risk, credit risk, and operational risk.

The FRM certification is highly regarded in the banking, investment, and insurance sectors, as these industries require professionals with specialized knowledge in risk management. To earn the FRM certification, candidates must pass two exams that cover topics like risk modeling, risk management tools, and financial markets. FRM-certified professionals are in demand in financial institutions, hedge funds, and insurance companies, where risk management plays a critical role in their operations.

Conclusion

Specialized certifications in accounting can provide significant career advantages, allowing professionals to carve out niches in specialized areas, stay competitive in the job market, and pursue advanced roles in their chosen fields. These certifications offer individuals the opportunity to build expertise in a particular area of accounting and distinguish themselves as specialists with unique skill sets.

While the CPA and CMA remain the most popular and widely pursued certifications, pursuing other specialized certifications such as the CIA, CFE, or CISA can be a strategic move for those looking to build careers in areas like internal auditing, fraud prevention, IT auditing, or risk management. Ultimately, choosing the right certification depends on an individual's interests, career goals, and the specific area of accounting they wish to pursue.

In the competitive field of accounting, professional certifications are not just credentials—they are a reflection of expertise, commitment to continued learning, and dedication to excelling in one's career. As you navigate your path to becoming an accountant, consider these certifications as a way to enhance your skills, expand your professional opportunities, and position yourself for success in a dynamic and evolving industry.

CHAPTER IV
Career Opportunities in Accounting

4.1 Entry-Level Positions

4.1.1 Staff Accountant

As one of the most common entry-level positions in the field of accounting, the role of a Staff Accountant is crucial to the financial health and operation of any organization. This position serves as the foundation upon which many accounting careers are built. Whether you are just starting out in the field or considering a shift into accounting, understanding the responsibilities, skill set, and growth potential of a staff accountant role will help you navigate your career path effectively.

What Does a Staff Accountant Do?

A Staff Accountant is responsible for a wide range of essential accounting tasks. These tasks are integral to ensuring that financial operations within a company are running smoothly and accurately. The specific responsibilities of a staff accountant can vary depending on the organization, but typically include:

- *Bookkeeping and General Ledger Management:* Staff accountants are responsible for maintaining the general ledger, which is the central repository of a company's financial transactions. This includes ensuring that all journal entries are accurate and categorized properly.

- *Account Reconciliation:* Reconciliation involves verifying that the company's records match the actual bank and credit card statements. This is a crucial task for ensuring the accuracy of financial reporting and preventing any discrepancies in accounts.

- *Financial Reporting:* A key part of the staff accountant's job is assisting with the preparation of financial statements, such as balance sheets, income statements, and cash flow statements. They may be responsible for compiling data and preparing reports that are used for both internal decision-making and external audits.

- *Payroll Processing:* In smaller companies, staff accountants may also be responsible for processing payroll, ensuring employees are paid on time and that tax withholdings are accurate. This includes calculating wages, benefits, and bonuses.

- *Assisting with Tax Filings:* Staff accountants often assist senior accountants or tax specialists with the preparation and filing of tax returns. They help ensure that the company complies with federal, state, and local tax regulations.

- *Auditing Support:* During an audit, staff accountants often assist in collecting and preparing the necessary documentation to ensure compliance with accounting standards. This may include verifying financial statements and supporting documents required by auditors.

Skills and Qualifications for a Staff Accountant

To succeed in an entry-level position as a staff accountant, certain technical and soft skills are necessary. These competencies not only help you perform well in your day-to-day responsibilities but also prepare you for career advancement.

- *Technical Skills:*

 - *Proficiency in Accounting Software:* Familiarity with accounting software such as QuickBooks, Xero, or Sage is essential for staff accountants. Larger companies may require knowledge of Enterprise Resource Planning (ERP) systems like SAP or Oracle.

 - *Microsoft Excel:* Advanced Excel skills, including functions like VLOOKUP, pivot tables, and financial modeling, are a must-have. Excel remains one of the most widely used tools in accounting, so mastering it is crucial.

 - *Understanding of Accounting Principles:* A solid grasp of Generally Accepted Accounting Principles (GAAP) or International Financial Reporting Standards (IFRS) is critical for ensuring that financial statements are accurate and compliant with legal standards.

 - *Attention to Detail:* Accuracy is paramount in accounting. Staff accountants must be able to identify discrepancies and ensure the integrity of the data being handled.

- Soft Skills:

- Analytical Thinking: The ability to analyze financial data, identify trends, and provide insights is essential for the role of a staff accountant.

- Time Management: Staff accountants are often responsible for managing multiple tasks simultaneously. Strong organizational and time management skills are necessary to meet deadlines, especially during high-pressure periods like tax season or financial reporting cycles.

- Communication Skills: A staff accountant must be able to explain complex financial data to both non-financial colleagues and senior management in a clear and concise manner.

- Problem-Solving Abilities: When errors occur or discrepancies are found, staff accountants must be able to identify the source of the issue and work towards a resolution.

- Education and Certifications:

- A bachelor's degree in Accounting, Finance, or Business Administration is typically required for an entry-level staff accountant position.

- While certification is not always necessary at this stage, obtaining certifications like Certified Public Accountant (CPA) or Certified Management Accountant (CMA) can set you apart from others in the field. These certifications often require additional coursework and experience, but they can significantly enhance career prospects.

- Internships and part-time work during college can also help gain practical experience and make a resume stand out.

Work Environment for a Staff Accountant

Staff accountants can work in various industries, including public accounting firms, private corporations, nonprofit organizations, and government agencies. The work environment may differ depending on the size and nature of the company:

- Public Accounting: In a public accounting firm, staff accountants often work with multiple clients, providing accounting, audit, and tax services. This may involve a high level of client interaction and can include traveling to client sites.

- Corporate Accounting: Staff accountants in corporate settings are typically focused on internal financial operations. They may work within finance departments of companies, handling accounts payable, accounts receivable, payroll, and budgeting.

- Government and Nonprofit: Staff accountants in these sectors typically deal with government funds or nonprofit budgets. While the day-to-day tasks may be similar to those in corporate accounting, they are often subject to stricter regulations and compliance rules.

Regardless of the setting, the role of a staff accountant is often office-based, requiring long hours spent at a desk working with financial data. Some positions may also offer remote work opportunities, especially as cloud-based accounting software becomes more prevalent.

Salary Range for Staff Accountants

The salary for a staff accountant can vary depending on factors such as location, industry, and level of experience. However, here are some general salary ranges:

- United States:

- The median salary for a staff accountant in the U.S. is approximately **$54,000 per year.**

- Entry-level staff accountants typically start with salaries ranging from **$45,000 to $55,000** annually, depending on the company and geographic location.

- In larger cities like New York or San Francisco, salaries may be higher, with some staff accountants earning between **$60,000 and $70,000** at the entry level.

- United Kingdom:

- The average salary for a staff accountant in the UK is around **£28,000 to £35,000** per year.

- In larger cities such as London, salaries can reach up to **£40,000 to £45,000** annually.

- Canada:

- In Canada, staff accountants can expect to earn an average of **CAD 50,000 to CAD 60,000** annually.

- Again, salaries may be higher in major cities such as Toronto or Vancouver.

Salaries tend to increase as staff accountants gain more experience, earn certifications, and take on more responsibilities. In addition, many companies offer benefits such as health insurance, retirement plans, and performance bonuses.

Career Path and Advancement Opportunities

Starting as a staff accountant provides numerous opportunities for career advancement. Here's a look at the typical progression in the accounting field:

- *Junior Accountant*: The first step for most people entering the accounting profession is as a junior or staff accountant. During this time, you'll learn the basics of financial management, reporting, and data analysis.

- *Senior Accountant:* After gaining experience (usually 2–4 years), many staff accountants are promoted to senior accountant roles. Senior accountants handle more complex financial tasks, such as managing larger accounts, preparing detailed financial reports, and overseeing junior staff.

- *Accounting Manager*: After further experience (often 5–7 years), a senior accountant may be promoted to an accounting manager role. Here, they oversee a team of accountants, ensuring that all financial records are accurate and compliant with regulations.

- *Controller*: A controller is typically responsible for overseeing the entire accounting department, managing financial reporting, budgeting, and internal controls.

- *Chief Financial Officer (CFO):* The ultimate goal for many accountants is to become a CFO. CFOs are responsible for overseeing the financial operations of an entire organization, including financial planning, risk management, and strategic decision-making.

Additionally, staff accountants can specialize in areas such as tax accounting, forensic accounting, or internal auditing, which can lead to more lucrative and specialized roles within the profession.

Conclusion

A position as a staff accountant is a promising entry point into the accounting profession. It offers a broad range of responsibilities that will give you invaluable experience and prepare you for career advancement. With the right skills, qualifications, and determination, you can move up the ranks and find success in accounting, with opportunities to specialize and explore leadership roles in the future.

By starting your career in an entry-level staff accountant position, you will gain the expertise and experience needed to excel in the field of accounting, ultimately positioning yourself for growth and long-term career success.

4.1.2 Junior Auditor

Introduction to the Role of a Junior Auditor

A Junior Auditor is typically an entry-level position within the accounting and auditing profession. It serves as an important starting point for individuals aspiring to pursue a long-term career in auditing, public accounting, or corporate finance. As a Junior Auditor, you will be working closely with senior auditors to perform audits on financial statements and ensure that companies comply with regulatory standards and laws.

Junior Auditors are commonly employed by accounting firms, particularly public accounting firms, or within the internal audit departments of corporations. This role is essential in the auditing process, as it supports the organization in maintaining financial transparency and accountability, which is crucial for the success of businesses, governmental bodies, and nonprofits alike.

Key Responsibilities of a Junior Auditor

The responsibilities of a Junior Auditor will vary depending on the size and type of the organization they work for. However, there are common tasks that most Junior Auditors are expected to carry out:

1. Assisting in Financial Audits:

  - One of the core tasks is to assist in the preparation and execution of financial audits. This includes verifying financial records, reconciling bank statements, and ensuring that financial statements align with the generally accepted accounting principles (GAAP) or International Financial Reporting Standards (IFRS).

  - Junior Auditors help in collecting data for audit files, reviewing balance sheets, income statements, and cash flow statements to identify discrepancies and report findings to senior team members.

2. Testing Internal Controls:

- Junior Auditors examine internal controls in financial reporting processes to ensure the company's financial data is accurate and reliable. This involves performing test transactions, evaluating internal policies and procedures, and identifying areas where there might be inefficiencies or vulnerabilities.

3. Documenting Audit Findings:

- Part of the job is ensuring that all findings, notes, and observations are documented accurately. This may include writing audit reports, preparing working papers, and tracking audit progress.

- These reports are submitted to senior auditors and managers for review and final conclusions.

4. Compliance Verification:

- Junior Auditors play a key role in verifying whether the company adheres to tax laws, financial regulations, and company policies. They often assist in conducting tax audits to ensure that financial transactions are in line with applicable local, state, or international tax codes.

5. Risk Assessment:

- Auditors assess the risk of misstatements in financial records, looking for errors or fraud. Junior Auditors often use various software tools and analytical methods to assess risk and help senior auditors understand where potential issues could arise.

6. Communicating with Clients:

- Junior Auditors may also communicate with clients to collect necessary documents, clarify discrepancies, and discuss audit findings. Effective communication skills are essential in building rapport with clients, ensuring the audit process runs smoothly, and addressing any concerns or questions.

Skills Required for a Junior Auditor

A Junior Auditor must possess a combination of technical accounting skills, analytical abilities, and soft skills to succeed in this role. Key skills include:

1. Technical Accounting Knowledge:

- A strong understanding of accounting principles, such as GAAP and IFRS, is vital for auditing financial records and preparing accurate audit reports.

- Familiarity with auditing procedures and techniques is crucial, including the ability to use specialized software tools for audit management.

2. Analytical Skills:

- The ability to analyze financial data, identify trends, and detect irregularities is essential. Junior Auditors should have an eye for detail, as small errors in financial reporting can have large consequences.

3. Problem-Solving Abilities:

- Junior Auditors must be able to think critically and troubleshoot problems that arise during the audit process, from identifying discrepancies in reports to proposing solutions to address those problems.

4. Attention to Detail:

- Auditing requires precision. A Junior Auditor must be meticulous and able to spot errors or issues that others might overlook in large volumes of data.

5. Communication Skills:

- Strong written and verbal communication skills are necessary for interacting with clients, reporting audit findings, and collaborating with senior auditors and other departments.

6. Time Management:

- Auditors are often given strict deadlines for audit completion. The ability to manage multiple tasks, prioritize work, and meet deadlines is essential in this role.

Educational Requirements and Certifications

Typically, a Junior Auditor position requires a bachelor's degree in accounting, finance, or a related field. Some positions may also accept degrees in business administration or economics. The foundation of accounting principles taught during university prepares aspiring auditors for their future work.

In addition to a degree, Junior Auditors may benefit from certifications such as:

- Certified Public Accountant (CPA): While a Junior Auditor may not be required to have CPA certification initially, working towards this certification is highly beneficial for career advancement. Obtaining a CPA license demonstrates a high level of expertise and is often required for more senior roles in auditing.

- Certified Internal Auditor (CIA): For those specifically interested in internal auditing roles, the CIA certification may be pursued to enhance credibility and expertise in internal audit functions.

- Other Relevant Certifications: Junior Auditors may pursue additional certifications or specialized training, such as in forensic accounting, IT auditing, or fraud examination, to broaden their skillset and improve career prospects.

Career Path and Opportunities for Growth

While the role of a Junior Auditor is an entry-level position, it provides excellent opportunities for career progression. With experience and further education, Junior Auditors can move into more advanced auditing roles or specialize in areas such as tax auditing, fraud investigation, or forensic accounting. Over time, a Junior Auditor can grow into one of the following positions:

1. Audit Senior: After gaining a few years of experience, Junior Auditors can move into the role of an Audit Senior, where they will take on more responsibility in managing audit teams, reviewing audit procedures, and making decisions on audit findings.

2. Managerial and Specialized Roles: With further experience, a Junior Auditor may transition into managerial roles, overseeing larger audit teams and working directly with clients to ensure compliance. There are also opportunities to specialize in specific areas of auditing, such as environmental auditing or tax auditing.

3. Partner or Director at a Public Accounting Firm: The ultimate goal for many auditors is to work their way up to a senior leadership position, such as becoming a Partner or Director at a public accounting firm. In these roles, auditors manage entire departments, provide strategic advice to clients, and lead large-scale audits of multinational corporations.

Salary Range and Job Outlook

The salary for a Junior Auditor varies based on location, the size of the company, and individual qualifications. On average, Junior Auditors in the United States can expect the following salary range:

- Average Salary: $50,000 - $65,000 per year

- Entry-Level Salary: $45,000 - $55,000 per year

- Experienced Junior Auditor Salary: $60,000 - $70,000 per year

In major cities or at top-tier accounting firms, salaries may be higher due to increased demand and the cost of living. For example, Junior Auditors working in New York or San Francisco can expect salaries closer to the higher end of this range.

The job outlook for auditors, including Junior Auditors, is positive. According to the U.S. Bureau of Labor Statistics, the employment of accountants and auditors is projected to grow by 6% from 2021 to 2031, which is about as fast as the average for all occupations. This growth is driven by the increasing complexity of financial regulations, the need for auditing services, and the rise of cybersecurity and fraud detection in the digital age.

Conclusion

The Junior Auditor position is an excellent starting point for those interested in pursuing a career in accounting, auditing, or finance. With a solid foundation in accounting principles, a strong work ethic, and the right set of skills, Junior Auditors can move up the career ladder to more advanced and specialized roles, such as Audit Senior, Manager, or even Partner. With a competitive salary and promising career growth, auditing is a highly rewarding and intellectually stimulating field for those who enjoy solving problems, analyzing financial data, and working in a collaborative environment.

The role of Junior Auditor is an essential part of the financial ecosystem, contributing to the transparency, integrity, and accuracy of financial reporting in organizations worldwide.

4.2 Mid-Level and Specialized Roles

4.2.1 Financial Analyst

A Financial Analyst plays a pivotal role in evaluating and interpreting financial data to assist businesses in making informed decisions. As one of the most in-demand roles in the accounting and finance field, financial analysts are essential in a wide range of industries, from corporate finance and banking to investment management and public sector organizations. If you're considering a mid-level accounting role, becoming a financial analyst can be an exciting and rewarding career path.

Key Responsibilities of a Financial Analyst

Financial analysts are tasked with scrutinizing a company's financial data, helping management make well-informed decisions. Some of the core responsibilities include:

1. Budgeting and Forecasting: A significant part of a financial analyst's role is working on the budgeting process, predicting the financial trajectory of a company, and providing forecasts based on historical data and market trends. This may involve constructing detailed financial models to simulate future scenarios, assessing the impact of potential business decisions, and advising on resource allocation.

2. Data Analysis and Reporting: Analysts must analyze financial statements, identify trends, and offer insights. They may work with profit and loss statements, balance sheets, and cash flow reports to evaluate a company's financial health. The ability to convert data into actionable insights is a critical aspect of the role. This often includes using financial tools such as Excel, specialized financial modeling software, or even programming languages like Python to enhance data analysis and reporting capabilities.

3. Investment Analysis: Financial analysts often specialize in evaluating investment opportunities. This involves examining potential investments, stocks, bonds, real estate, or entire business portfolios. They assess risk, return potential, and market conditions to recommend profitable ventures or avoid potential losses.

4. Financial Risk Management: Financial analysts are also responsible for assessing risk exposure and implementing strategies to mitigate those risks. This could involve analyzing financial products, operational activities, or market conditions that could harm the company's bottom line. For instance, an analyst may evaluate market volatility and advise senior leadership on how to hedge or safeguard investments.

5. *Regulatory Compliance and Reporting:* Compliance with local, national, and international regulations is paramount in financial reporting. Analysts ensure that financial data complies with accounting principles, tax laws, and industry-specific regulations. They prepare financial reports that meet regulatory standards and help avoid any legal or financial penalties.

6. *Strategy and Advisory:* A financial analyst also plays a key advisory role within the organization, offering insights on financial strategy. This could involve analyzing mergers, acquisitions, and other major business transactions. They help senior leaders make strategic decisions that drive the company's growth and profitability.

Skills Required for Financial Analysts

To succeed as a financial analyst, one needs to possess a combination of technical, analytical, and interpersonal skills. These include:

- Financial Modeling and Analysis: The ability to build and interpret complex financial models is essential. Financial analysts must be adept at using tools like Microsoft Excel, as well as more advanced financial modeling software like SAS, Oracle Financial Services Analytical Applications, and Bloomberg Terminal.

- Quantitative and Analytical Abilities: Strong numerical and analytical skills are crucial for identifying patterns in financial data, making accurate forecasts, and solving complex problems. Financial analysts are expected to be detail-oriented and meticulous.

- Communication Skills: As a financial analyst, you will often be required to communicate complex financial concepts to non-financial stakeholders, such as senior executives or clients. The ability to present findings clearly and concisely, both in writing and verbally, is a must.

- Problem-Solving: Financial analysts often face challenging problems that require innovative thinking and strategic solutions. The ability to approach issues from various angles and develop effective solutions is crucial.

- Attention to Detail: Financial data must be accurate and precise. A keen eye for detail helps ensure that financial reports are error-free and reliable for decision-making.

- Knowledge of Accounting and Financial Principles: A strong understanding of accounting principles, such as GAAP (Generally Accepted Accounting Principles), and financial concepts is necessary. Analysts should also be familiar with tax regulations and industry-specific standards.

- Time Management and Organization: Financial analysts are often tasked with handling multiple projects simultaneously, so the ability to prioritize tasks, meet deadlines, and manage time effectively is critical.

Path to Becoming a Financial Analyst

The journey to becoming a financial analyst typically involves several stages, starting with education and progressing through certifications and work experience.

1. Education: Most financial analysts hold at least a bachelor's degree in accounting, finance, economics, or a related field. Some may pursue a master's degree, such as a Master of Business Administration (MBA) with a concentration in finance, to increase their job prospects and earning potential.

2. Certifications: While not always required, certifications can significantly enhance a financial analyst's qualifications. The Chartered Financial Analyst (CFA) credential is one of the most prestigious certifications in the field. This certification requires passing a series of exams and demonstrating experience in financial analysis. Additionally, certifications such as the Financial Risk Manager (FRM) or Certified Management Accountant (CMA) can also boost an analyst's career.

3. Work Experience: Entry-level positions in accounting or finance often serve as stepping stones toward a career in financial analysis. Many analysts start in roles such as junior accountant, finance assistant, or financial assistant, gaining valuable experience in financial reporting, budgeting, and analysis before transitioning to full-time analyst positions.

4. Continuing Education: The finance field is constantly evolving, and staying up to date on new regulations, technologies, and financial instruments is vital. Ongoing professional development and continuing education can help analysts remain competitive in the job market.

Job Opportunities and Industries for Financial Analysts

Financial analysts are in demand across various industries, including:

- Investment Banks: Analysts in this field typically focus on evaluating investment opportunities, conducting financial modeling, and providing buy/sell recommendations.

- Corporate Finance: In corporations, financial analysts help companies plan for long-term growth by advising on capital investment, risk management, and budgeting.

- Insurance Companies: Insurance companies employ financial analysts to evaluate risk, manage investments, and determine the profitability of policies.

- Government Agencies: Analysts in government sectors may be responsible for budgeting, forecasting, and managing public funds, ensuring financial transparency and efficiency.

- Nonprofit Organizations: Financial analysts in the nonprofit sector help these organizations manage their finances, ensure transparency, and allocate resources for maximum impact.

Estimated Salary Range for Financial Analysts

The salary of a financial analyst can vary based on factors such as experience, location, industry, and level of education. On average, the following are typical salary ranges:

- Entry-Level: For those just starting, salaries typically range from **$50,000 to $70,000** per year. This range can be influenced by factors such as location and whether the role is in a high-demand industry like investment banking.

- Mid-Level: With several years of experience, financial analysts can expect to earn between **$70,000 and $100,000** annually. Analysts with specialized skills, such as in risk management or financial modeling, tend to earn salaries at the higher end of the range.

- Senior-Level: Experienced financial analysts with 5 to 10 years of experience may earn between **$100,000 and $130,000** annually. This can increase significantly with promotions to senior analyst or managerial roles.

- Top-Tier Roles: At the highest levels, such as a Senior Financial Analyst in investment banking or corporate finance, salaries can range from **$130,000 to $150,000** or more, particularly with bonuses and other forms of compensation.

Career Outlook for Financial Analysts
The demand for financial analysts is expected to remain strong in the coming years. According to the U.S. Bureau of Labor Statistics (BLS),

the employment of financial analysts is projected to grow by 9% from 2022 to 2032, which is faster than the average for all occupations. This growth is driven by an increasingly complex financial landscape, the need for businesses to make informed decisions, and the continued reliance on financial analysis in both public and private sectors.

As more companies adopt advanced technologies like artificial intelligence (AI) and machine learning for financial modeling and forecasting, financial analysts will be expected to adapt by learning how to work with these tools to stay relevant in the field.

In summary, becoming a financial analyst offers a dynamic and rewarding career path in the accounting profession. It requires a solid educational foundation, analytical skills, and the ability to adapt to new technologies. With strong demand for skilled financial analysts across multiple industries, it's a career that promises growth, variety, and competitive compensation.

4.2.2 Tax Specialist

Tax specialists, often referred to as tax accountants or tax advisors, play a crucial role in helping individuals, businesses, and organizations navigate the complex landscape of tax laws. Their primary responsibility is to ensure that their clients or employers comply with tax regulations while also identifying opportunities to minimize tax liabilities. This role offers a diverse range of opportunities and is critical to both businesses and individuals, as taxes are a significant part of the financial landscape.

Role and Responsibilities

A tax specialist is responsible for understanding and interpreting various tax codes and regulations to help clients prepare their tax returns accurately. This process includes reviewing financial records, preparing tax returns, advising on tax strategies, and ensuring compliance with federal, state, and local tax laws. The role of a tax specialist can vary depending on whether they work for a corporation, government agency, or as an independent consultant. Below are the primary responsibilities of a tax specialist:

1. Tax Return Preparation

Tax specialists prepare individual, business, and corporate tax returns. This involves collecting financial data, identifying deductions and credits, and ensuring that all tax forms are filed accurately and on time.

2. Tax Planning and Strategy

One of the core functions of a tax specialist is to develop tax strategies that help clients minimize their tax liabilities. This can include advising on business structures, recommending investments, and suggesting ways to defer taxes or take advantage of tax credits and deductions.

3. Tax Research

Tax laws are constantly changing, and a tax specialist must stay up-to-date on new tax laws, regulations, and case law. This requires ongoing research to ensure compliance and to advise clients effectively.

4. Audit Support

If a client is audited by tax authorities, a tax specialist may be called upon to represent the client and provide necessary documentation to support the tax returns. This could involve preparing for an audit, interacting with auditors, and providing explanations of tax filings.

5. International Tax Considerations

For clients or businesses with international operations, tax specialists may help navigate cross-border tax issues, including tax treaties, transfer pricing, and international tax compliance.

6. Client Consultation

Tax specialists work closely with clients to explain complex tax issues, answer questions, and provide recommendations. They must be able to break down complex tax concepts into easy-to-understand language.

Key Skills Required

To be successful in the role of a tax specialist, one must possess a blend of technical accounting skills, legal knowledge, and the ability to communicate effectively with clients. Some of the most important skills required include:

1. In-Depth Knowledge of Tax Laws and Regulations

A strong understanding of federal, state, and local tax laws is essential. Tax specialists must be aware of both current tax regulations and upcoming changes in tax law.

2. Attention to Detail

Tax filings require a high degree of accuracy, as even small mistakes can result in costly penalties. Tax specialists must be meticulous in their work, ensuring that every piece of data is correctly entered and that every opportunity for tax savings is identified.

3. Analytical Skills

A tax specialist must have strong analytical skills to interpret complex financial data, identify discrepancies, and recommend strategies that benefit clients. The ability to analyze tax codes and apply them to different financial situations is crucial.

4. Communication Skills

Tax specialists must explain complex tax concepts in a way that clients can understand. Strong communication skills are necessary to build relationships with clients and to explain tax strategies clearly and persuasively.

5. Organizational Skills

Tax preparation often involves managing multiple clients with varying deadlines. Tax specialists must be organized, able to prioritize tasks, and ensure that all deadlines are met without compromising the quality of their work.

6. Ethical Judgment

Given the sensitive nature of financial information, tax specialists must demonstrate high ethical standards. They are often trusted with confidential client data and must ensure that all actions taken are in compliance with tax laws.

7. Problem-Solving Abilities

Tax specialists often encounter complex situations that require innovative solutions. Whether it's resolving a tax dispute with a client or finding a creative way to minimize tax liabilities, problem-solving is a key skill in this role.

Educational and Professional Requirements

To become a tax specialist, individuals typically need a combination of formal education, professional certifications, and relevant experience. Here are the key steps to entering the field:

1. Education

A bachelor's degree in accounting, finance, or a related field is usually the minimum requirement. Some tax specialists also pursue additional coursework in taxation to deepen their understanding of the subject. Some universities offer specialized programs in tax accounting, which can provide an excellent foundation for a career in this field.

2. Certifications

While certification is not always required, many tax specialists pursue professional designations to enhance their credentials and increase their job prospects. The most common certification for tax specialists is the Certified Public Accountant (CPA) designation. To become a CPA, individuals must pass the Uniform CPA Examination and meet state-specific licensing requirements.

Another relevant certification is the Enrolled Agent (EA) designation, which is granted by the IRS to individuals who have passed a comprehensive exam covering all aspects of tax law. This certification allows tax specialists to represent clients before the IRS.

3. Experience

Most tax specialists start their careers in entry-level positions, such as tax preparers or junior tax accountants, where they gain hands-on experience in preparing tax returns, assisting clients, and researching tax laws. Over time, they may transition into more specialized roles as they gain expertise in specific areas of tax law.

4. Continuing Education

Given the constantly changing nature of tax law, continuing education is essential for tax specialists. Many states require CPAs and EAs to complete continuing professional education (CPE) courses regularly to maintain their certifications.

Career Growth and Opportunities

Tax specialists have various career paths available to them. With experience, tax specialists can move into mid-level and senior roles such as tax manager, tax director, or even partner in a public accounting firm. Additionally, tax specialists may choose to specialize in particular areas of taxation, such as international tax, mergers and acquisitions, or estate planning.

Some tax specialists also move into related fields such as financial consulting, corporate finance, or management positions in tax departments within large corporations. Given the broad application of tax knowledge in business, tax specialists have the flexibility to shift across industries.

Salary Range and Job Outlook

The salary for a tax specialist can vary depending on factors such as location, experience, industry, and education level. Below is a general estimate of salary ranges for tax specialists:

- Entry-Level Tax Specialist (0-2 years of experience):

 Salary range: *$50,000 - $70,000* per year

- Mid-Level Tax Specialist (3-5 years of experience):

 Salary range: *$70,000 - $100,000* per year

- Senior Tax Specialist (5+ years of experience):

 Salary range: *$100,000 - $150,000* per year

- Tax Manager/Director:

 Salary range: *$120,000 - $200,000* per year

For tax specialists working in large cities or with specialized expertise, salaries may be higher. For example, tax specialists in metropolitan areas such as New York, Chicago, or Los Angeles often earn salaries at the higher end of these ranges due to the higher cost of living and demand for tax services.

In terms of job outlook, the demand for tax specialists remains strong, as businesses and individuals continue to rely on tax professionals to navigate the complexities of tax laws. The Bureau of Labor Statistics (BLS) reports that the employment of accountants and auditors, which includes tax specialists, is projected to grow by 6% from 2021 to 2031, which is about as fast as the average for all occupations.

Conclusion

Becoming a tax specialist is an excellent career path for those who enjoy working with numbers, solving complex problems, and staying up-to-date with the ever-changing tax laws. With strong job demand, excellent salary potential, and ample room for career growth, a career in tax accounting offers stability and a wide variety of opportunities. Whether you work for a public accounting firm, a corporation, or as an independent consultant, the role of a tax specialist is an integral part of the accounting profession and provides valuable expertise to businesses and individuals alike.

4.3 Advanced Positions and Leadership

4.3.1 Controller

A Controller is a key leadership position within the accounting department of any business, responsible for overseeing financial operations and ensuring that financial reporting is accurate and compliant with laws and regulations. Often seen as the highest accounting position in a company, the role of a Controller requires a deep understanding of accounting principles, financial analysis, and management skills. The Controller plays an integral part in managing the company's finances, maintaining budget controls, and providing strategic direction for financial planning.

The Role of a Controller

The Controller's role varies depending on the size and structure of the organization. In smaller companies, the Controller might be responsible for overseeing all accounting operations, whereas, in larger corporations, they may oversee a team of accountants and financial professionals. Typically, the Controller reports directly to the Chief Financial Officer (CFO) or the company's upper management.

Key responsibilities of a Controller include:

- *Financial Reporting:* One of the most important duties of a Controller is overseeing the preparation and accuracy of financial statements. This includes income statements, balance sheets, and cash flow statements. The Controller ensures that these documents adhere to Generally Accepted Accounting Principles (GAAP) or International Financial Reporting Standards (IFRS), depending on the company's location and requirements.

- *Internal Controls and Auditing:* The Controller is responsible for maintaining effective internal controls within the company. They ensure that there are no errors or fraud in the financial reporting process. This often involves conducting internal audits and overseeing external audits.

- *Budgeting and Forecasting:* Another critical responsibility is managing the company's budget. Controllers work closely with the CFO to establish budgets, track actual performance against those budgets, and forecast future financial outcomes. They may also be involved in financial analysis to identify trends, risks, and opportunities that could affect the company's financial health.

- *Compliance and Regulatory Requirements:* Ensuring the company is in compliance with tax laws, corporate regulations, and financial reporting standards is a fundamental aspect of the role. Controllers must keep up-to-date with changing regulations to ensure the company adheres to them and avoids legal issues.

- *Team Leadership and Development:* In larger companies, Controllers often oversee a team of accountants and financial analysts. They are responsible for mentoring and training their team, providing feedback, and helping with career development. As a leader, the Controller ensures that the team is motivated, productive, and aligned with the company's financial goals.

- *Strategic Financial Planning:* Controllers also play a role in long-term financial planning, working with senior management to set financial goals, improve efficiencies, and support strategic initiatives. They analyze financial data to offer recommendations that drive business growth and profitability.

Skills and Qualifications

To excel in the role of Controller, a combination of technical accounting knowledge and soft skills is required. Some of the most important skills and qualifications include:

- *Advanced Accounting Knowledge:* A deep understanding of accounting principles, financial reporting, tax laws, and corporate finance is essential for a Controller. They must be able to interpret financial data and ensure its accuracy.

- *Leadership Skills:* Controllers need strong leadership abilities, as they often manage teams of accountants. They should be able to communicate effectively, delegate tasks, and motivate staff to perform at their best.

- *Analytical Thinking:* The Controller must be able to analyze complex financial data and provide insights that help in decision-making. This requires proficiency in financial modeling, forecasting, and trend analysis.

- *Attention to Detail:* Since Controllers are responsible for ensuring the accuracy of financial reports, attention to detail is crucial. Small errors can lead to significant financial discrepancies.

- *Problem-Solving:* Controllers are often called upon to identify financial problems, propose solutions, and implement corrective actions. They should be able to make quick, informed decisions in high-pressure situations.

- *Proficiency with Accounting Software:* Knowledge of accounting software is a must. Many organizations use enterprise resource planning (ERP) systems, such as SAP, Oracle, or Microsoft Dynamics. Experience with financial software like QuickBooks, Excel, and other data management tools is also beneficial.

- *Communication Skills:* As Controllers work closely with senior management, auditors, and sometimes the board of directors, strong verbal and written communication skills are essential. They must be able to explain complex financial information to non-financial stakeholders.

- *Certifications and Education:* Most Controllers hold a bachelor's degree in Accounting, Finance, or a related field. Many also pursue advanced qualifications such as a Certified Public Accountant (CPA) or Certified Management Accountant (CMA) designation. In addition, many Controllers have an MBA or other advanced business degrees.

Career Path to Becoming a Controller

The typical career progression to a Controller position generally begins with entry-level roles in accounting, such as a Junior Accountant or Staff Accountant. Over time, professionals advance through mid-level positions, including Senior Accountant and Accounting Manager, before achieving the role of Controller.

Here's a general outline of the steps involved:

1. Bachelor's Degree in Accounting or Finance: The first step is to earn a bachelor's degree in accounting, finance, or a related field. This provides the foundational knowledge required for the role.

2. Entry-Level Accounting Experience: After graduation, professionals typically begin in entry-level accounting positions such as Staff Accountant or Junior Auditor. These roles provide hands-on experience in managing financial records, preparing reports, and understanding compliance regulations.

3. Professional Certification (CPA or CMA): Earning a professional certification, such as a CPA (Certified Public Accountant) or CMA (Certified Management Accountant), can significantly boost one's chances of advancing to a Controller position. These certifications demonstrate expertise and commitment to the profession.

4. Mid-Level Management Roles: After gaining experience and credentials, professionals often move into mid-level management roles such as Senior Accountant, Accounting

Manager, or Financial Analyst. These positions provide experience in supervising teams, managing budgets, and developing financial strategies.

5. Controller: Once a professional has gained sufficient experience, leadership skills, and technical knowledge, they can move into a Controller role. The journey to this position often takes 5-10 years, depending on the size of the company and the individual's career progression.

Salary Range for Controllers

The salary for a Controller can vary significantly depending on factors such as location, company size, and experience. On average, here are the estimated salary ranges:

- Entry-Level Controller: *$70,000 - $90,000* per year

- Mid-Level Controller: *$90,000 - $120,000* per year

- Experienced Controller: *$120,000 - $180,000+* per year

In larger companies or industries with complex financial needs, the salary can be even higher. Additionally, many Controllers receive bonuses, profit-sharing, or stock options as part of their compensation package.

Job Outlook for Controllers

The demand for skilled accounting professionals, including Controllers, is expected to remain strong. According to the U.S. Bureau of Labor Statistics (BLS), the employment of accountants and auditors is projected to grow by 6% from 2021 to 2031, which is about as fast as the average for all occupations.

Controllers are essential to ensuring that companies manage their finances efficiently and comply with financial regulations, so their role is unlikely to become obsolete. However, it is important for future Controllers to stay up-to-date with advancements in technology, such as automation and artificial intelligence, as these tools are becoming more integrated into the accounting profession.

Conclusion

The Controller is a critical role within an organization, offering both leadership opportunities and high earning potential. This position is ideal for individuals who are passionate about accounting, possess strong leadership and analytical skills, and aspire to play a strategic role in the financial management of a business. For those who are ready to take on the challenges of overseeing financial operations and leading a team of accountants, becoming a Controller can be a highly rewarding career choice.

4.3.2 Chief Financial Officer (CFO)

The Chief Financial Officer (CFO) is one of the highest-ranking executives in an organization, responsible for overseeing the financial operations, strategic financial planning, risk management, and overall financial health of the company. This leadership position plays a critical role in shaping the financial future of the organization, guiding its growth, and ensuring compliance with financial regulations. The CFO is often a key member of the executive team, working closely with the CEO (Chief Executive Officer) and other senior leaders to make strategic decisions that affect the entire company.

For young professionals considering a career path that could lead to the CFO role, it's important to understand the qualifications, skills, and career trajectory required to reach this prestigious position. In this section, we'll explore the responsibilities, required skills, typical career path, and estimated salary range for a CFO.

Responsibilities of a CFO

The CFO is responsible for a wide range of functions that are crucial for the financial stability and success of the company. Here are the key areas of responsibility for a CFO:

1. Financial Strategy and Planning:

The CFO leads the development of financial strategies to help the company meet its long-term goals. This includes overseeing budgeting, forecasting, financial modeling, and risk management. They ensure that the company has a clear financial direction and allocate resources efficiently.

2. Financial Reporting:

A CFO is responsible for ensuring accurate and timely financial reporting to external stakeholders, such as investors, regulators, and auditors. This includes preparing quarterly and annual reports, financial statements, and disclosures. The CFO ensures that these reports comply with generally accepted accounting principles (GAAP) and other regulatory standards.

3. Risk Management:

Identifying financial risks and implementing risk mitigation strategies is another crucial role of the CFO. They evaluate market risks, operational risks, and financial risks to ensure the company's stability and growth. The CFO often develops contingency plans and stress-test financial models to prepare for unexpected situations, such as market downturns or economic shifts.

4. Capital Management:

Managing the company's capital structure is a key responsibility. This involves deciding on the mix of debt, equity, and internal funding used for investment purposes, acquisitions, or operational expansion. The CFO must maintain an optimal capital structure to support the company's goals while minimizing financial risk.

5. Leadership and Team Management:

The CFO often oversees the finance department, managing teams responsible for accounting, financial analysis, budgeting, and auditing. As a leader, the CFO needs to ensure that the finance team is aligned with the company's overall strategy and that they have the necessary resources, skills, and training to perform their duties effectively.

6. Investor Relations:

The CFO is often the main point of contact for investors, analysts, and shareholders. They communicate the financial health of the company, addressing any concerns or questions from stakeholders and building trust in the company's financial outlook. In times of financial turbulence or major business decisions, the CFO plays a key role in managing public perception and guiding the company through challenges.

7. Mergers and Acquisitions (M&A):

In larger organizations, the CFO often plays an integral role in evaluating potential mergers, acquisitions, and other strategic investments. They analyze the financial viability of these opportunities, oversee due diligence, and structure the financial aspects of these deals. The CFO may also be involved in negotiating terms and managing the post-acquisition integration process.

Key Skills and Qualifications for a CFO

Reaching the CFO position requires a combination of technical expertise, leadership abilities, and business acumen. Here are the skills and qualifications that are typically expected from a successful CFO:

1. Financial Expertise:

A deep understanding of financial management, accounting principles, and financial analysis is essential. CFOs must be experts in budgeting, financial reporting, and financial modeling. They should have advanced knowledge of accounting software and enterprise resource planning (ERP) systems.

2. Strategic Thinking:

As a member of the executive team, the CFO must think strategically and contribute to the overall direction of the company. They should have the ability to balance long-term financial growth with short-term financial management, aligning the financial strategy with the company's goals.

3. Leadership Skills:

The CFO leads large teams and often manages multiple departments. Strong leadership skills, including the ability to inspire and motivate teams, are essential. The CFO must also have excellent communication skills to present complex financial information to non-financial stakeholders and make decisions that impact the entire organization.

4. Risk Management:

A strong understanding of risk management and the ability to anticipate, assess, and mitigate financial risks are critical skills. CFOs need to have the experience and tools to navigate economic uncertainty, market fluctuations, and financial crises.

5. Negotiation Skills:

CFOs are frequently involved in high-level negotiations, whether they are managing capital investments, securing loans, or overseeing mergers and acquisitions. Strong negotiation skills are necessary to achieve favorable outcomes for the company.

6. Technological Proficiency:

As technology continues to transform the financial sector, CFOs must be proficient with the latest tools and software used for financial management, analytics, and reporting.

Knowledge of big data, artificial intelligence, and financial technology (fintech) can provide a competitive edge.

7. Industry Knowledge:

CFOs need a solid understanding of the specific industry in which their company operates. This includes being aware of industry trends, regulatory changes, and the competitive landscape. A CFO's ability to adapt to changes within their industry and apply financial strategies accordingly is vital for long-term success.

8. Education and Certification:

Most CFOs hold at least a bachelor's degree in accounting, finance, economics, or business administration. However, many have advanced degrees such as an MBA (Master of Business Administration) or a Master's in Finance. Certification as a CPA (Certified Public Accountant) or CMA (Certified Management Accountant) is often preferred, and many CFOs also hold additional certifications in financial management.

Career Path to Becoming a CFO

The path to becoming a CFO is typically a long and gradual journey that requires years of experience, education, and demonstrated leadership ability. Here's an overview of a typical career progression for someone aspiring to become a CFO:

1. Early Career:

Most CFOs begin their careers in entry-level accounting or finance roles, such as a Staff Accountant or Junior Auditor. In these roles, they gain foundational knowledge of financial statements, auditing practices, and reporting. During this stage, professionals typically pursue further education and certifications, such as the CPA or CMA.

2. Mid-Level Roles:

After gaining experience in entry-level roles, many professionals move into mid-level positions, such as Financial Analyst or Senior Accountant. In these positions, they begin to take on more responsibility, including financial analysis, budgeting, and reporting. This is also when they may begin to specialize in areas such as tax accounting, corporate finance, or internal auditing.

3. Managerial Roles:

As individuals gain experience and develop their leadership abilities, they often transition into managerial roles. Positions such as Finance Manager, Controller, or Accounting Director are common stepping stones to the CFO position. In these roles, professionals oversee entire departments, manage teams, and make strategic decisions related to financial planning and operations.

4. Executive Leadership:

The final step to becoming a CFO is transitioning into executive leadership roles, such as Vice President of Finance or Chief Accounting Officer (CAO). At this stage, individuals are expected to manage the financial operations of the company at a strategic level and contribute to overall business decisions.

Salary Range for CFOs

The salary of a CFO can vary greatly depending on factors such as the size of the organization, the industry, geographic location, and the individual's level of experience. Here's a general breakdown of the salary range for CFOs:

- Entry-Level CFOs (0–5 years of experience): *$150,000 – $250,000* per year

- Mid-Career CFOs (5–15 years of experience*): $250,000 – $400,000* per year

- Experienced CFOs (15+ years of experience): *$400,000 – $1,000,000+* per year

In addition to base salary, many CFOs receive bonuses, stock options, and other forms of compensation that can significantly increase their overall earnings. CFOs at large, publicly traded companies or in highly competitive industries, such as finance or technology, may earn even higher compensation packages.

Conclusion

Becoming a CFO is the pinnacle of many accounting and finance careers, and the role comes with a great deal of responsibility. The path to becoming a CFO requires a combination of technical expertise, leadership skills, and a strategic mindset. For young professionals, it is essential to develop a strong foundation in accounting, pursue continuous education, and gain experience in progressively senior roles. The rewards, both financially and professionally, are considerable, and the role of CFO offers the opportunity to make a significant impact on an organization's success and future.

CHAPTER V
Day in the Life of an Accountant

5.1 Working in Public Accounting

Public accounting is one of the most exciting and dynamic areas of the accounting profession, offering a wide range of services and an unparalleled opportunity to work with a diverse array of clients. Whether it's auditing a multinational corporation or providing tax advice to a small business owner, public accounting provides an excellent foundation for anyone pursuing a career in the field.

As a young accountant, the idea of working in public accounting might seem daunting due to its fast-paced and challenging nature, but it can be one of the most rewarding career paths you can take. In this section, we'll take a deeper look at what it's like to work in public accounting, the various roles and responsibilities, the work environment, and the skills you'll need to thrive.

What is Public Accounting?

Public accounting refers to firms or practices that offer accounting services to a broad range of clients, including individuals, corporations, government agencies, and non-profit organizations. Public accountants provide services such as auditing, tax preparation, consulting, and advisory services. These firms can range in size from small local firms to large global ones, such as the "Big Four" accounting firms—Deloitte, PwC, EY, and KPMG.

Unlike private accountants, who work for a single company or organization, public accountants are employed by firms that provide services to multiple clients. This provides an exciting variety of experiences and exposure to different industries, making it a unique career choice for young professionals.

Daily Responsibilities and Tasks

A typical day for an accountant working in public accounting will depend on their role and the specific department they're assigned to. The key areas of public accounting that you might work in include:

- *Audit*

- *Tax*

- *Consulting/Advisory*

- *Forensic Accounting*

- *Financial Reporting*

Each of these areas has distinct roles and requires specialized knowledge and skills, but all of them share a core requirement: attention to detail and strong communication skills.

Audit

Auditors in public accounting are responsible for examining and verifying the financial records of clients to ensure accuracy and compliance with regulations and laws. A typical day for an auditor can include:

- Reviewing financial statements and accounting records.

- Performing tests on client transactions to ensure compliance with financial regulations.

- Communicating findings and recommendations to clients.

- Collaborating with team members to prepare audit reports and present results.

- Visiting client sites to observe operations and gather evidence.

Auditors typically work in teams, with each member focusing on specific areas of a client's financial records. The work can be intense, especially during peak audit season, which often aligns with the financial year-end of many businesses. While it may involve long hours, it provides a deep dive into the workings of different industries, allowing you to develop a broad understanding of business operations.

Tax

Tax accountants in public accounting help clients manage their tax liabilities by preparing tax returns, advising on tax strategies, and ensuring compliance with local, state, and federal tax laws. A typical day for a tax accountant might look like:

- Reviewing and preparing corporate, personal, and partnership tax returns.

- Researching tax laws and regulations to provide up-to-date advice to clients.

- Advising clients on tax planning strategies to reduce tax liabilities.

- Communicating with tax authorities on behalf of clients.

- Preparing financial statements in accordance with tax standards.

Tax accountants often specialize in certain types of taxation, such as corporate tax, estate tax, or international tax. Working in tax can be especially rewarding if you enjoy problem-solving and understanding the complexities of tax codes. Like audit, tax accounting also involves significant busy seasons, particularly around tax filing deadlines.

Consulting and Advisory

Consultants in public accounting firms offer strategic advice to businesses on how to improve their financial performance, operations, and systems. A consultant's day might involve:

- Analyzing financial data to identify trends and issues.

- Working with clients to develop strategies to improve profitability.

- Advising on mergers and acquisitions.

- Helping clients implement new accounting systems or technologies.

Consulting offers variety in that each day can look completely different depending on the client's needs. If you're someone who enjoys working with clients to help solve their problems and providing solutions to improve their businesses, consulting might be the right path for you.

Skills You Need to Succeed in Public Accounting

Working in public accounting requires a combination of technical and soft skills. To excel, you will need:

- *Technical Skills:* A solid understanding of accounting principles (such as GAAP and IFRS), tax laws, auditing standards, and financial regulations. Knowledge of accounting software, spreadsheets, and data analysis tools is also crucial.

- *Attention to Detail:* Public accountants need to ensure accuracy in all financial reports and transactions. Small mistakes can have big consequences, so a sharp eye for detail is essential.

- *Communication Skills:* Public accountants often need to explain complex financial information to clients, who may not have a strong accounting background. Clear communication is essential, whether you're writing a report or having a conversation with a client.

- *Time Management:* Accountants in public accounting must handle multiple clients and projects at once, especially during peak seasons. Managing time effectively and meeting deadlines is crucial in this environment.

- *Problem-Solving Skills:* Whether it's resolving a client's tax issue or finding discrepancies during an audit, being able to think critically and find solutions is key to success in public accounting.

The Work Environment

Public accounting firms vary greatly in size, culture, and work environment. However, there are some general trends that most accountants will experience.

Office Culture

Most public accounting firms, particularly the larger ones, have a professional, fast-paced environment. You'll likely spend a significant amount of time working in an office, collaborating with other accountants, or working directly with clients. While the work can be demanding, there is also a strong culture of teamwork and support.

Firms may have a hierarchical structure, with junior accountants reporting to senior accountants or managers, who in turn report to partners. Despite the hierarchy, many firms encourage a collaborative work environment where all team members contribute ideas and help each other.

Work Hours and Busy Seasons

Working in public accounting can mean long hours, particularly during peak seasons such as tax season or year-end audit time. You may find yourself working overtime, including weekends, to meet deadlines. However, the busy seasons are balanced out by quieter periods where the workload is more manageable.

The work hours may vary depending on the firm's culture and the department you work in. Large firms may have a more rigorous schedule, while smaller firms may offer more flexibility. While the hours can be demanding, many public accountants find the variety and challenges to be rewarding, and the pay can be lucrative, especially after earning promotions.

Career Advancement

One of the greatest advantages of working in public accounting is the potential for career growth. Public accounting firms offer structured career paths that lead to rapid advancement for hard-working professionals. Starting as an associate or junior accountant, you can move up to a senior role, and eventually become a manager or partner in the firm.

Many accountants use their time in public accounting as a springboard to move into other roles, such as corporate accounting, financial analysis, or even starting their own firms. The broad exposure to different industries and clients also provides a great foundation for anyone considering a specialized career in tax, audit, or consulting.

Is Public Accounting Right for You?

Working in public accounting can be both challenging and rewarding. It's perfect for individuals who enjoy working with numbers, solving complex problems, and providing valuable insights to clients. Public accountants also enjoy diverse career opportunities and a chance to grow professionally at a rapid pace.

If you are someone who thrives in fast-paced environments, has a strong attention to detail, and is willing to put in the effort during peak seasons, then public accounting may be the perfect fit for you. However, it's important to understand the demands of the job, especially in terms of time commitment, and whether you're ready for a career that often requires working long hours under tight deadlines.

Ultimately, public accounting can provide an excellent foundation for anyone pursuing a career in accounting, offering valuable experience that can open doors to a wide range of career paths in the future.

5.2 Life in Corporate Accounting

Corporate accounting plays a pivotal role in the financial health and success of any business, from multinational corporations to small startups. If you've ever wondered what it's like to work in the accounting department of a company, this section will give you an inside look at the day-to-day life of a corporate accountant. Whether you're considering a career in corporate accounting or simply exploring your options, understanding the nature of this role can help you decide if it's the right fit for your career aspirations.

What is Corporate Accounting?

Corporate accounting refers to the management of a company's financial records, ensuring that all transactions are accurately documented and that financial statements reflect the true state of the organization's financial health. Corporate accountants are responsible for various financial tasks, from bookkeeping to preparing reports for management, investors, and regulatory bodies.

Unlike public accounting, where firms offer services to a wide range of clients, corporate accountants work exclusively for one company. They are often part of the company's internal accounting or finance department and are integral to decision-making processes within the organization. Their work ensures that financial transactions comply with accounting standards and laws, and it provides the necessary information for stakeholders to assess the company's performance.

Corporate accounting can be divided into different functions, each of which contributes to the overall financial operations of the organization. These functions may include:

- *General Accounting*: Responsible for maintaining the company's general ledger, ensuring accurate record-keeping of all transactions.

- *Cost Accounting:* Analyzing and controlling costs associated with the production of goods or services.

- *Financial Reporting:* Preparing financial statements, such as income statements, balance sheets, and cash flow statements, in accordance with regulatory guidelines.

- *Internal Controls:* Implementing systems to prevent fraud, ensure accuracy, and comply with laws and regulations.

- *Tax Accounting:* Managing the company's tax obligations, ensuring compliance with tax laws, and minimizing the company's tax liability.

A Day in the Life of a Corporate Accountant

A typical day in the life of a corporate accountant can vary depending on the size of the company, the industry it operates in, and the specific role within the accounting department. However, many of the tasks performed by corporate accountants share common characteristics. Here's a general overview of what you might expect:

1. Morning: Starting the Day with Financial Monitoring

The day often begins with reviewing the financial activities from the previous day. Corporate accountants may log into the company's financial software to monitor transactions, check the accounts payable and receivable systems, and ensure that all records are up to date. This early morning check-up can include:

- Verifying that all transactions from the previous day have been entered correctly.

- Reviewing any discrepancies or issues from prior reports.

- Ensuring that the company's cash balance is properly reconciled, and preparing for any upcoming payments or deposits.

In larger organizations, this task may be performed by accounting clerks or assistants, but it's still an important part of the daily routine for corporate accountants, especially those involved in financial reporting or analysis.

2. Midday: Preparing Reports and Analyzing Financial Data

After completing the initial financial check, corporate accountants spend a significant portion of their day preparing various financial reports. These reports can range from monthly financial statements to budget forecasts, cash flow analysis, and performance reports for different departments or product lines. Common tasks include:

- Creating Financial Statements: One of the primary responsibilities of corporate accountants is the preparation of accurate financial statements, including income statements, balance sheets, and cash flow statements. These reports help management understand the company's financial performance and make informed decisions.

- Budgeting and Forecasting: Corporate accountants are often involved in the process of creating budgets for various departments or the entire company. They work closely with department heads to understand their financial needs and project future expenses and revenues. They also update forecasts throughout the year to adjust for any unexpected changes in the business environment.

- Variance Analysis: Corporate accountants regularly compare actual financial results with the company's budget and forecasts to identify any significant variances. This analysis helps to spot potential issues or areas for improvement, such as cost overruns or underperforming product lines.

In some cases, corporate accountants may also conduct more complex analysis, such as break-even analysis, return on investment (ROI) calculations, and financial ratios to evaluate business performance.

3. Afternoon: Collaborating with Other Departments

While corporate accountants are primarily responsible for handling financial matters, they also work closely with other departments in the company. Collaboration is key to ensuring that financial operations align with business goals. Corporate accountants often have to:

- Work with the Operations Team: If the company produces goods or services, corporate accountants will regularly collaborate with the operations team to understand the cost structure, track inventory, and optimize cost controls. For example, they might analyze production costs to ensure they are within budget and identify areas where efficiency can be improved.

- Partner with Human Resources (HR): Payroll is an important area where accounting and HR intersect. Corporate accountants work with HR to ensure that employee compensation is processed correctly, taxes are deducted properly, and benefits are accounted for.

- Communicate with Management: Corporate accountants often serve as financial advisors to company executives and department heads. They may participate in meetings to provide insights into the company's financial status, help with decision-making, and recommend strategies for improving financial performance.

4. Late Afternoon: Closing the Books and Preparing for Audit

As the day progresses, corporate accountants focus on closing the books for the day or week. This process can involve reviewing journal entries, reconciling accounts, and ensuring that all transactions have been properly recorded. The closing process also includes:

- Bank Reconciliations: Accountants verify that the company's bank records match the internal records, ensuring that no discrepancies exist between what has been recorded and what is actually in the bank.

- Internal Audits: Corporate accountants often perform internal audits to ensure that the company's financial operations are accurate and compliant with accounting standards. This could involve checking for compliance with regulatory standards, verifying the accuracy of transactions, and ensuring the integrity of financial data.

- Preparing for External Audits: At the end of each financial year, the company may undergo an external audit by a public accounting firm. Corporate accountants help prepare for these audits by ensuring that all financial records are complete and accurate, and by answering any questions auditors may have.

Challenges and Rewards of Corporate Accounting

Working in corporate accounting can be challenging, but it also offers a range of rewards. The nature of the work can vary greatly depending on the company, industry, and specific role, but here are some key factors to consider:

Challenges:

- Tight Deadlines: Many corporate accountants work under strict deadlines, especially during the end-of-month or end-of-quarter reporting periods. The pressure to ensure that financial data is accurate and submitted on time can be stressful.

- Complex Regulations: Accounting standards, tax laws, and financial reporting requirements can be complicated and constantly changing. Corporate accountants must stay up to date with the latest regulations to ensure compliance.

- Workload Peaks: During certain times of the year, such as the end of the fiscal year or tax season, corporate accountants may experience a spike in workload. This can lead to long hours and tight schedules.

Rewards:

- Career Stability: Corporate accounting offers a high level of job stability, as every company, regardless of its size or industry, needs accounting professionals. The demand for skilled accountants remains strong, and the career outlook for corporate accountants is positive.

- Growth Opportunities: There is significant potential for career advancement within corporate accounting. Accountants can move up the ranks, transitioning from entry-level positions to managerial roles and eventually to senior leadership positions, such as Chief Financial Officer (CFO).

- Diverse Career Paths: Accounting is a highly transferable skill. After gaining experience in corporate accounting, you may find opportunities to move into other areas of finance, such as financial analysis, auditing, or tax management.

- Variety of Industries: Corporate accountants can work in almost any industry, from technology to healthcare, retail, finance, and more. This offers flexibility and the opportunity to work in an industry that aligns with personal interests and values.

Conclusion

A career in corporate accounting can be both challenging and rewarding. It requires attention to detail, strong analytical skills, and the ability to work under pressure. However, it also offers opportunities for growth, stability, and career advancement. By understanding the daily life of a corporate accountant, you can determine if this career path aligns with your interests and strengths. Whether you are drawn to the idea of working with financial data, collaborating with other departments, or helping companies succeed financially, corporate accounting offers a fulfilling career for those who enjoy problem-solving and working with numbers.

5.3 Nonprofit and Government Accounting

When most people think of accountants, they often picture professionals working in large corporations, preparing financial statements or tax returns. However, accounting is just as essential in the nonprofit sector and within government organizations. While the core principles of accounting, such as accuracy, transparency, and compliance, apply to all fields, nonprofit and government accounting come with their own set of unique challenges and requirements. In this section, we will explore the roles, responsibilities, and key differences associated with nonprofit and government accounting, providing you with a comprehensive understanding of what a day in the life of an accountant looks like in these fields.

1. Understanding the Differences: Nonprofit vs. Government Accounting

While both nonprofit and government accounting aim to ensure transparency and accountability in the handling of funds, they operate under different frameworks and have unique purposes.

Nonprofit Accounting

Nonprofit organizations, unlike for-profit businesses, do not distribute profits to shareholders or owners. Instead, any surplus revenue is reinvested into the organization's mission. Nonprofit organizations can include charities, educational institutions, foundations, and healthcare providers, among others.

The main difference between nonprofit accounting and for-profit accounting is the emphasis on the organization's mission over profit generation. Nonprofits must follow strict regulations regarding how they account for donations, grants, and funds generated from fundraising efforts. Their financial statements are generally categorized into different types of funds (restricted, unrestricted, and temporarily restricted) to maintain accountability to donors, government agencies, and the public.

Government Accounting

Government accounting is similarly mission-driven, focusing on the stewardship of public funds. Government entities at the federal, state, and local levels must adhere to specific accounting standards designed to ensure the efficient use of taxpayer money. In contrast to businesses, the goal of government accounting is not profit maximization but providing services to citizens in a transparent and efficient manner.

Government accounting also differs significantly from the private sector in terms of regulatory requirements. The Governmental Accounting Standards Board (GASB) sets the guidelines for government accounting, while nonprofit organizations typically adhere to standards outlined by the Financial Accounting Standards Board (FASB). This difference means that accountants working in these fields must understand and apply distinct sets of accounting principles and practices.

2. A Day in the Life of a Nonprofit Accountant

Nonprofit accountants often work in small to medium-sized teams, depending on the size of the organization. Their responsibilities revolve around ensuring that the nonprofit adheres to regulations and remains compliant with financial reporting standards. Their duties include preparing financial reports, managing funds, and working closely with management to ensure that the nonprofit's financial decisions align with its mission and strategic objectives.

Key Responsibilities of Nonprofit Accountants:

- *Tracking Donations and Grants:* Nonprofit accountants are responsible for tracking and categorizing donations, grants, and other sources of funding. These funds must be properly allocated and used in accordance with donor restrictions (e.g., some donations can only be used for specific programs or services).

- *Preparing Financial Statements:* Nonprofits must prepare various financial reports, including balance sheets, income statements, and cash flow statements. These reports must clearly show how funds were spent and whether the organization is fulfilling its mission within the allocated budget.

- *Fund Accounting:* A critical aspect of nonprofit accounting is fund accounting, which helps organizations track revenues and expenditures by category. This is especially important for nonprofit organizations that receive donations for specific purposes, such as grants for particular projects or programs. Fund accounting ensures that each dollar is used for its intended purpose.

- *Tax-Exempt Status Compliance:* Many nonprofit organizations are tax-exempt, meaning they are not required to pay taxes on certain income. However, maintaining this status requires compliance with specific regulations, such as the filing of annual reports like the IRS Form 990. Nonprofit accountants ensure that all paperwork is completed accurately and submitted on time to preserve tax-exempt status.

- *Internal Controls and Fraud Prevention:* Just as in for-profit businesses, nonprofit organizations must establish strong internal controls to protect against fraud and mismanagement of funds. Nonprofit accountants may also be responsible for conducting internal audits and helping to ensure that financial practices remain in line with ethical and legal standards.

Challenges Faced by Nonprofit Accountants:

Nonprofit accountants face some unique challenges that accountants in other industries may not encounter. These challenges include:

- *Revenue Variability:* Many nonprofits rely on donations and grants, which can fluctuate year to year. Accountants must work with uncertain and unpredictable revenue streams and ensure that financial planning accounts for these variations.

- *Donor Restrictions:* Nonprofits often receive funds with specific restrictions, such as grants that can only be used for a particular project. Managing and reporting these funds requires careful tracking and clear documentation.

- *Resource Limitations:* Nonprofit organizations may not have the same resources or access to sophisticated accounting software that for-profit businesses do. As a result, nonprofit accountants often need to be resourceful, managing finances with limited staff and tools.

3. A Day in the Life of a Government Accountant

Government accountants play a crucial role in managing taxpayer dollars and ensuring that public resources are used efficiently. Whether working at the federal, state, or local government level, government accountants are responsible for tracking revenue and expenditures, preparing financial statements, and ensuring compliance with regulatory guidelines.

Key Responsibilities of Government Accountants:

- Budgeting and Financial Reporting: Government accountants are involved in creating and managing budgets that reflect the priorities and needs of the community. They help governments allocate funds to different sectors, such as education, healthcare, and infrastructure, and ensure that these funds are spent appropriately.

- Compliance and Auditing: Government entities must comply with strict accounting standards, which include not only following generally accepted accounting principles (GAAP) but also meeting requirements specific to governmental accounting. Government accountants often perform audits to ensure that departments and agencies are spending taxpayer money in accordance with the law.

- Preparing Governmental Financial Statements: Government accountants prepare a variety of financial statements, including reports that show how public funds are being used. These statements must be transparent and easily understandable for both policymakers and the public.

- Managing Federal and State Grants: Many government accountants are responsible for managing federal and state grants, ensuring that the funds are used in accordance with their designated purposes and that detailed records are kept for future audits.

Challenges Faced by Government Accountants:

While the job of a government accountant is stable and offers meaningful work, it also comes with its own set of challenges:

- Public Scrutiny: Government accountants work in a highly transparent environment, where every dollar spent is subject to public scrutiny. This requires meticulous attention to detail and strict adherence to compliance standards.

- Political Influence: Government spending is often influenced by political decisions. Accountants working in government may find themselves navigating changing priorities and political climates that can impact budget allocation and financial reporting.

- Complex Regulations: Government accounting is governed by a labyrinth of regulations, and the application of these rules can be highly complex. Government accountants must stay up-to-date on changes to these regulations, especially when they involve things like tax laws or the funding of government projects.

4. The Work-Life Balance in Nonprofit and Government Accounting

Accounting in nonprofit and government sectors is often perceived as less demanding than in the private sector, and there is a strong emphasis on work-life balance in many of these organizations. However, this doesn't mean that these professionals don't face challenges. While the hours may not be as intense as those in corporate accounting, deadlines can still be tight, particularly during tax season, audit preparation, or the end of the fiscal year. Nonprofit and government accountants typically have more predictable schedules and may enjoy a better work-life balance compared to those working in private accounting firms or large corporations.

Benefits of Work-Life Balance in Nonprofit and Government Accounting:

- Standard Business Hours: Many nonprofit and government organizations operate within standard business hours, often Monday through Friday, which can allow for more consistent and predictable schedules.

- Fewer Overtime Demands: While some overtime is inevitable, especially during the tax season or audit preparation, accountants in these sectors generally work fewer hours than their counterparts in for-profit sectors.

- Mission-Driven Work: Many accountants in nonprofit and government sectors find fulfillment in their work because it directly supports public good or contributes to causes they care about. This sense of purpose can help reduce stress and create a healthier work-life balance.

Conclusion

Nonprofit and government accounting offer unique and fulfilling career paths for those interested in making a difference in society. While the work can be challenging, it also provides accountants with the opportunity to contribute to meaningful projects that benefit communities and the public at large. Whether you are helping a nonprofit stay true to its mission or ensuring that taxpayer dollars are spent efficiently, accountants in these fields play a vital role in maintaining transparency, accountability, and financial integrity.

In this section, we have explored what a typical day looks like for an accountant working in nonprofit and government sectors, the challenges they face, and the rewards that come with this work. As you consider your career in accounting, these fields may be an excellent choice if you value public service, stability, and the opportunity to contribute to positive   change.

5.4 Work-Life Balance in Accounting

One of the most significant aspects of any profession, and one that often dictates job satisfaction, is the ability to maintain a healthy work-life balance. For young professionals considering a career in accounting, it is essential to understand what work-life balance looks like in this field. Accounting, like many other professions, has its demands, but it also offers unique opportunities for achieving equilibrium between career and personal life. In this section, we will explore what work-life balance looks like for accountants, how it varies by sector, and practical strategies for managing work and personal life.

Understanding Work-Life Balance in Accounting

Work-life balance refers to the ability to effectively manage one's professional responsibilities and personal life without one area overwhelming the other. In accounting, this can be particularly challenging during peak seasons, such as tax season or fiscal year-end, when demands on accountants' time increase dramatically. However, outside of these peak times, many accounting professionals enjoy the flexibility that comes with the job.

Accounting roles vary widely, from public accounting firms to corporate finance departments to nonprofit organizations. Each sector has its own culture and expectations regarding work hours, workload, and flexibility, so understanding the nuances of each is crucial when considering a career in accounting.

Work-Life Balance in Public Accounting

Public accounting is often considered one of the most demanding sectors in the accounting profession. Firms like the "Big Four" (Deloitte, PwC, EY, and KPMG) are well-known for their rigorous work schedules, especially for entry-level staff and auditors. During busy seasons, such as tax season or audit season, public accountants may work long hours, sometimes even extending into the weekend or late nights. This can significantly impact their work-life balance.

Despite the challenges, many public accounting firms are taking steps to improve work-life balance. Some firms offer flexible hours, remote work options, and paid time off to help employees recharge. These changes have become even more common in the wake of the COVID-19 pandemic, which pushed many firms to embrace remote and hybrid work arrangements.

Moreover, public accounting provides opportunities for career advancement that are not always available in other sectors. Junior accountants often work their way up to senior positions, and those who make partner can enjoy increased control over their schedules. For some, the trade-off of long hours early in their careers is worth the potential rewards of higher positions and salaries later on. However, it's crucial for young accountants to set boundaries and maintain open communication with supervisors about their work-life needs.

Work-Life Balance in Corporate Accounting

Corporate accounting offers a more predictable and less demanding work schedule compared to public accounting. Accountants working in corporations often follow the company's business calendar, which includes regular working hours and less unpredictability. While quarterly and year-end financial reporting periods can still involve long hours, corporate accountants generally experience fewer of the intense work bursts that public accountants face.

One key advantage of working in corporate accounting is the stability of the workload. Many companies offer their employees regular office hours (9 to 5, Monday through Friday), which makes it easier to plan personal activities outside of work. Corporate accountants can also take advantage of employee benefits, such as vacation days, sick leave, and paid holidays, which provide greater opportunities for rest and personal time.

In addition, corporate accounting departments often emphasize collaboration and teamwork, which can foster a more supportive work environment. This collaborative nature of corporate accounting allows for better resource sharing, enabling employees to better manage workloads during high-demand periods.

However, while corporate accounting may provide a more stable work-life balance, there is still the potential for increased demands depending on the size and complexity of the organization. For instance, accountants working in multinational corporations may face the pressure of managing international accounts, which could involve coordination with teams in different time zones. Therefore, although corporate accounting offers more consistency, balancing work and life still requires effective time management and the ability to navigate challenges that may arise during busy periods.

Work-Life Balance in Nonprofit and Government Accounting

Nonprofit and government accounting roles tend to offer a more balanced work-life dynamic compared to the private sector. These organizations, while still maintaining high standards of financial accountability, often prioritize work-life balance for their employees. Nonprofit organizations, in particular, are known for offering more flexible work schedules and a strong emphasis on employee well-being. Employees are often encouraged to take time off, work remotely, or adjust their hours when necessary, making it easier for individuals to balance family responsibilities or personal interests.

Government accountants, on the other hand, typically work within regular government hours, such as 9 to 5, Monday through Friday. There is also a strong focus on maintaining regular hours and achieving work efficiency within those hours. Government jobs often come with benefits like pension plans, generous leave policies, and health insurance, which can contribute to a better overall work-life balance.

Because the workload in nonprofit and government accounting does not fluctuate as intensely as in the corporate or public accounting sectors, employees in these fields often experience fewer instances of burnout. Additionally, many individuals in nonprofit and government accounting find their work deeply rewarding because they contribute to the public good. This sense of purpose can positively impact overall well-being and job satisfaction, further promoting work-life balance.

Strategies for Achieving Work-Life Balance in Accounting

While some sectors of accounting may be more demanding than others, achieving a healthy work-life balance ultimately depends on the individual. Here are several strategies that accountants can implement to manage their workload and personal time effectively:

1. *Time Management Skills:* Effective time management is essential in any accounting role. This involves setting clear goals, prioritizing tasks, and avoiding procrastination. Using tools like calendars, to-do lists, and project management software can help accountants stay organized and on track.

2. *Setting Boundaries:* It's crucial for accountants to set clear boundaries with clients and colleagues. This includes not answering emails or taking calls outside of work hours unless absolutely necessary. Communicating expectations early on and adhering to boundaries is a key component of managing work-life balance.

3. *Delegation and Teamwork:* Accountants should learn to delegate tasks when appropriate and leverage their team's strengths. By sharing responsibilities, accountants can reduce the burden of individual workload during busy times and maintain a better work-life balance.

4. *Taking Breaks and Vacations:* Accountants, especially those working in high-pressure environments, should prioritize taking breaks throughout the day to recharge. Taking

time off for vacations and personal events is essential to prevent burnout and maintain mental health.

5. Remote Work Options: Many accounting professionals now have the option to work from home or take advantage of flexible schedules. If available, remote work can significantly improve work-life balance by eliminating commuting time and allowing for a more comfortable, personalized workspace.

6. Health and Wellness Practices: Maintaining physical and mental health is essential to managing work-life balance. Regular exercise, a healthy diet, and practices such as mindfulness or yoga can help accountants manage stress and stay energized throughout the workday.

7. Communicating with Supervisors: It's important to have open conversations with supervisors about workload and work-life balance needs. A supportive work environment encourages employees to express their concerns and request accommodations when necessary.

8. Knowing When to Ask for Help: If work pressures become overwhelming, accountants should not hesitate to ask for help from colleagues, supervisors, or even professional counselors. Recognizing when it's time to ask for assistance is a sign of strength, not weakness.

Conclusion

Work-life balance in accounting can vary greatly depending on the sector, the specific company culture, and the individual's approach to managing their time. While public accounting may present more challenges in terms of long hours and seasonal demands, corporate accounting, nonprofit, and government accounting roles offer more predictable schedules and less intense work spikes. Ultimately, achieving work-life balance in accounting requires proactive effort, strong time management skills, and the ability to set clear boundaries.

As the accounting profession continues to evolve, with more flexible work arrangements and remote options becoming the norm, the prospect of balancing work with personal life is becoming more achievable for accountants at all levels. For young professionals entering the field, understanding the demands of the profession and implementing strategies to manage work-life balance will be key to sustaining a fulfilling career in accounting.

CHAPTER VI
Networking and Building a Professional Brand

6.1 The Importance of Networking

Networking is not just about collecting business cards or following people on LinkedIn—it's about building meaningful, reciprocal relationships that can help you throughout your career. As you grow in your profession, these relationships will become vital assets, opening doors to job opportunities, new projects, and professional collaborations that might not have been possible otherwise.

As a young aspiring accountant, understanding the value of networking early on will give you a significant advantage. It allows you to connect with experienced professionals who can share their wisdom, provide career guidance, and even recommend you for job openings when the time comes. Additionally, it helps you stay current with industry trends, technological advancements, and best practices, which are constantly evolving in the accounting field.

One of the most effective ways to start building your network is by attending conferences and events. In this section, we'll explore how these events can help you make meaningful connections and why you should prioritize them as part of your career-building strategy.

6.1.1 Attending Conferences and Events

Attending conferences and industry events can be one of the most powerful ways to expand your professional network in the accounting field. These events provide an invaluable opportunity to meet like-minded individuals, from fellow aspiring accountants to seasoned professionals and even industry leaders. Here, we will delve into the numerous benefits of attending conferences and events, how to maximize the experience, and how to follow up on the connections you make.

Why Conferences and Events Matter

1. Exposure to Industry Leaders

One of the primary benefits of attending conferences and events is the chance to meet and interact with industry leaders, many of whom may be difficult to approach in other settings. These are the professionals who can provide you with insights into the latest developments in the accounting field, career advice, and even potential job opportunities. Often, these leaders are featured as keynote speakers or panelists, offering insights on topics like accounting trends, regulatory changes, and the future of the profession.

2. Access to Current Trends and Innovations

Accounting is a dynamic field with constant changes, especially in areas such as taxation, financial reporting standards, and technology. Attending conferences and events gives you direct access to the latest trends and innovations that may affect your future career. Whether it's new software tools that streamline bookkeeping processes or changes in international financial reporting standards, these events provide a first-hand look at what's coming next, helping you stay ahead of the curve.

3. Building a Personal Brand

Networking at conferences is an excellent way to build and promote your personal brand. When you attend industry events, you're essentially positioning yourself as someone who is serious about your professional growth. People at these events are looking for connections, and making a strong impression by engaging with others, asking thoughtful questions, and showing enthusiasm for your career can help you stand out in a crowded field.

4. Learning Opportunities

Conferences and events are also an excellent opportunity for learning. Whether through formal workshops or informal conversations, you will gain practical insights into the field that will enhance your knowledge base. The accounting profession, with its broad scope and depth, demands continuous learning, and attending these events helps you acquire new skills and deepen your understanding of specialized areas within accounting.

5. Expanding Your Reach

In the digital age, the people you meet at conferences can often become long-term contacts and collaborators. With platforms like LinkedIn and professional association memberships, you can maintain relationships with conference attendees long after the event ends. You'll find that some of these relationships evolve into collaborative projects, joint ventures, or even future job opportunities, making the connections you build at conferences some of the most valuable in your career.

How to Maximize Your Conference Experience

1. Do Your Research Before Attending

To make the most of any event, it's essential to prepare ahead of time. Start by researching the speakers, sessions, and attendees. What are the key topics being discussed? Who are the influencers or thought leaders at the event? By understanding the focus of the conference and identifying the individuals you want to connect with, you can tailor your approach, making your networking efforts more targeted and efficient.

2. Set Clear Goals

Before attending a conference, think about what you hope to achieve. Are you looking for a mentor? Do you want to learn more about a specific accounting specialty, such as forensic accounting or tax planning? Setting clear goals for the event will help you prioritize your time and energy, ensuring that you leave with the information or connections that matter most to you.

3. Engage Actively in Sessions

Simply attending a conference and sitting through sessions isn't enough to make the most of the event. Actively participate in discussions, ask questions, and interact with speakers and other attendees during breaks. Engaging with the material and the people around you demonstrates that you're not just there to learn—you're there to contribute to the conversation and make valuable connections.

4. Bring Business Cards and Digital Networking Tools

Even in the digital age, business cards remain an important tool for networking. While you can connect online through social media or LinkedIn later, having a business card handy ensures that you leave a tangible reminder of your conversation with the people you meet. Some conferences also use event-specific apps that allow attendees to connect digitally. Make sure to download these apps, and don't be shy about exchanging contact information with those you meet.

5. Be Approachable and Authentic

When networking at conferences, be yourself. People appreciate authenticity and are more likely to connect with someone who is genuine. Rather than trying to impress with your knowledge, focus on building relationships. Be a good listener and show interest in what others have to say. Networking is not just about what you can take from others—it's also about how you can contribute and offer value in return.

6. Follow Up After the Event

After the conference, don't let your new connections fade into the background. Take the time to follow up with the people you met. Send a personalized message on LinkedIn or through email, referencing something specific from your conversation. This not only reinforces the connection but also keeps you on their radar for future opportunities. Make it a habit to check in every few months, sharing updates about your professional journey, asking for advice, or simply keeping in touch.

Overcoming the Challenges of Networking at Conferences

While attending conferences offers many benefits, it can also come with challenges. It's easy to feel overwhelmed in a room full of professionals, especially if you're new to the field. Here are some tips to overcome common challenges:

- *Feeling Out of Place:* Remember, everyone at the event is there to network and learn, just like you. It's okay to feel nervous, but don't let it stop you from approaching others. Start with simple questions like, "What brought you to this conference?" or "What session did you find most interesting?"

- *Fear of Rejection:* Networking can sometimes feel intimidating, and you may worry about rejection. Keep in mind that most professionals at conferences are open to making new connections. If someone doesn't seem interested, don't take it personally—just move on and continue meeting new people.

- *Time Management:* Conferences can be packed with sessions, workshops, and social events. Plan your time wisely to ensure that you attend the most relevant sessions while also leaving room for networking. Don't be afraid to step out of a session if you feel like you've learned what you needed and want to make a connection in the networking area.

Conclusion

Networking at conferences and events is a vital part of building a successful career in accounting. These events provide opportunities to learn, connect with professionals, and stay informed about the latest developments in the industry. By preparing effectively, engaging with others, and following up after the event, you can create a strong professional network that will support your career growth and help you achieve long-term success in the accounting field.

In the next section, we will explore another critical aspect of networking—joining professional associations—and how these memberships can offer you ongoing support, development, and connections throughout your accounting career.

Example: Networking at an Accounting Conference

Background:

Imagine you're a young accounting student named Sarah, and you've just started your journey into the accounting profession. You've heard a lot about the importance of networking, but you're unsure how to begin. You decide to attend the "Annual Accounting & Finance Summit," a well-known conference for accountants, auditors, tax professionals, and financial analysts.

The conference will feature key industry leaders, breakout sessions on various accounting specialties, and numerous networking events aimed at connecting professionals. While you feel nervous about meeting so many experienced professionals, you're determined to make the most of this opportunity.

Sarah's Experience at the Conference:

1. Research and Preparation:

Before attending, Sarah does her homework. She checks the conference website and reviews the list of speakers, panel discussions, and breakout sessions. She notices that there will be a panel on "Emerging Trends in Forensic Accounting," which piques her interest, as she's considering this specialty for her future career. She also reads up on some of the key influencers in the accounting field who will be attending, such as the CEO of a top forensic accounting firm and a prominent professor in accounting technology.

2. Setting Goals:

Sarah sets clear goals for the conference. First, she wants to gain a deeper understanding of forensic accounting. Second, she aims to network with at least five professionals, including a few who work in forensic accounting, to get a better idea of the field. Lastly, she hopes to gather some useful insights from established professionals on what it takes to succeed in the accounting industry.

3. Engaging Actively in Sessions:

On the first day of the conference, Sarah attends the panel on "Emerging Trends in Forensic Accounting." During the discussion, a senior forensic accountant mentions the rising role of technology in fraud detection. Sarah, eager to learn more, raises her hand and asks a question about how technology has impacted forensic accounting and whether she should focus on tech skills. The panelist answers her question thoughtfully, giving Sarah valuable advice about the growing demand for accounting professionals who can combine accounting expertise with tech knowledge.

After the session, Sarah approaches the panelist, introduces herself, and thanks him for his insights. She asks if he has any advice for someone just starting out in forensic accounting. The panelist offers to connect with her on LinkedIn and invites her to send a follow-up email for further discussion.

4. Networking During Breaks and Social Events:

During lunch, Sarah strikes up a conversation with a fellow attendee, John, who works as an internal auditor. They discuss the differences between auditing and financial accounting, and Sarah shares her interest in forensic accounting. John mentions that his company often hires forensic accountants for certain cases and offers to introduce Sarah to his HR team when the time is right. Sarah takes note of his contact details and thanks him for his generosity.

In the evening, there's a networking reception. Sarah is initially hesitant about mingling in such a large crowd but remembers that she's there to build relationships. She introduces herself to a few professionals at the event, including Laura, an experienced tax accountant who has been in the field for over 15 years. Laura shares her career journey and offers advice about the importance of continuous learning and certifications like the CPA. They exchange business cards, and Laura invites Sarah to attend a local chapter of the American Institute of CPAs (AICPA), where she can continue learning and networking with other professionals.

5. Following Up After the Conference:

The day after the conference, Sarah follows up with the panelist from the forensic accounting session, sending a personalized email expressing her appreciation for his insights and offering a brief update on her career progress. She also connects with him on LinkedIn, attaching a brief message referencing their conversation.

Similarly, Sarah sends follow-up messages to John and Laura, thanking them for their time and the helpful advice they shared. She mentions specific points they discussed during their conversations, which helps personalize the message and strengthen the relationship.

Sarah also takes action on Laura's invitation to join the AICPA chapter. By the end of the month, she attends her first meeting, where she meets several other young professionals and learns more about the resources available to students and early-career accountants.

Outcome:

By attending the conference and engaging with the right people, Sarah gains valuable insights into the field of forensic accounting, makes meaningful connections with professionals, and even receives an invitation to join a professional association. These new relationships give Sarah a sense of direction in her career, as well as practical advice on navigating the challenges she will face as a young accountant. Additionally, the conference helps her stay up-to-date with industry trends, which will be crucial as she progresses in her career.

As Sarah continues to build her network, she finds that the connections she made at the conference become important mentors, sources of guidance, and even job leads in the future. Her experience at the conference demonstrates the power of networking in the accounting field and how a single event can shape the trajectory of an entire career.

6.1.2 Joining Professional Associations

As you begin your journey into the world of accounting, one of the most powerful steps you can take to develop your career is to become a member of a professional association. These associations are not just for experienced accountants; they offer valuable opportunities for students and young professionals as well. Joining an association can be a transformative move that accelerates your career growth, builds your professional network, and keeps you updated on industry trends and developments.

In this section, we will explore the significance of joining professional accounting associations, the benefits they provide, how to choose the right one for your career goals, and how to maximize your membership to make the most of this important resource.

What Are Professional Associations?

Professional associations are organizations that bring together individuals who share common interests, goals, and a professional background in a particular field. In the case of accounting, these associations typically consist of certified public accountants (CPAs), auditors, tax professionals, financial analysts, and other specialists within the broader accounting profession. The primary purpose of these associations is to advance the knowledge, standards, and ethics of the profession, as well as to provide members with ongoing education, advocacy, and networking opportunities.

Some of the most prominent accounting associations include:

- The American Institute of Certified Public Accountants (AICPA): One of the largest and most well-known organizations for CPAs in the United States, offering resources for education, certification, and career development.

- The Association of Chartered Certified Accountants (ACCA): A global body for professional accountants, focusing on providing members with skills, knowledge, and qualifications.

- The Institute of Management Accountants (IMA): Specializing in management accounting, IMA provides resources for professionals in managerial roles within accounting.

- The Chartered Institute of Management Accountants (CIMA): A UK-based association that focuses on business accounting and management practices.

Many countries have their own national and regional associations that cater to local standards, regulations, and industries. Additionally, there are specialized organizations that focus on niches within accounting, such as forensic accounting, government accounting, and internal auditing.

Why Join a Professional Association?

There are several compelling reasons to join a professional accounting association early in your career. While many may think that such memberships are reserved for seasoned professionals, joining an association at the beginning of your career can be incredibly beneficial. Here are some of the main advantages:

1. Networking Opportunities

Professional associations are excellent venues for connecting with other accounting professionals. As a member, you will have access to a broad network of accountants, including people with experience in areas that interest you. Networking is one of the most effective ways to gain career insights, find mentorship opportunities, and even discover job openings. The connections you make through these organizations can be crucial in helping you land your first job or advancing your career to the next level.

2. Educational Resources and Training

Most professional associations offer a wealth of educational resources to their members. This can include access to webinars, workshops, conferences, and training programs designed to enhance your technical and soft skills. These resources are tailored to current industry standards and trends, so you will be equipped with the latest knowledge, keeping you ahead in your career.

Many associations also provide access to certification courses or offer discounts on certification exams, which is particularly beneficial if you're planning to pursue advanced qualifications like the Certified Public Accountant (CPA) or Certified Management Accountant (CMA).

3. Career Development and Job Search Support

One of the most significant advantages of joining a professional association is the career support they offer. Many associations have job boards where employers post open positions exclusively for members. They also often offer career coaching, resume reviews, and interview preparation services to help you navigate the job market more effectively. If you're unsure of your career path, professional associations can provide valuable guidance on how to specialize or explore various accounting niches.

In addition, membership in an association can increase your credibility and attractiveness to potential employers. Being affiliated with a respected professional body shows your commitment to your career and ongoing professional development, which can give you an edge over other candidates.

4. Staying Updated on Industry Trends

The accounting profession is constantly evolving. Changes in tax laws, financial regulations, and industry standards can have a significant impact on your work. By joining a professional association, you gain access to publications, newsletters, and industry reports that keep you informed about new developments in accounting. Staying current with industry trends is crucial, especially as technology continues to transform the accounting landscape.

Professional associations often organize conferences and seminars where experts discuss emerging topics in the field. By attending these events, you can stay up-to-date with new tools, techniques, and methodologies that will enhance your skill set.

5. Advocacy and Representation

Many professional associations advocate for the rights and interests of accounting professionals on a national or international level. They work with government bodies and regulatory agencies to influence policy decisions that affect the profession. As a member, you can participate in these advocacy efforts and help shape the future of the industry.

Being part of an association also means you have access to industry standards, ethics guidelines, and best practices that can enhance your professional reputation and ensure that you adhere to the highest ethical standards.

6. Recognition and Credibility

Membership in a respected accounting association adds credibility to your resume and professional profile. It signals to potential employers and clients that you are committed to maintaining high standards in your work. As you gain more experience and move up in your career, your membership in an association may also open doors for leadership and volunteer roles within the organization, providing further recognition and opportunities for career advancement.

How to Choose the Right Professional Association

With so many professional associations available, it can be challenging to determine which one is right for you. Here are a few tips to help you make the right choice:

1. Consider Your Career Goals and Interests

If you're still exploring different areas of accounting, joining a broad association like the AICPA or ACCA can give you access to a wide range of resources. However, if you know you want to specialize in a particular area—such as tax accounting, forensic accounting, or internal auditing—it may be worth joining an organization that focuses specifically on that field.

2. Look for Local and Global Opportunities

Consider whether you want to be part of a global association or one that focuses on your local region or country. Some associations have a global reach and offer international networking opportunities, while others focus on local laws, regulations, and job markets.

3. Evaluate Membership Benefits

Review the benefits offered by each association. Compare the types of educational resources, career services, and networking opportunities they provide. Some associations may offer mentorship programs, access to exclusive job postings, or discounts on certification exams, while others might have a stronger focus on conferences and networking events.

4. Consider Membership Costs

While the benefits of professional association membership can be invaluable, it's essential to weigh the membership costs against the resources provided. Most associations charge an annual fee, which can vary depending on the level of membership and the services offered. Be sure to understand the cost and whether it aligns with the benefits you'll receive.

Maximizing Your Membership

Once you've joined a professional association, it's important to make the most of your membership. Here are some tips to help you get the most out of your experience:

1. Participate Actively

Attend association events, webinars, and conferences to learn from industry experts and expand your network. Take advantage of any leadership or volunteer opportunities that may arise within the organization. Actively participating in these activities will help you gain visibility and build relationships with other professionals in your field.

2. Seek Mentorship

Many associations offer mentorship programs where you can connect with experienced professionals who can provide career advice, guidance, and support. Mentorship is an invaluable tool for personal and professional growth, and it can give you insights that will help you navigate the challenges of your accounting career.

3. Use Resources Regularly

Take advantage of the educational materials, job boards, and career development tools offered by the association. Set aside time each week or month to engage with these resources to stay informed and keep building your skills.

Joining a professional accounting association is a powerful step in building your career. By providing you with networking opportunities, educational resources, career support, and industry insights, these organizations can help you grow both personally and professionally. As you progress through your accounting career, your association membership will be a valuable asset that enables you to stay competitive, connect with like-minded professionals, and continuously develop your skills.

6.2 Building Your Personal Brand

6.2.1 Creating a LinkedIn Profile

In today's professional world, having a strong online presence is no longer optional—it's a necessity. One of the most powerful platforms for building and showcasing your personal brand is LinkedIn. As the world's largest professional network, LinkedIn offers a unique space for individuals to connect, share ideas, seek advice, and, most importantly, present themselves as valuable assets to potential employers, clients, and colleagues. For aspiring accountants, LinkedIn is a game-changer that can help you stand out in a competitive field.

Why LinkedIn Matters for Aspiring Accountants

LinkedIn is more than just an online resume; it's an opportunity to showcase your skills, expertise, and professional persona to a global audience. More than 700 million people across the world use LinkedIn to network, search for job opportunities, and build their careers. For young professionals interested in accounting, LinkedIn serves as a vital tool for career development in the following ways:

1. Visibility: Potential employers, recruiters, and clients often turn to LinkedIn when seeking candidates. A well-crafted LinkedIn profile increases your chances of being noticed.

2. Networking: LinkedIn enables you to connect with industry professionals, accounting firms, and thought leaders. These connections can lead to mentorship, collaborations, and even job offers.

3. Knowledge Sharing: The platform allows you to stay up-to-date with industry trends, accounting practices, and financial regulations. By following companies, groups, and influencers in the accounting space, you can grow your knowledge base and stay relevant.

Now that we understand why LinkedIn is important, let's look at how to create a compelling LinkedIn profile that reflects your aspirations and potential as an accountant.

1. Start with a Professional Profile Picture

The first thing anyone will notice on your LinkedIn profile is your profile picture. This photo is your first impression, so it's important to make it count. While LinkedIn isn't a platform for casual photos, you don't need to have a studio-shot image. Here are some tips for selecting the perfect professional profile picture:

- Dress Professionally: Wear business attire appropriate for your industry. For accounting, a suit or smart business outfit is typically a good choice.

- Smile and Look Approachable: A friendly expression can make you seem more approachable. A smile will help others connect with you better.

- Choose a Neutral Background: Opt for a clean, simple background that doesn't distract from you. A solid color or a blurred background of an office or library works well.

- Good Lighting: Ensure your face is clearly visible with sufficient lighting. Avoid dark or overly bright images.

This profile photo will be the visual representation of you as a professional, so it's crucial to make it look polished and business-ready.

---

2. Write a Compelling Headline

Your LinkedIn headline is a key piece of real estate in your profile. It's one of the first things people see when they search for you, and it's a vital opportunity to capture attention. By default, LinkedIn uses your current job title as your headline, but that may not fully convey your aspirations or skills. Consider customizing your headline to better reflect who you are and what you want to achieve.

Here's how to make your LinkedIn headline more impactful:

- Be Specific: Instead of a generic headline like "Accounting Student," consider something more specific, such as "Aspiring Accountant | Passionate About Financial Analysis and Tax Planning." This gives a clearer sense of your goals and interests.

- Highlight Your Skills: If you have any specific skills or certifications, such as "Certified QuickBooks ProAdvisor" or "Experienced in Tax Preparation," include these to demonstrate your expertise.

- Use Keywords: Think about what recruiters and employers might be searching for when looking for young accounting talent. Use relevant keywords like "Accounting," "Financial Reporting," "Tax Services," or "Auditing."

A strong headline will help you attract the right opportunities and encourage viewers to explore your profile further.

3. Craft a Compelling Summary (About Section)

Your LinkedIn summary is where you can tell your story—why you chose accounting, what you're passionate about, and what sets you apart from others. This section allows you to dive deeper than your headline and give visitors a sense of your personality, goals, and expertise. It's important to make this part engaging and reflective of your professional journey.

Here's a guide to creating a powerful summary:

- Start with an Engaging Hook: Begin with an attention-grabbing sentence that draws the reader in. For example, you could say, "As a young aspiring accountant with a passion for numbers and problem-solving, I'm eager to bring my skills to the financial world."

- Explain Your Journey: Share your background, education, and why you decided to pursue accounting. Mention any relevant experience or internships you've had that gave you practical exposure to the field.

- Highlight Your Skills: Briefly mention the key skills you've developed, such as financial analysis, bookkeeping, tax preparation, or familiarity with accounting software like QuickBooks or Excel.

- State Your Career Goals: Share what you hope to achieve in your accounting career. For example, "I'm excited to contribute to an accounting firm where I can expand my knowledge in tax accounting and develop my auditing skills."

- Show Personality: While professionalism is important, it's also good to let your personality shine through. Write in the first person to make your summary more personal and relatable.

A well-written summary gives recruiters and potential employers a comprehensive view of who you are as a professional and why you stand out.

---

4. Highlight Your Education and Certifications

For young professionals in accounting, education plays a central role in your career path. LinkedIn allows you to showcase your academic achievements, which can help establish credibility and demonstrate your dedication to the profession.

Here's how to highlight your education effectively:

- Include Your Degree(s): List your major (e.g., Accounting, Finance) and any relevant coursework that showcases your knowledge of financial principles, tax law, or auditing.

- Mention Certifications: If you've earned any certifications such as CPA (Certified Public Accountant) or CMA (Certified Management Accountant), make sure to list them. These credentials show that you're committed to advancing in your profession.

- Highlight Extracurricular Activities: Many students and young professionals gain valuable experience outside the classroom. If you've been part of an accounting club, volunteered for tax assistance programs, or participated in relevant workshops, include these activities in your education section.

These details not only demonstrate your academic qualifications but also highlight your proactive approach to learning and growing in your field.

---

5. Experience and Internships

While you may not yet have years of professional experience, it's still important to highlight any internships, part-time jobs, or volunteer experiences you've had in the accounting field. This section helps recruiters and potential employers understand how you've applied your learning in real-world settings.

When listing your experience, consider the following:

- Internships: If you've interned at an accounting firm or within an accounting department, include details about the tasks you were responsible for, such as preparing financial reports, assisting with audits, or managing client accounts.

- Part-time Roles: If you've held part-time positions that required you to use your analytical skills, such as working in a retail job that involved inventory management or bookkeeping, mention these experiences.

- Achievements: Don't just list your duties—highlight any specific accomplishments or projects that demonstrate your ability to succeed in the accounting world.

---

6. Recommendations and Endorsements

One of the most powerful features on LinkedIn is the ability to gather recommendations and endorsements. These serve as testimonials from colleagues, supervisors, professors, or anyone else who can vouch for your skills and character.

- Request Recommendations: Ask professors, internship supervisors, or mentors to write you a recommendation that highlights your skills, work ethic, and potential as an accountant.

- Endorse Skills: On LinkedIn, your connections can endorse the skills you've listed on your profile, such as "Financial Reporting" or "Tax Accounting." Endorsements provide social proof of your abilities and can help you stand out.

---

7. Engage with Content

Finally, a key part of building your LinkedIn brand is engaging with relevant content. Sharing articles, commenting on posts, and publishing your own thoughts can help establish you as a thought leader in your field, even at a young age.

- Share Relevant Articles: Share articles related to the accounting industry, such as updates on tax regulations, changes in financial reporting standards, or trends in accounting software. Add your thoughts to spark discussions and show your expertise.

- Publish Posts or Articles: If you feel comfortable, consider writing original content, such as blog posts or articles, discussing your experiences with accounting coursework, or sharing tips for young accountants.

- Participate in Groups: Join LinkedIn groups related to accounting and finance. Engaging in these communities will help you expand your network and demonstrate your commitment to the profession.

Conclusion

Building a LinkedIn profile isn't just about filling out fields and uploading a picture. It's about strategically positioning yourself as a professional ready to take on the challenges of the accounting industry. By carefully crafting your profile, highlighting your skills and experiences, and engaging with relevant content, you'll be able to create a personal brand that reflects your potential as a future accountant. A strong LinkedIn profile will not only help you stand out to recruiters and employers but will also serve as a tool to expand your network, learn from industry leaders, and advance your career in accounting.

6.2.2 Developing a Resume and Cover Letter

When you're just starting out in your career, having a resume and cover letter that accurately reflect your skills, qualifications, and potential is essential. These documents serve as your first introduction to a potential employer, and in many cases, they can make the difference between landing an interview or being passed over. While they both serve the same purpose—getting you noticed—your resume and cover letter need to be tailored for specific roles, ensuring that your personal brand is conveyed clearly and effectively.

Crafting Your Resume

A resume is your personal marketing tool—it highlights your qualifications, experience, and accomplishments in a concise format. In the field of accounting, the details matter. You need to demonstrate both your technical skills and your ability to work within a professional setting. Your resume should be a reflection of your potential as an accountant and show that you are capable of handling the responsibilities of the job you're applying for. Here are some key components to consider when crafting your resume:

1. Contact Information

At the top of your resume, include your name, phone number, email address, and LinkedIn profile URL. Make sure your email address is professional—avoid using addresses like "coolguy123@gmail.com" or "partyanimal@aol.com." Instead, opt for something more professional, like "john.doe@email.com." A professional email address can make a significant difference in the impression you give.

2. Professional Summary or Objective

This section briefly summarizes who you are as a professional and what you aim to achieve in your career. A strong objective statement can set the tone for the rest of your resume. If you're applying for a role as a junior accountant, for instance, your objective might look something like this:

"Detail-oriented and proactive recent graduate with a degree in accounting, seeking an entry-level accounting position to utilize strong analytical skills, technical knowledge, and passion for financial management. Eager to contribute to a dynamic team while continuing to grow professionally within the accounting field."

Keep it short and impactful, showing enthusiasm and a clear focus.

3. Skills

Highlight the technical skills and soft skills that are relevant to the position you're applying for. For accounting, this would include skills like:

- Financial reporting and analysis

- Proficiency in accounting software (e.g., QuickBooks, Microsoft Excel, SAP)

- Knowledge of tax laws and accounting regulations

- Attention to detail and accuracy

- Organizational and time management skills

- Strong communication and interpersonal skills

Make sure the skills you list match those required in the job description, as many employers use applicant tracking systems (ATS) to scan resumes for keywords.

4. Education

Your educational background is crucial, especially early in your career. List your degree(s), the school(s) you attended, and your graduation year. If you've earned any additional certifications, such as CPA, CMA, or any other accounting-related qualifications, include those as well. For example:

"Bachelor of Science in Accounting, XYZ University, Graduated: 2023"

"Certified Public Accountant (CPA), In Progress, Expected Completion: 2025"

If you have a strong GPA or academic achievements, consider including them, but only if they are above 3.5 or otherwise noteworthy.

5. Experience

Even if you don't have direct professional experience in accounting, there are ways to demonstrate your skills through internships, part-time jobs, volunteer work, or academic projects. For each position, include the following:

- Job title

- Company name

- Dates of employment

- Bullet points describing your responsibilities and achievements

Quantify your achievements wherever possible. For example, instead of saying "Assisted with budget planning," say "Assisted in preparing quarterly budget reports for a team of 5, improving budgeting accuracy by 15%." Use numbers to show your impact.

6. Additional Sections

Depending on your experiences and the role you're applying for, you may include additional sections like:

- Certifications: Include any certifications or licenses, such as CPA or CMA, or courses you have completed that are relevant to the job.

- Projects: If you've worked on accounting-related projects (such as a tax preparation project or an analysis of company financials), include those here.

- Languages: If you are bilingual or multilingual, list those languages and your proficiency level.

- Awards and Honors: Include any academic, professional, or volunteer awards you have received.

Writing a Compelling Cover Letter

While your resume showcases your qualifications, your cover letter allows you to tell your story. It's your opportunity to show your personality, explain why you're interested in the specific role, and demonstrate how your skills and experiences align with the company's needs. A great cover letter helps personalize your application and allows the employer to see your enthusiasm and fit for the position. Below are some key tips for writing an effective cover letter:

1. Format and Structure

A cover letter should always begin with a formal greeting, ideally addressed to a specific person (such as the hiring manager). If you're unsure of the name, "Dear Hiring Manager" is an acceptable alternative. Next, include an introductory paragraph where you introduce yourself and express your interest in the role. The body of the letter should detail your relevant skills and experiences, while the closing paragraph should thank the employer for considering your application and express your interest in discussing the position further. Lastly, end with a formal closing like "Sincerely" or "Best Regards."

2. Opening Paragraph

In the opening paragraph, briefly introduce yourself and explain why you're excited about the position. For example:

"Dear [Hiring Manager's Name],

I am writing to express my interest in the Junior Accountant position at [Company Name], as advertised on your website. I am a recent graduate with a Bachelor's degree in Accounting from XYZ University, and I am eager to apply my analytical skills and attention to detail in a dynamic accounting role."

3. Body Paragraph(s)

In the body of your cover letter, focus on specific skills and experiences that make you an ideal fit for the job. Show that you understand the company's needs and explain how you can contribute to its success. Mention any relevant academic projects, internships, or previous jobs. Highlight your technical skills (like familiarity with accounting software) and soft skills (like communication or teamwork). For example:

"During my internship at ABC Accounting Firm, I assisted in preparing financial statements, reconciled accounts, and worked closely with senior accountants on tax filing for clients. My ability to handle complex tasks under tight deadlines, combined with my strong technical skills in Excel, has prepared me well for this position."

4. Closing Paragraph

The closing paragraph should express gratitude for the opportunity to apply and indicate your desire for an interview. It should also provide your contact information in case the hiring manager needs to reach you.

"I would love the opportunity to discuss how my skills and experience align with the needs of your team. Thank you for considering my application, and I look forward to the possibility of speaking with you further. Please feel free to contact me at [phone number] or [email address]."

5. Tone and Style

Your cover letter should be professional, but it should also convey your enthusiasm. Avoid using overly formal or robotic language. Keep the tone conversational but respectful, and ensure that your personality shines through while remaining appropriate for a professional context.

In summary, developing a strong resume and cover letter is one of the most important steps you can take to build your personal brand as an aspiring accountant. These documents are your first opportunity to make a lasting impression on potential employers, and with careful attention to detail, they can set you apart from the competition. By clearly highlighting your skills, experiences, and passion for accounting, you'll be well on your way to landing your first job in the field.

Sure! Below is a detailed, practical example of how to craft a resume and cover letter for an aspiring accountant. These examples will help you understand how to structure and format your resume and cover letter, making them stand out in the competitive field of accounting.

Example Resume:

Jane Doe

1234 Accounting Lane, Cityville, NY 12345

Phone: (555) 123-4567 | Email: janedoe@email.com

LinkedIn: linkedin.com/in/janedoe

Professional Summary

Detail-oriented and highly motivated accounting graduate with a strong understanding of financial analysis, tax laws, and accounting principles. Proficient in accounting software including QuickBooks and Microsoft Excel. Seeking an entry-level accounting position to apply technical skills and contribute to the growth of a dynamic team.

Skills

- Financial Reporting & Analysis

- General Ledger Reconciliation

- Tax Preparation & Compliance

- Microsoft Excel (Advanced Functions)

- QuickBooks & Accounting Software

- Strong Attention to Detail

- Excellent Communication Skills

- Time Management & Multitasking

Education

Bachelor of Science in Accounting

XYZ University, Cityville, NY

Graduated: May 2023

- GPA: 3.8/4.0

- Relevant Coursework: Financial Accounting, Managerial Accounting, Corporate Taxation, Auditing, Business Law

Certifications

- Certified Public Accountant (CPA) – In Progress (Expected Completion: 2025)

Experience

Accounting Intern

ABC Accounting Firm, Cityville, NY

June 2022 – August 2022

- Assisted with the preparation of financial statements for small businesses, ensuring accuracy and compliance with GAAP.

- Performed account reconciliations, identifying discrepancies and correcting errors, resulting in a 10% decrease in reconciliation time.

- Supported senior accountants with tax preparation, including filing tax returns and gathering supporting documentation for clients.

- Utilized Microsoft Excel to create reports and analyze financial data, improving decision-making for clients.

Part-Time Bookkeeper

XYZ Restaurant, Cityville, NY

September 2021 – May 2022

- Managed the daily financial records, including accounts payable and receivable, for a local restaurant.

- Processed payroll for 20 employees, ensuring timely and accurate payments.

- Developed a new filing system that reduced document retrieval time by 30%.

Projects

Financial Statement Analysis – XYZ University

- Conducted a comprehensive analysis of the financial statements of a public company, identifying key financial trends, profitability, and liquidity ratios.

- Presented findings to a group of professors and peers, receiving positive feedback for clarity and insight.

Languages

- English (Fluent)

- Spanish (Intermediate)

Example Cover Letter:

Jane Doe

1234 Accounting Lane, Cityville, NY 12345

Phone: (555) 123-4567 | Email: janedoe@email.com

[Date]

Hiring Manager

XYZ Accounting Firm

5678 Finance Avenue, Cityville, NY 12345

Dear Hiring Manager,

I am writing to express my interest in the Junior Accountant position at XYZ Accounting Firm, as advertised on your website. As a recent graduate with a Bachelor's degree in

Accounting from XYZ University and a strong foundation in financial reporting and tax preparation, I am eager to contribute my skills and passion for accounting to your team.

During my internship at ABC Accounting Firm, I had the opportunity to assist with preparing financial statements, perform account reconciliations, and support tax filing for clients. I became proficient in using QuickBooks and Excel to analyze financial data and generate reports that informed key decisions for small businesses. This hands-on experience helped me develop strong technical skills, attention to detail, and the ability to work effectively in a fast-paced environment.

In addition to my technical skills, I have a strong commitment to professionalism and client satisfaction. I understand the importance of maintaining confidentiality, adhering to deadlines, and working collaboratively with team members and clients. I am excited about the prospect of working at XYZ Accounting Firm, where I can contribute my skills while continuing to grow as an accounting professional.

I would be thrilled to discuss how my background and skills align with the needs of your team. Thank you for considering my application. I look forward to the possibility of speaking with you in further detail. Please feel free to contact me at (555) 123-4567 or janedoe@email.com.

Sincerely,

Jane Doe

Breakdown of the Resume and Cover Letter:

Resume:

1. Professional Summary:

  - Starts with a concise statement about who the candidate is, highlighting key skills and qualifications. It shows what the candidate aims to achieve and what value they can bring to the role.

2. Skills:

- Includes both technical and soft skills. The technical skills are related to accounting software, financial analysis, and tax laws, while soft skills emphasize communication, attention to detail, and time management. These are all essential for a career in accounting.

3. Education:

- Lists the degree obtained, along with relevant coursework. This is particularly important for someone just starting their career, as their educational background will be the primary qualification.

4. Experience:

- Provides details of previous internships or work experience, even if not directly related to accounting. The key is to focus on transferable skills (e.g., attention to detail, using software, handling financial data).

5. Certifications:

- Shows an ongoing commitment to professional development by listing certifications like CPA, which signals that the candidate is serious about their career in accounting.

Cover Letter:

1. Introduction:

- The letter begins by introducing the candidate and stating the specific position being applied for. This is where the candidate shows enthusiasm for the role and the company.

2. Body Paragraphs:

- The candidate details relevant experience, explaining how it aligns with the job description. The body emphasizes both technical accounting skills (such as preparing financial statements and using accounting software) and soft skills (such as working in a team and maintaining confidentiality).

3. Closing Paragraph:

- The letter ends with a polite expression of interest in an interview and a thank you for considering the application. It includes contact details, making it easy for the hiring manager to follow up.

By using this resume and cover letter structure, the candidate can effectively showcase their qualifications, demonstrate their understanding of the accounting profession, and express their enthusiasm for the role. Both documents are clear, professional, and tailored to the position, significantly increasing the candidate's chances of securing an interview.

6.3 Mentorship and Learning from Others

The Value of Mentorship in Accounting

Mentorship is a crucial component of professional development, especially in a field as dynamic and detail-oriented as accounting. As a young individual stepping into the world of accounting, it can be overwhelming to navigate the complex landscape of certifications, career choices, industry standards, and client relationships. This is where mentorship plays a vital role. Having a mentor to guide you through these early stages of your career can provide invaluable insights, helping you avoid mistakes, develop your skills faster, and navigate the challenges of the profession more confidently.

Mentorship, at its core, is about learning from someone who has walked the path you are starting to walk. A mentor is an experienced professional who is willing to invest time and energy into helping you succeed. They offer guidance, encouragement, and advice that are tailored to your individual needs, helping you build a solid foundation for your career in accounting.

In the accounting profession, mentorship can take many forms. It can be a formal relationship through a structured mentorship program or an informal connection with someone you respect in the field. Regardless of the format, mentorship provides you with several benefits:

- Guidance on career choices: A mentor can help you identify the best career paths within accounting, whether that means specializing in tax accounting, pursuing a career in forensic accounting, or becoming a corporate accountant.

- Feedback on your work: Constructive feedback on your performance can be the difference between stagnation and improvement. A mentor can provide valuable insights into how you can enhance your skills and work habits.

- Personal development: Beyond technical accounting skills, mentors also help you improve your soft skills, such as communication, leadership, and problem-solving abilities.

- Networking opportunities: Mentors often introduce their mentees to influential contacts, helping them expand their professional network and open doors to new opportunities.

How to Find a Mentor in Accounting

Finding the right mentor is a pivotal step in your professional journey. The ideal mentor should be someone whose experience and skills align with your career goals and values. Here are several strategies for finding a mentor in accounting:

1. Leverage your educational connections

Many educational institutions offer mentorship programs that connect students with experienced professionals in their chosen field. If you're currently studying accounting, take advantage of these resources. Professors, career counselors, and alumni networks can also be great sources of mentorship. Professors with extensive industry experience can provide insight into both the technical aspects of accounting and the broader business world.

2. Join professional associations

Professional organizations, such as the American Institute of Certified Public Accountants (AICPA), the Chartered Institute of Management Accountants (CIMA), or other regional and global accounting bodies, often have mentorship programs in place. By joining these associations, you gain access to a pool of experienced professionals who are eager to support the next generation of accountants.

3. Participate in industry events

Attending conferences, seminars, webinars, and other networking events is another way to meet potential mentors. These events are a great opportunity to interact with industry leaders and experienced accountants who can offer you mentorship. Make sure to introduce yourself to key people, share your aspirations, and express a genuine interest in learning from their experience.

4. Networking through LinkedIn and other platforms

LinkedIn is an excellent tool for finding mentors. Start by following influential accountants and thought leaders in the industry. Engage with their posts, share relevant content, and reach out to them with a thoughtful message expressing your interest in learning from their career experiences. Many professionals are open to offering advice, especially if you approach them respectfully and express a genuine desire to learn.

5. Reach out to senior colleagues or supervisors

If you're already working in an accounting role, consider reaching out to a senior colleague or supervisor to ask for mentorship. Many professionals are happy to share their knowledge and provide guidance, especially when they see you are motivated to grow in your career.

How to Make the Most of Mentorship

Once you've identified a potential mentor, it's important to approach the relationship with respect and a willingness to learn. Here are some tips to make the most of your mentorship:

1. Set clear goals

Be clear about what you want to achieve through the mentorship. Are you seeking guidance on a specific accounting topic, such as tax planning or auditing techniques? Do you need help navigating your career path or preparing for certifications like the CPA? Clearly defined goals will help both you and your mentor stay focused and make the relationship more productive.

2. Be proactive and show initiative

While your mentor is there to guide you, you need to be proactive in your learning. Ask questions, seek advice, and take the initiative to apply the knowledge you gain. Be open to receiving constructive criticism and use it as a learning opportunity to improve your skills.

3. Be respectful of their time

Mentors are busy professionals, so be mindful of their time. Schedule regular meetings, but don't overwhelm them with requests for immediate help. Be punctual for meetings and come prepared with specific questions or topics you'd like to discuss.

4. Be open to feedback

A good mentor will challenge you and offer constructive feedback. Embrace these opportunities to grow, even when the feedback is tough to hear. Remember, your mentor's goal is to help you succeed, and their criticism is meant to help you improve.

5. Maintain a long-term relationship

Mentorship doesn't have to end once you've reached your immediate goals. As you progress in your career, continue to stay in touch with your mentor and seek advice as needed. A strong mentor-mentee relationship can last throughout your career, offering support during different phases of your professional journey.

The Power of Learning from Others

Mentorship is just one aspect of learning in the accounting profession. The industry is full of learning opportunities from a variety of sources, and it's crucial to be open to different avenues of knowledge. Here are some ways to continue learning from others:

1. Peer Learning

Don't underestimate the value of learning from your peers. Fellow students or junior colleagues can often provide fresh perspectives on complex issues. Peer learning can also be a great way to stay updated on trends or practices that may not yet be common knowledge among more senior accountants.

2. Workshops and Training Programs

Accounting is a field that constantly evolves, with new regulations, technologies, and practices emerging regularly. Participating in workshops, webinars, and formal training programs can help you stay ahead. Many professional organizations offer training sessions and workshops for new accountants, which are designed to build both technical and soft skills.

3. Online Communities and Forums

Online platforms such as Reddit, professional Facebook groups, and forums dedicated to accounting can be a treasure trove of information. Engaging with these communities allows you to learn from people across the globe who may have different experiences and insights to offer.

4. Volunteering and Internships

One of the best ways to learn from others is through hands-on experience. By participating in internships or volunteer opportunities, you expose yourself to real-world accounting challenges, often under the guidance of more experienced professionals.

These opportunities allow you to build practical skills while also learning valuable lessons from those who have been in the industry longer.

5. Reading Books, Articles, and Journals

The accounting profession has a wealth of literature that can deepen your understanding of technical topics and industry trends. Reading books by respected accountants, industry journals, and blogs written by thought leaders helps you stay informed and develop a well-rounded understanding of the profession.

Conclusion

Mentorship and learning from others are essential components of career growth in accounting. A mentor can provide invaluable guidance, share industry knowledge, and open doors to new opportunities. At the same time, it's crucial to seek learning opportunities from a variety of sources, including peers, online communities, and professional networks. By building strong relationships with experienced professionals and continuously seeking knowledge, you'll be well-equipped to navigate the complexities of the accounting profession and build a successful and fulfilling career.

CHAPTER VII
Preparing for Your First Job

7.1 Building a Competitive Resume

In today's competitive job market, your resume is often the first impression you make on a potential employer. It's crucial to ensure that your resume stands out, effectively communicates your abilities, and highlights your potential as an aspiring accountant. While academic qualifications and experience are essential, recruiters are also looking for the right skills that will make you an asset to their team. Whether you're a recent graduate, an internship applicant, or a young professional, presenting your skills and experiences in a clear, organized, and compelling manner will increase your chances of landing the job you want.

7.1.1 Highlighting Skills and Experience

One of the most vital sections of your resume is the way you present your skills and experience. Since accounting is a field that requires both technical and soft skills, your resume should highlight a balance of both. Below is a guide on how to effectively highlight your skills and experience in a way that will appeal to hiring managers in the accounting profession.

1. Categorizing Your Skills

When building your resume, it is important to categorize your skills in a way that aligns with the role you're applying for. Start by dividing your skills into two major categories: technical skills and soft skills. Both are critical for an accountant, but they serve different purposes.

Technical Skills

Technical skills refer to the hard skills you've learned through education, training, and experience that are directly related to the job. These are measurable skills that you can demonstrate with examples. For an accountant, these may include:

- Accounting Software Proficiency: Experience with accounting software such as QuickBooks, SAP, Oracle, or Microsoft Excel is highly valued. Specify the software you are familiar with and how you've used it in your coursework or internships to perform tasks like data entry, financial reporting, and account reconciliation.

- Financial Reporting: Emphasize your ability to prepare financial statements, balance sheets, and profit and loss statements. Be specific about the types of reports you've created or worked with, the volume of data you handled, and how you contributed to analysis or decision-making.

- Tax Knowledge: Highlight any experience or coursework that focused on tax preparation and compliance. This could include familiarity with tax regulations, preparing tax returns, or assisting clients with tax-related queries.

- Data Analysis and Financial Modeling: Showcase any projects or internships where you've analyzed financial data, identified trends, or worked on financial forecasting. Mention tools or techniques you used, such as Excel for financial modeling or pivot tables for data analysis.

- Audit and Compliance: If you've had any experience in auditing, either through internships or college projects, highlight it. Mention the kinds of audits you participated in (e.g., internal or external audits), and describe how your work contributed to the success of the project.

Soft Skills

Soft skills are just as important in accounting as technical skills. In fact, many employers prioritize soft skills as they demonstrate how well you will fit within their team and company culture. Some key soft skills for an accountant include:

- Attention to Detail: This is one of the most critical soft skills for an accountant. It demonstrates your ability to catch errors, ensure accuracy, and maintain precision in your work. Provide specific examples from your coursework, internships, or part-time jobs where attention to detail was essential to success.

- Communication Skills: As an accountant, you'll often need to explain complex financial data in simple terms to clients or team members who may not have a financial background. Emphasize your written and verbal communication skills. You can demonstrate this by mentioning presentations, reports, or meetings where you communicated financial information clearly and effectively.

- Problem-Solving: Accountants frequently encounter problems that require analytical thinking and problem-solving. Share specific instances where you solved complex accounting problems, whether it was resolving discrepancies in financial data or figuring out a way to streamline processes in an accounting system.

- Time Management: Deadlines are a crucial part of the accounting profession, and managing multiple tasks or projects efficiently is essential. Highlight your ability to prioritize tasks, meet deadlines, and stay organized, especially in high-pressure situations. Mention any instances when you had to juggle different accounting assignments during your studies or in an internship.

- Teamwork: Even though accountants often work independently, they must also collaborate with colleagues and clients. Show that you're able to work well in a team setting by providing examples from group projects or team-oriented work experiences.

2. Using Action-Oriented Language

To make your skills and experience stand out, use action-oriented language. Instead of saying "I was responsible for managing accounts," use action verbs like "managed," "oversaw," or "led." These stronger verbs demonstrate your active involvement and your ability to drive results. For example:

- Weak: Assisted with the preparation of tax returns.

- Strong: Prepared and filed tax returns for individual and corporate clients, ensuring full compliance with tax laws and regulations.

By using action verbs and specific details, you can highlight your achievements and responsibilities in a way that grabs the recruiter's attention.

3. Tailoring Your Skills and Experience to the Job Description

No two accounting jobs are identical, and neither should your resume be. Every time you apply for a job, tailor your resume to the specific role by carefully reviewing the job description. Highlight the skills and experiences that align with the job requirements.

For instance, if the job requires experience with financial forecasting, ensure that you emphasize any relevant projects or internships where you worked with financial projections or budgeting. If the position calls for strong communication skills, mention experiences where you worked with clients or presented financial reports to senior management.

4. Providing Context to Your Experience

When listing your experience, providing context is crucial. Don't just mention your job responsibilities; instead, show how you made a difference in the organization or project you were involved with. You should include numbers and specifics where possible, as quantifiable achievements make your experience more impactful.

For example:

- Weak: Responsible for financial reporting.

- Strong: Managed the preparation and analysis of monthly financial reports, improving accuracy by 15% and reducing reporting time by 20%.

The more concrete your accomplishments, the better.

5. Gaining Experience Through Internships, Volunteering, and Freelancing

If you're early in your accounting career and don't have much professional experience, consider gaining experience through internships, volunteering, or freelance work. Many young job seekers think they need a full-time job to gain experience, but internships and volunteer opportunities provide valuable, hands-on learning that you can showcase on your resume.

For example, if you worked on a tax filing project for a non-profit or handled bookkeeping tasks for a small business, these experiences still count and can demonstrate your ability to take on real-world accounting tasks.

By focusing on these aspects and tailoring your resume, you'll effectively highlight your skills and experience, making you a more competitive candidate for accounting roles. Your resume should clearly communicate that you not only have the necessary qualifications but also the initiative, creativity, and drive to succeed in the field of accounting.

In the next section, we will discuss tips for formatting your resume to ensure it is visually appealing and easy to navigate.

7.1.2 Formatting Tips

Creating a well-formatted resume is an essential aspect of the job application process, especially in the field of accounting. As a young candidate starting out, your resume is often the first opportunity to make a strong impression on hiring managers, so it's important to get it right. A clean, clear, and professional format ensures that your skills, qualifications, and experiences are communicated effectively. In this section, we will explore the key elements of resume formatting, offering practical advice and tips to ensure your resume stands out for all the right reasons.

Why Resume Formatting Matters

First, let's discuss why formatting is so important. When employers receive a stack of resumes, they often spend only a few seconds scanning each one before deciding whether or not to give it further attention. This means that clear, concise formatting can make a difference between your resume being noticed or ignored. A well-structured document conveys professionalism, helps guide the reader's eye, and highlights your qualifications in a way that's easy to digest. In short, a resume that's both visually appealing and logically organized will allow your potential employer to see the best version of you within those few moments of review.

Key Principles of Resume Formatting

Let's break down the most important principles of resume formatting.

1. Consistency

Consistency is critical throughout your resume. This includes things like font choices, spacing, margin alignment, and the use of bullet points. Ensuring your formatting is consistent throughout demonstrates your attention to detail—an important trait for an accountant. If you use one font for your headings, stick with it throughout the document. Similarly, if you use a particular style for your bullet points, ensure it's uniform across all sections.

2. Simplicity and Clean Layout

While it's tempting to add graphics, colors, or flashy fonts to make your resume stand out, simplicity is often the key to success. A cluttered resume is hard to read, and hiring managers may overlook important details. Use clean, professional fonts such as Arial, Calibri, or Times New Roman. Keep the font size between 10-12 points for the body text and slightly larger for headings (14-16 points). Avoid using too many fonts—one or two is sufficient.

White space is another crucial aspect of clean formatting. Proper use of margins and line spacing makes the document more readable. A resume that looks crowded or cramped can be overwhelming and might cause the reader to skip over important details. By ensuring there is ample white space, you're making your resume easy on the eyes and allowing key information to stand out.

3. Clear Section Headings

Each section of your resume should be clearly labeled, so the hiring manager can quickly find the information they're looking for. Use bold or slightly larger font for your section titles, such as "Education," "Work Experience," and "Skills." You can also use lines or boxes to separate sections, but don't go overboard—just enough to make the layout easy to follow.

Headings can also guide the reader's focus and signal what's most important. For instance, for an entry-level accounting position, the "Skills" section might be more important than your work experience, so place the most relevant section toward the top, or give it extra prominence.

4. Bullet Points for Key Details

Bullet points are a great way to break down information into digestible pieces. In the "Work Experience" and "Skills" sections, use bullet points to list your responsibilities, accomplishments, and abilities. Bullets help your resume stand out by giving it a clean and professional look, and they make it easier for the hiring manager to scan your document quickly.

However, avoid overuse of bullet points. Each point should be concise—no more than one or two lines. If you have several bullet points that all list similar tasks, try to consolidate them into a few key accomplishments that best showcase your skills.

5. One or Two Pages?

One of the most debated topics in resume formatting is whether your resume should be one page or two. The general rule is that for entry-level positions, especially for those just beginning their career, a one-page resume is ideal. This forces you to focus on the most important and relevant information. However, if you have a significant amount of experience, such as internships, relevant coursework, volunteer work, or projects, you may extend to two pages. Keep in mind that employers have limited time, so be as concise as possible, highlighting your most valuable qualifications for the job.

6. Sections to Include

Your resume should be structured in a way that allows a hiring manager to easily find your relevant skills and experience. Here are the core sections you should include in your accounting resume:

1. Contact Information: At the top of your resume, clearly list your full name, phone number, professional email address, and LinkedIn profile (optional). Ensure your email is professional and avoids any overly casual usernames.

2. Objective or Summary (Optional): A short statement that outlines your career goals and why you're interested in the accounting profession can provide context. For entry-level candidates, an objective may be useful to show your enthusiasm and focus.

3. Education: List your academic credentials, including the name of the institution, degree earned, and graduation date. If you have relevant coursework or honors, this can be included under this section. For example, if you completed courses in financial reporting, tax accounting, or auditing, be sure to mention them.

4. Work Experience (or Relevant Experience): Highlight any internships, part-time jobs, or volunteer work related to accounting or finance. Use bullet points to describe your achievements and specific responsibilities.

5. Skills: This is the section where you can list technical skills like proficiency in accounting software (e.g., QuickBooks, Excel, SAP), knowledge of financial analysis, and any certifications you hold. For accounting positions, familiarity with Generally Accepted Accounting Principles (GAAP) is often a must, so be sure to list this if applicable.

6. Certifications and Professional Development: If you are pursuing or have completed certifications like the CPA (Certified Public Accountant) or CMA (Certified Management Accountant), make sure to include them in this section.

7. Additional Sections: Depending on your experience, you might want to add sections for languages, awards, leadership roles, or relevant projects. If you've contributed to a team project that resulted in improved financial performance or worked with budgeting software, this is the place to include it.

7. Tailoring Your Resume

Once you have a general resume format that works for you, it's essential to tailor it to the specific job you're applying for. Carefully read the job description and ensure that your resume highlights the skills and experiences that align with what the employer is looking for. If a job posting emphasizes the importance of financial analysis, for example, ensure that you draw attention to your expertise in this area by adjusting your resume.

Customizing your resume to each job application demonstrates your attention to detail and commitment to the role. Even small changes to the wording of your bullet points or adding relevant achievements can help you stand out from other candidates.

8. Proofreading and Final Checks

After formatting your resume, it's time for a final review. Proofreading is a critical step in the process. Hiring managers will quickly notice any typos or grammatical errors, which can diminish your chances of landing an interview. Here are some things to check:

- Spelling and Grammar: Even the most minor mistakes can be enough to make you seem unprofessional. Make sure you proofread your resume multiple times and, if possible, ask a mentor, friend, or family member to review it as well.

- Consistency: Ensure that your formatting is consistent throughout. For example, if you use bullet points in one section, make sure they're the same style in other sections.

- Accuracy: Double-check all your dates, job titles, and other details for accuracy. Ensure that any numbers or financial figures you've listed are correct.

Conclusion

In conclusion, resume formatting plays a vital role in creating a competitive job application. By following these best practices, you'll craft a resume that is clear, concise, and easy to read. Whether you're applying for your first accounting job or an internship, a well-formatted resume can significantly improve your chances of making a great first impression. Take the time to create a professional, polished resume, and you'll be well on your way to landing your first job in the accounting field.

7.2 Interviewing for Accounting Roles

One of the most crucial steps in your career journey is preparing for an interview. Whether you're applying for a role in public accounting, corporate accounting, tax accounting, or any other specialized field, interviews are your opportunity to demonstrate your skills, knowledge, and passion for accounting. Understanding what to expect in these interviews and how to prepare will set you apart from other candidates and position you as a strong contender for the job.

This section will guide you through common interview questions in accounting, how to approach them, and tips to make the best impression

7.2.1 Common Interview Questions

When preparing for an accounting interview, it's important to anticipate the types of questions that may be asked. Below, we've highlighted some of the most common questions you may face, along with tips on how to answer them.

1. Tell me about yourself.

This is a common opening question that allows interviewers to get to know you on a personal and professional level. Although it may seem straightforward, it's your opportunity to set the tone for the rest of the interview. Avoid rambling and focus on a brief overview of your background, education, and why you're passionate about accounting.

Example Answer:

"I recently graduated with a degree in Accounting from [University]. During my studies, I developed a strong interest in financial analysis and auditing, which I pursued through internships and coursework. I'm particularly drawn to the precision and problem-solving aspects of accounting, and I'm excited to apply my skills in a professional setting, helping organizations manage their finances efficiently and accurately."

2. Why do you want to work in accounting?

This question helps interviewers gauge your motivation for choosing this career path. Accounting is a demanding field, so they want to see that you have a genuine interest in the profession and not just a job.

Example Answer:

"I've always been fascinated by numbers and how they can tell a story about a company's financial health. Accounting gives me the chance to use my analytical skills to solve problems and contribute to an organization's success. Additionally, the variety of career paths in accounting, such as tax, audit, and financial reporting, excites me because it allows for continuous learning and growth."

3. What do you know about our company?

This question tests how much research you've done on the organization. Before your interview, thoroughly research the company's background, culture, and values. Understand what they do, their mission, and any recent news or developments. This shows that you're genuinely interested in the role and not just looking for any job.

Example Answer:

"I've done some research on [Company], and I was impressed by your commitment to providing innovative financial solutions to clients. Your recent expansion into new international markets shows a forward-thinking approach that resonates with my own career aspirations. I admire your emphasis on integrity and transparency in financial reporting, and I would love to contribute to such a values-driven organization."

4. Can you explain the difference between financial accounting and managerial accounting?

As an aspiring accountant, you should be able to clearly explain basic accounting concepts. This question tests your technical knowledge and understanding of the different areas within accounting.

Example Answer:

"Financial accounting focuses on creating financial statements, such as income statements and balance sheets, that are used by external stakeholders like investors, creditors, and regulators. It follows standardized rules, such as Generally Accepted Accounting Principles (GAAP). On the other hand, managerial accounting deals with internal decision-making processes. It involves budgeting, cost analysis, and performance evaluation, helping managers make informed decisions for the company's growth and profitability."

5. How do you prioritize tasks and manage deadlines?

In accounting, you'll often have multiple tasks to handle, such as preparing reports, auditing accounts, or preparing tax filings. This question tests your time management and organizational skills. Employers want to know that you can manage workloads efficiently, especially during busy periods like tax season or year-end close.

Example Answer:

"I prioritize tasks based on deadlines and the level of importance. For instance, if I'm preparing a financial report that's due at the end of the week, I'll break the project into smaller tasks and work on the most time-sensitive ones first. I also use tools like calendars and project management software to track my tasks and ensure I'm staying on track. I find that maintaining clear communication with my team is also key to making sure we meet deadlines effectively."

6. Tell me about a time when you worked under pressure to meet a deadline.

This question assesses your ability to handle stress and manage time effectively in high-pressure situations. When answering this question, use the STAR method (Situation, Task, Action, Result) to provide a clear and structured response.

Example Answer:

"During my internship at [Company], I was assigned to assist in preparing the monthly financial statement. One month, the team encountered delays due to technical issues, and we were at risk of missing the deadline. I took the initiative to reorganize the tasks, reallocated responsibilities to my teammates, and worked overtime to ensure the report was completed on time. As a result, we not only met the deadline but also caught a small discrepancy in the accounts that had gone unnoticed earlier."

7. How do you stay updated with changes in accounting regulations and standards?

The field of accounting is constantly evolving, with changes in tax laws, financial reporting standards, and technology. Interviewers want to know that you're committed to ongoing learning and staying current with these changes.

Example Answer:

"I make a habit of reading industry publications such as Accounting Today and the Journal of Accountancy. I also attend webinars and participate in professional accounting associations like [local CPA association] to stay informed. Additionally, I take continuing education courses to keep up with updates to regulations like GAAP or IFRS and other industry best practices."

8. How do you ensure accuracy in your work?

As an accountant, attention to detail and accuracy are crucial. This question assesses your commitment to quality and your approach to minimizing errors.

Example Answer:

"Accuracy is vital in accounting, so I take a methodical approach to ensure my work is precise. First, I double-check all calculations and review the data for inconsistencies. I also take advantage of tools like accounting software, which helps reduce human error. If I'm preparing a report or statement, I often take a short break after finishing a draft, then review it with fresh eyes to catch any mistakes before submitting it."

9. What are your long-term career goals in accounting?

This question helps interviewers understand your ambitions and whether they align with the opportunities the company can provide. It's important to demonstrate that you have a clear vision for your career, but also that you're flexible and open to growth within the company.

Example Answer:

"My long-term goal is to become a Certified Public Accountant (CPA) and eventually move into a managerial or leadership role, such as a financial controller or CFO. I'm eager to gain a broad range of experience in different accounting areas, such as auditing and tax, to develop a well-rounded skill set. I see this role as an excellent opportunity to grow and learn from experienced professionals."

10. Why should we hire you?

This is your chance to sell yourself. Focus on what sets you apart from other candidates, such as your education, skills, and enthusiasm for the job.

Example Answer:

"I believe my strong academic background in accounting, combined with my hands-on experience during internships, makes me a great fit for this role. I'm detail-oriented, dedicated to producing accurate work, and have a strong understanding of accounting principles. Additionally, I'm a quick learner, a team player, and excited to contribute to your company's success."

Conclusion

Preparing for common interview questions in accounting roles will give you the confidence to perform well and stand out to potential employers. By anticipating questions and practicing your responses, you can demonstrate your expertise, enthusiasm, and professionalism during the interview. Remember, the interview is not only a chance for the company to learn more about you, but also for you to learn about the company and assess if it aligns with your values and career goals.

Being prepared, practicing your answers, and staying calm and composed will greatly increase your chances of landing your first job in accounting.

7.2.2 Professional Etiquette

Professional etiquette during an accounting interview is crucial for creating a lasting impression. Not only does it reflect your personal professionalism, but it also communicates your respect for the company and the hiring process. In the competitive field of accounting, where attention to detail and communication skills are paramount, mastering interview etiquette can set you apart from other candidates.

This section will guide you through the essential aspects of professional etiquette in an accounting interview, helping you navigate this critical step in your career journey.

1. Dressing Appropriately for the Interview

First impressions are powerful, and your attire is one of the first things an interviewer will notice. As an accountant, you are expected to maintain a professional appearance that aligns with the values of precision, responsibility, and reliability. For most accounting firms and corporate settings, business formal attire is expected.

- *For Men:* A well-fitted suit in neutral colors (black, navy, or gray) paired with a dress shirt and a conservative tie is ideal. Ensure that your clothes are clean, pressed, and fit properly. Avoid flashy colors or excessive patterns that could distract from the professionalism you want to convey.

- *For Women:* A business suit or professional dress paired with closed-toe shoes is a safe choice. Like men's attire, neutral tones such as black, navy, or dark gray work best. Avoid overly casual clothing such as jeans, and make sure that your outfit is neither too revealing nor too casual. Accessories should be minimal, and makeup should be natural.

It's important to remember that overdressing is always better than underdressing. Even if you're unsure about the company's dress code, it's better to err on the side of formality.

2. Punctuality is Key

In accounting, time is money. Being punctual not only reflects your time management skills but also demonstrates your commitment and respect for the opportunity. Arriving late for an interview is one of the most unprofessional mistakes you can make and can hurt your chances before the conversation even begins.

- *Arrive Early:* Aim to arrive at least 10-15 minutes before your scheduled interview time. This gives you a buffer in case of unforeseen circumstances such as traffic delays. It also shows that you are organized and conscientious.

- *Plan Ahead:* If your interview is at a company you haven't visited before, make sure to check the location in advance. Consider using a GPS app to get an accurate estimate of travel time and allow for any possible delays. Factor in parking time, as well, to avoid arriving flustered.

3. Greeting the Interviewer

When you first meet your interviewer, offer a firm handshake, smile, and make eye contact. A handshake should be confident but not too forceful. This gesture is an important part of your professional etiquette because it sets the tone for the entire interaction. Remember, you're not just trying to showcase your accounting skills – you're also trying to show that you're a good fit for the company culture.

- *Introduce Yourself Politely:* In addition to a handshake, introduce yourself with your full name and express your gratitude for the opportunity to interview. For instance, "Hello, I'm [Your Name], and I'm really excited to be here today. Thank you for taking the time to meet with me."

- *Eye Contact and Posture:* Maintain steady eye contact throughout the conversation and sit up straight. Good posture indicates confidence and engagement, both of which are important for an accounting professional.

4. Active Listening

One of the most important aspects of professional communication is active listening. In an interview, it's essential that you listen carefully to the interviewer's questions, comments, and instructions. Active listening ensures that you understand the question before responding, allowing you to provide thoughtful and relevant answers.

- *Avoid Interrupting:* Let the interviewer finish their thoughts before you respond. Interrupting can come across as impatient or disrespectful, which can create a negative impression.

- *Acknowledge the Speaker:* Nod occasionally to show that you are paying attention. After the interviewer finishes speaking, take a moment to collect your thoughts before answering. This brief pause will give you a chance to respond more effectively and thoughtfully.

5. Clear and Concise Communication

In an accounting interview, you are likely to be asked a series of technical questions, along with behavioral and situational questions. While your answers should demonstrate your knowledge and skills, they should also be clear and concise.

- *Avoid Over-Explaining:* While it's important to elaborate on your experience, avoid rambling. Interviewers value candidates who can get straight to the point without unnecessary elaboration. Keep your answers focused on the question and ensure that your responses are relevant.

- *Use Simple Language:* While you may have advanced knowledge of accounting terms, remember that the person interviewing you may not be familiar with complex terminology. It's essential to communicate in a way that's easy to understand while still demonstrating your expertise.

- *Tailor Your Answers:* In an interview, you'll likely be asked about past experiences, and you should tailor your responses to the company and role. When answering questions, provide specific examples from your background that are relevant to the job. For instance, if asked about teamwork, mention a specific situation where you collaborated with others to solve a problem.

6. Mind Your Body Language

Your body language plays a significant role in the way you're perceived during an interview. Positive body language can convey confidence and enthusiasm, while negative body language can create a sense of discomfort or disinterest.

- *Maintain Open Body Language:* Keep your arms uncrossed and your hands visible. This shows that you are open and engaged. Leaning slightly forward during the conversation can also convey interest and attentiveness.

- *Avoid Fidgeting:* Fidgeting with your hands, hair, or clothing can be distracting and may suggest nervousness. Try to remain calm and composed throughout the interview.

- *Facial Expressions:* Your facial expressions should reflect your engagement in the conversation. Smile when appropriate and maintain a neutral expression when listening to questions. Avoid looking disinterested or distracted.

7. Ask Thoughtful Questions

At the end of the interview, you will typically be asked if you have any questions. This is a critical part of the interview, as it demonstrates your interest in the company and the role.

- *Prepare Questions in Advance:* Before the interview, think of a few questions that demonstrate your understanding of the company and the industry. For example, you could ask about the team structure, growth opportunities, or how the company stays ahead in an evolving industry.

- *Focus on the Role:* Avoid asking questions that could be answered by looking at the company's website or job posting. Instead, inquire about the day-to-day responsibilities of the role or what the interviewer likes best about working at the company.

- *Avoid Salary and Benefits Early On:* While salary is important, it's best to avoid discussing compensation during the first interview unless the interviewer brings it up. Focusing on the role and culture early on is a better way to demonstrate your enthusiasm.

8. Closing the Interview

When the interview comes to a close, express your gratitude for the opportunity once again. This not only demonstrates professionalism but also reinforces your genuine interest in the position.

- *Reaffirm Your Interest:* Before leaving, you should briefly express your excitement about the role and how your skills align with the company's needs. A simple statement such as, "I'm really excited about the opportunity to contribute to your team and bring my skills to your company," can leave a positive final impression.

- *Thank You Note:* After the interview, send a personalized thank-you note or email. Thank the interviewer for their time and express your continued interest in the position. This is a small but powerful gesture that shows professionalism and appreciation.

Conclusion

Mastering professional etiquette in an accounting interview is essential for making a strong impression and improving your chances of landing your first job. By following these guidelines – from dressing appropriately and being punctual to maintaining good posture and active listening – you will present yourself as a confident, competent, and well-rounded candidate. Remember, professional etiquette is about more than just manners; it's about showing respect for the opportunity and the people you are interacting with, and it's a key step toward launching a successful career in accounting.

7.3 Negotiating Your First Job Offer

Negotiating your first job offer can feel intimidating, especially if you're just starting out in your career. However, it's an essential skill that can set the stage for your professional success and financial security. Many young professionals hesitate to negotiate, thinking that accepting the first offer is the norm. However, being prepared to negotiate with confidence can help you secure a fair compensation package, work conditions, and benefits that align with your goals and needs. This section will guide you through the critical steps in negotiating your first accounting job offer.

Understanding the Job Offer

Before you enter negotiations, it's essential to fully understand the terms of the offer. Take the time to carefully review the compensation package, benefits, job responsibilities, and any additional perks that come with the job. In many cases, job offers may include:

- Salary: The base pay you'll receive for performing your job.

- Bonuses and Incentives: Performance-related bonuses, sign-on bonuses, or incentives.

- Benefits: Health insurance, retirement plans, paid time off, and other fringe benefits.

- Job Title and Responsibilities: The role you're being offered and the expectations related to the job.

- Work Schedule and Flexibility: Hours, remote work policies, and work-life balance options.

Take the time to assess each element of the offer and how it aligns with your needs, both personally and professionally. If any area raises questions or concerns, these are the aspects you should focus on during negotiations.

Step 1: Do Your Research

Effective negotiation begins with research. Understanding industry standards and salary expectations for entry-level accounting roles in your geographic area is key. Researching salary ranges on websites like Glassdoor, Payscale, or Indeed can give you a clearer picture of what others in your field are earning. Make sure to consider factors such as:

- Industry: The accounting industry has different pay scales depending on the sector (public accounting, corporate accounting, government, nonprofit, etc.).

- Location: Pay rates may vary depending on the region or city, with higher salaries often found in major metropolitan areas.

- Company: Large firms may offer higher salaries and more benefits, while smaller companies or startups may offer a different balance of compensation, flexibility, or career development opportunities.

- Education and Experience: Although you are negotiating your first job, the more experience you have (e.g., internships, academic achievements), the more leverage you may have during negotiations.

Armed with this information, you can develop a clear idea of what is fair and reasonable in your situation.

Step 2: Determine What You Need and Want

Negotiation is not only about getting more money; it's about ensuring that the offer meets your needs and long-term goals. To negotiate effectively, you must have a clear understanding of what you value most. Here are some factors to consider:

- Salary Expectations: Determine what salary you need to meet your financial needs. Consider factors like student loans, cost of living, and your financial goals.

- Benefits: Health insurance, retirement savings plans, and paid time off can significantly impact your overall job satisfaction. Understand what benefits are included and whether they meet your needs.

- Career Growth and Development: Does the job offer opportunities for professional growth? Will the company invest in your development, offering things like training, mentorship, or sponsorship for further certifications (like CPA)? These can be just as important as salary.

- Work-Life Balance: If a healthy work-life balance is essential to you, look at the company's policies on flexible work arrangements, vacation time, and sick leave.

- Job Responsibilities: Ensure that the duties outlined in the offer align with your career goals and interests. If the job description isn't clear, this is a good point to clarify during the negotiation.

By identifying your needs and wants, you can better determine what is negotiable and what is non-negotiable.

Step 3: Approach the Negotiation Professionally

Approaching the negotiation process with professionalism is key to achieving a positive outcome. You want to demonstrate that you are confident, but also respectful and flexible. Here are some tips to help you navigate the conversation:

- Be Confident but Not Aggressive: Express your excitement about the offer while highlighting areas where you feel there could be improvements. Be confident in your request, but avoid being confrontational or demanding.

- Timing Matters: Negotiate after receiving a formal job offer, but before signing the contract. This is when you have the most leverage. If the employer is eager to have you on board, they may be open to negotiating.

- Express Gratitude: Begin by thanking the employer for the offer and expressing your enthusiasm for the role. This sets a positive tone for the negotiation.

- State Your Case Clearly: Present the data you've gathered and explain why you believe an adjustment is warranted. Be specific about what you would like changed, whether it's the salary, benefits, or job title.

- Use "I" Statements: Frame your requests in a way that reflects your personal situation. For example, "Based on my research, the typical salary for a first-year accountant in this region is around $X, and I believe my academic background and internship experience align with this range."

Step 4: Consider Other Benefits Beyond Salary

While salary is often the focal point of negotiation, there are other factors that could enhance your overall compensation package. These may include:

- Bonuses and Incentives: Ask if there are performance-based bonuses or signing bonuses available, especially if the salary offer is non-negotiable.

- Remote Work and Flexible Hours: Many companies offer flexibility in terms of work location and hours, especially in today's changing work environment. This is particularly important if you value work-life balance.

- Professional Development: Inquire about the company's willingness to support your continued education or certification pursuits, such as paying for CPA exam fees or offering training opportunities.

- Additional Time Off: If the salary is non-negotiable, ask about additional vacation days or the option for flexible scheduling.

Be creative and open to considering a broader set of benefits to improve your overall job satisfaction.

Step 5: Handle the Employer's Response

Once you've made your case, the employer may either accept, decline, or offer a compromise. Here's how to handle the various responses:

- Acceptance: If the employer agrees to your requests, thank them and proceed to the next steps in the hiring process. Ensure that any agreed-upon changes are clearly documented in the formal offer.

- Compromise: If the employer is willing to make some concessions but not everything you requested, carefully evaluate whether the modified offer still meets your needs. If it does, it may be worth accepting. However, be sure to clarify any details and ensure that all agreements are written into the contract.

- Decline: If the employer is unwilling to negotiate or meet your requests, take time to carefully consider whether the offer is still in line with your career goals. You may choose to politely decline the offer if it does not meet your minimum requirements.

Step 6: Finalizing the Agreement

Once you've reached a mutually agreeable solution, it's important to ensure that everything is documented in writing. The employer should send you an updated offer letter outlining the revised salary, benefits, and job responsibilities. Review the document carefully to ensure all changes are included.

Once you've received and reviewed the revised offer, you can formally accept the job. Express your gratitude, sign the offer letter, and prepare for your exciting new role in accounting!

Conclusion

Negotiating your first job offer may feel like a daunting task, but with the right preparation and approach, it can be a rewarding experience that sets you up for a successful career. Remember to research, be clear about your needs, maintain professionalism, and consider all aspects of the offer—not just salary. By negotiating effectively, you can ensure that your first step into the accounting profession is a positive one, with a fair and competitive compensation package that supports your long-term goals.

CHAPTER VIII
Long-Term Career Growth and Specialization

8.1 Advancing in Accounting

8.1.1 Seeking Promotions

In the field of accounting, career advancement is often structured and predictable, with clear steps to reach higher levels. However, simply putting in the hours and performing your daily duties is rarely enough to ensure promotion. Success in accounting is as much about developing a proactive mindset, networking, building relationships, and pursuing continuous personal and professional growth as it is about technical skills. If you're an accountant aiming for a promotion, here are some strategies and tips to help you progress in your career.

Understand the Path to Promotion

The first step toward seeking promotion is to understand the career path in accounting. Many accounting careers follow a hierarchical structure, with clear stages for advancement. These might include moving from entry-level positions to mid-level roles and eventually to senior management or partner positions in public accounting firms.

- Entry-Level: Most accounting professionals begin as staff accountants or junior auditors. These roles focus on foundational tasks like preparing financial statements, conducting audits, or analyzing financial records.

- Mid-Level: As you gain experience, you may be promoted to roles such as senior accountant, auditor, or financial analyst. In these positions, you'll take on more responsibility, handle complex projects, and begin to mentor junior staff.

- Senior-Level: Beyond mid-level roles, senior accountants often step into managerial positions, such as accounting manager, controller, or tax manager. Here, you may be responsible for overseeing teams, managing client relationships, and implementing policies.

- Executive/Partner-Level: At the top of the accounting hierarchy are executive positions such as Chief Financial Officer (CFO) or partner in a public accounting firm. These roles involve strategic decision-making, leading financial operations, and guiding the direction of the company.

By understanding this progression, you can develop a clear plan for how to navigate the steps to promotion. It's important to know where you are on the career ladder and what it will take to reach the next step.

Take Initiative and Demonstrate Leadership

One of the most effective ways to seek a promotion is to demonstrate leadership potential, even if you're not in a formal leadership role. While accounting is often seen as a technical profession, leadership qualities are essential for moving up in the field. Here are a few ways to exhibit leadership:

1. Take Initiative: Look for opportunities to go above and beyond your current job responsibilities. Volunteering for challenging projects or taking ownership of tasks outside your regular duties will show that you're capable of handling more responsibility. Whether it's leading a team for a specific project or volunteering to help your department meet a deadline, these actions show that you're ready to take on more.

2. Show Problem-Solving Skills: Accountants who can identify problems and offer solutions are highly valued. Being proactive in resolving issues within your team, department, or even for clients shows that you are a critical thinker who can contribute to the overall success of the company.

3. Support Senior Leadership: Demonstrate that you can be trusted by senior managers or executives. This could involve assisting in reporting processes, giving presentations, or helping solve larger issues. Taking on this level of responsibility proves that you are capable of managing larger projects and being a valuable asset to leadership.

4. Mentor Junior Staff: Offering guidance and mentorship to new accountants or interns is an excellent way to show that you have the skills and mindset needed to manage teams.

Mentoring allows you to build strong relationships and demonstrate your ability to support and develop others in the organization.

Build and Nurture Relationships

The importance of networking and building professional relationships cannot be overstated in accounting. Whether you're working in public accounting, corporate finance, or another sector, relationships can play a pivotal role in your career advancement. Here's how to leverage your network for promotions:

1. Seek a Mentor: A mentor in the accounting field can provide invaluable insight into how to climb the career ladder. Find someone with more experience, ideally in a role you aspire to, and ask them for guidance. They can help you navigate the challenges of your current position and offer advice on how to stand out and secure a promotion.

2. Network Within the Organization: Your promotion might not always depend on just your performance; it can also be influenced by how well you've built relationships with senior leaders. Attend company events, participate in meetings, and look for informal ways to engage with decision-makers within your organization. Networking will ensure that you are visible and known by those who are responsible for promotions.

3. Connect with Other Departments: Especially in larger organizations, it's important to build relationships with people outside of the accounting department. Having a broad network across the business can help you understand the company's needs better, demonstrate your willingness to collaborate, and position you as someone who sees the bigger picture.

4. Build Client Relationships (For Public Accountants): If you work in public accounting, developing strong relationships with clients is critical. Clients who trust you are more likely to recommend you for higher positions or offer new responsibilities. In corporate accounting, building relationships with department heads and executives can give you greater visibility when promotion opportunities arise.

Demonstrate Your Value to the Organization

One key to advancing in accounting is proving that you are indispensable to your company. If your work is recognized as valuable, the chances of a promotion increase substantially. Here are some ways to demonstrate your value:

1. Deliver Consistent Results: In accounting, accuracy and reliability are key. Consistently delivering high-quality work, meeting deadlines, and maintaining attention to detail will make you a valued asset. Senior leaders want to promote individuals who can be trusted with critical tasks.

2. Add Value Beyond Your Core Responsibilities: Always look for ways to improve processes and help the company save time and money. Whether it's suggesting new software tools to streamline accounting tasks or offering insights into cost-saving measures, adding value outside of your core duties can make you stand out as someone who is not just executing tasks but contributing to the organization's growth.

3. Track Your Achievements: Keep a record of your achievements and successes. When the time comes to discuss a potential promotion, having specific examples of how you've contributed to the company's success will be crucial. Whether it's cost reductions, process improvements, or successful audits, your track record should speak for itself.

4. Take on Challenging Projects: Be the first to volunteer for difficult or high-profile projects. Successfully completing challenging assignments, particularly those that require innovation or complex problem-solving, will demonstrate your readiness for a more senior role.

Communicate Your Career Goals

To be considered for a promotion, it's essential to communicate your career goals with your manager. Being proactive about your ambitions shows that you are committed to growth and long-term success within the company. Here's how to approach this conversation:

1. Request Regular Performance Reviews: Annual or semi-annual performance reviews are an excellent opportunity to discuss your career progress with your supervisor. Use these reviews to highlight your achievements, ask for feedback, and express your desire for career advancement. Make sure to ask what steps you need to take to be considered for a promotion.

2. Have Career Development Conversations: Don't wait for your supervisor to bring it up. Schedule meetings to talk about your career aspirations and what you need to do to progress. Ask for specific feedback on what skills or experience you need to gain for a promotion.

3. Be Open to Constructive Criticism: Receiving feedback can be difficult, but it's an essential part of growing your career. If your manager gives you constructive criticism, accept it gracefully and work on improving the areas they highlight. Showing a willingness to learn and improve will demonstrate your commitment to advancing.

Patience and Persistence

Seeking a promotion takes time and persistence. The accounting profession often requires a combination of technical expertise, interpersonal skills, and strategic thinking, all of which take years to develop. It's important to be patient, especially when advancement seems slow. Continue to focus on your professional development, and opportunities will open up over time.

Promotions aren't always immediate, but staying consistent and dedicated to your growth will eventually lead to greater opportunities. As long as you show initiative, take on leadership responsibilities, and demonstrate your value to the company, your efforts will eventually be recognized.

Conclusion

Seeking promotions in accounting requires more than just technical expertise. It's about developing the right mindset, demonstrating leadership potential, building strong relationships, and constantly working to improve. By following the strategies outlined above and staying proactive, you'll be well on your way to advancing in your accounting career. Remember, career growth is a marathon, not a sprint, and with persistence and a clear plan, you'll see the results in due time.

8.1.2 Continuing Education

As you embark on your accounting career, continuing education will play a pivotal role in your long-term success. The field of accounting is dynamic, with evolving standards, technologies, and practices that demand accountants to stay ahead of the curve. Continuing education isn't just a necessity to meet licensure requirements; it's also a valuable way to enhance your skills, adapt to new challenges, and position yourself for growth within the profession.

The Importance of Continuing Education in Accounting

The accounting profession has undergone significant changes in the past few decades, driven by advancements in technology, globalization, and increasingly complex regulations. For instance, the rise of artificial intelligence (AI), cloud computing, and blockchain technology has reshaped the way accounting functions operate. As such, staying updated on the latest trends and tools is crucial for remaining competitive in the job market.

Moreover, accounting standards and regulations continue to evolve. For example, the shift from Generally Accepted Accounting Principles (GAAP) to International Financial Reporting Standards (IFRS) has created new opportunities and challenges for accountants worldwide. Those who invest in continuing education are better positioned to navigate these changes and remain valuable to employers.

Continuing education also helps you gain a broader understanding of accounting and related fields. This is especially important as you advance in your career and take on more responsibility. Whether it's understanding new accounting software, mastering complex tax laws, or learning about cutting-edge audit methods, education allows you to broaden your expertise and become more effective in your role.

Forms of Continuing Education

There are several ways you can pursue continuing education throughout your accounting career, ranging from formal academic programs to informal learning opportunities. Here's a look at some of the most common routes:

1. Professional Certifications and Licenses

Obtaining certifications is one of the most common and impactful ways to advance your education as an accountant. Some certifications are required for certain positions, while others can significantly enhance your qualifications and make you more competitive in the job market. Common certifications include:

- Certified Public Accountant (CPA): The CPA designation is arguably the most prestigious certification in accounting. It demonstrates that you have met rigorous educational and experience requirements, and that you are committed to maintaining high professional standards. Becoming a CPA opens doors to a wide range of job opportunities, from public accounting to corporate finance.

- Certified Management Accountant (CMA): If you are interested in management accounting, the CMA certification can be a valuable asset. It focuses on financial management, strategic planning, and decision-making. Holding this certification may help you land roles in financial planning, budgeting, or management accounting.

- Certified Internal Auditor (CIA): For those pursuing a career in internal auditing, the CIA certification is highly regarded. This credential highlights your proficiency in internal controls, risk management, and audit procedures, which are essential skills for roles in corporate governance and compliance.

- Certified Information Systems Auditor (CISA): With the increasing reliance on digital technologies, the CISA certification is becoming increasingly important for accountants interested in IT auditing. This certification covers areas such as information security, systems development, and auditing information systems.

2. Workshops and Seminars

Many professional accounting organizations, such as the American Institute of CPAs (AICPA) and the Institute of Management Accountants (IMA), offer workshops and seminars on a variety of accounting topics. These events are usually focused on specific areas of interest, such as tax law changes, new auditing techniques, or the use of accounting software.

Workshops and seminars offer an excellent opportunity to engage in hands-on learning, network with other professionals, and ask questions from experts in the field. They also often provide Continuing Professional Education (CPE) credits, which are required to maintain certain certifications.

3. Online Courses and Webinars

Online courses have become a popular and flexible way for accountants to continue their education. Platforms such as Coursera, LinkedIn Learning, and Udemy offer courses on a wide range of accounting topics, from basic bookkeeping to advanced financial modeling. Many of these courses are self-paced, allowing you to learn on your own schedule.

Additionally, webinars offer another convenient way to stay informed about current trends and developments in the accounting field. These online seminars can be a great option if you prefer short, focused learning sessions that can be attended from anywhere.

4. Postgraduate Degrees

For accountants who wish to pursue advanced career paths or specialize in particular areas of accounting, pursuing a master's degree may be a worthwhile investment. A Master of Accounting (MAcc) or Master of Business Administration (MBA) with a focus on accounting provides a deep dive into advanced accounting topics such as forensic accounting, advanced tax law, and financial strategy.

These advanced degrees often provide more in-depth training and education than what you received during your undergraduate studies, and they can position you for senior management or leadership roles. Many universities offer flexible, part-time options for working professionals, so you can continue to work while pursuing your degree.

5. Self-Study and Research

Apart from structured educational programs, self-study can also be an excellent way to enhance your knowledge. Reading books, subscribing to professional journals, and keeping up with accounting blogs or newsletters will allow you to stay current on industry trends and best practices.

Self-study is especially important for accountants who are seeking to specialize in a particular area, such as forensic accounting or environmental accounting. By dedicating time to research and learning, you can develop niche expertise that sets you apart from others in the field.

6. Mentorship and Peer Learning

While formal education is valuable, learning from others within the profession is also an essential part of your growth. Mentorship is an excellent way to gain insights into the practical side of accounting, as mentors can share their experiences, guide you through complex situations, and offer valuable career advice.

Peer learning groups are another informal yet effective method of continuing education. You can collaborate with colleagues to discuss challenging topics, share resources, or study for certifications together. Peer groups provide a sense of community and foster an environment of continuous improvement.

Funding Your Continuing Education

As you consider pursuing continuing education, it's important to remember that many educational opportunities come with a financial cost. However, there are various ways to fund your ongoing education:

- Employer Sponsorship: Many employers offer financial support for continuing education, particularly if it aligns with your job responsibilities. Some companies cover the costs of certification exams, seminars, and workshops. Be sure to check with your employer to see if they offer education reimbursement programs.

- Scholarships and Grants: Some professional accounting organizations offer scholarships or grants to help offset the costs of continuing education. These can be particularly helpful for young professionals or those pursuing advanced degrees.

- Tax Deductions: In some countries, continuing education costs related to your current profession may be tax-deductible. Check with a tax professional to see if this applies to you.

- Flexible Payment Plans: Many institutions offer flexible payment options, allowing you to spread the cost of courses or certifications over time. This can make continuing education more manageable financially.

The Long-Term Benefits of Continuing Education

Investing in continuing education brings numerous long-term benefits for your career in accounting. Here are a few reasons why it's worth the effort:

1. Increased Earning Potential

Accounting professionals with advanced certifications, specialized skills, and higher education levels typically earn more than their counterparts without these credentials. Continuing education can significantly enhance your salary prospects, especially as you move into more senior or specialized roles.

2. Career Advancement

Continuing education demonstrates your commitment to your career and your willingness to stay on top of industry changes. This can make you a more attractive candidate for promotions and new job opportunities. Employers value employees who invest in their professional development, as it shows initiative and dedication to quality work.

3. Personal Fulfillment

Beyond career advancement, continuing education provides a sense of personal accomplishment. Gaining new knowledge and skills can be rewarding in itself, and it can help you feel more confident and competent in your work.

4. Adaptability in a Changing Field

Accounting is constantly evolving due to technological advancements and changes in regulations. By committing to continuing education, you'll be better prepared to adapt to these changes, ensuring your relevance in the field.

In conclusion, continuing education is essential for long-term success in accounting. Whether you choose to pursue certifications, attend workshops, or pursue a postgraduate degree, investing in your education will enhance your skills, open up new career opportunities, and keep you competitive in the fast-paced accounting profession.

8.2 Exploring Specializations

8.2.1 Forensic Accounting

Forensic accounting is one of the most intriguing and dynamic fields within the accounting profession. It combines elements of accounting, auditing, investigative skills, and legal knowledge to uncover financial fraud, misconduct, or other forms of financial irregularities. This specialization is ideal for individuals who enjoy problem-solving, attention to detail, and working in environments that require analytical thinking.

In this section, we will explore the nature of forensic accounting, the qualifications and skills required, the job prospects, and the diverse range of opportunities within this fascinating field.

What is Forensic Accounting?

Forensic accounting is a specialized area of accounting that focuses on investigating financial discrepancies and disputes. The term "forensic" refers to the use of accounting techniques to investigate and solve legal issues, making it a hybrid between accounting and law enforcement. Forensic accountants are often tasked with uncovering fraud, embezzlement, money laundering, financial misstatements, and other forms of financial misconduct that may involve legal consequences.

Forensic accountants may be called upon to provide their findings in court as expert witnesses, where they are expected to explain their findings in a clear and concise manner, translating complex financial data into language that is easily understood by judges, lawyers, and juries.

Forensic accounting is not limited to criminal investigations. It also involves civil matters such as divorce settlements, business valuations, and insurance claims, where financial data needs to be examined to resolve disputes.

Key Responsibilities of Forensic Accountants

The primary responsibility of a forensic accountant is to examine financial records, transactions, and business practices to detect and investigate suspicious activities. Their work involves analyzing financial data in-depth to uncover irregularities or fraudulent behavior. Specific tasks often include:

- Investigating Financial Fraud: Forensic accountants are highly skilled at identifying fraud, whether it involves embezzlement, asset misappropriation, or financial statement manipulation. They conduct thorough audits of financial records to detect fraudulent transactions.

- Tracing Financial Transactions: Forensic accountants follow the trail of money, investigating where funds are coming from, where they are going, and identifying any discrepancies or unauthorized transactions.

- Litigation Support: Forensic accountants often provide litigation support by offering expert testimony in court. They might also assist attorneys with document review, deposition preparation, and trial strategy based on their analysis.

- Bankruptcy and Insolvency Investigations: Forensic accountants may be tasked with investigating cases of bankruptcy or insolvency to determine whether financial misconduct contributed to the failure of the business or individual.

- Investigating Money Laundering: Forensic accountants frequently work with law enforcement agencies to trace illegal money laundering activities. They analyze financial transactions that appear suspicious and work to uncover hidden assets.

- Identifying Asset Misappropriation: They are also skilled at investigating cases of employees or executives misappropriating company assets for personal gain. Forensic accountants use various techniques, including forensic data analysis, to trace stolen or misused assets.

Qualifications and Skills Required

Becoming a forensic accountant requires a solid foundation in accounting, investigative skills, and an understanding of legal procedures. It is a career path that blends traditional accounting knowledge with an in-depth understanding of criminal and civil law. Below are the key qualifications and skills that aspiring forensic accountants should develop:

Educational Requirements:

- Bachelor's Degree in Accounting or Related Field: A solid educational background in accounting is essential for entering the field of forensic accounting. Many forensic accountants start their careers with a bachelor's degree in accounting, finance, or a related field. This foundation equips them with the basic knowledge of financial reporting, auditing, and general accounting practices.

- Master's Degree (Optional but Beneficial): Although not mandatory, a master's degree in forensic accounting, finance, or business administration can enhance an accountant's job prospects. A master's degree often offers specialized knowledge in areas like financial fraud detection, investigative techniques, and the legal aspects of forensic accounting.

Certifications:

- Certified Public Accountant (CPA): A CPA designation is one of the most important certifications for a forensic accountant. While it is not strictly required for all forensic accounting roles, a CPA credential demonstrates a high level of expertise in accounting practices and is highly respected in the industry.

- Certified Fraud Examiner (CFE): The CFE designation, offered by the Association of Certified Fraud Examiners (ACFE), is essential for those pursuing a career in forensic accounting. The CFE designation validates an accountant's ability to investigate and detect fraud, making it a crucial credential for forensic accountants.

- Certified in Financial Forensics (CFF): Offered by the American Institute of CPAs (AICPA), the CFF credential is another important certification for forensic accountants. It focuses on specialized skills needed for financial investigations, including the ability to analyze complex financial records and trace hidden assets.

Skills and Competencies:

- Analytical Skills: Forensic accountants must have strong analytical abilities to interpret complex financial records, detect fraud, and identify discrepancies in data. They need to assess large volumes of information and extract key details that others may overlook.

- Attention to Detail: Given the nature of forensic accounting, attention to detail is essential. A small oversight could mean the difference between uncovering fraud or missing a critical piece of evidence.

- Investigative Skills: Forensic accountants need to think critically and approach problems from an investigative perspective. They must be adept at following financial trails and identifying patterns that could indicate illegal activity.

- Communication Skills: Forensic accountants must have excellent written and verbal communication skills. They need to prepare clear and concise reports for clients, colleagues, or legal teams. Additionally, they must be able to explain complex financial concepts in a way that non-financial experts, such as lawyers or judges, can understand.

- Legal Knowledge: While forensic accountants are not attorneys, a basic understanding of legal concepts is crucial. Forensic accountants often work closely with legal professionals and may need to present evidence in court.

- Technology Proficiency: In today's digital age, forensic accountants must be proficient in accounting software and forensic tools used to detect fraud and analyze financial data. Familiarity with data analysis software, Excel, and other advanced tools is essential for handling complex financial investigations.

Job Prospects and Opportunities in Forensic Accounting

Forensic accounting is a rapidly growing field with diverse opportunities. As businesses and governments become more concerned with financial fraud, corruption, and compliance, the demand for forensic accountants continues to rise. Forensic accountants can work in a variety of sectors, including public accounting firms, government agencies, private companies, and law enforcement agencies.

Career Opportunities:

- Public Accounting Firms: Many forensic accountants begin their careers at large public accounting firms, such as the "Big Four" (Deloitte, PwC, Ernst & Young, and KPMG). These firms have dedicated forensic accounting divisions and regularly handle large-scale fraud investigations.

- Government Agencies: Forensic accountants are often employed by government bodies, such as the FBI, IRS, and other regulatory agencies. These accountants investigate crimes like tax evasion, money laundering, and financial fraud committed by individuals or businesses.

- Corporate Roles: Large corporations often hire forensic accountants to safeguard against internal fraud, financial mismanagement, and compliance issues. Forensic accountants working in corporations help detect financial discrepancies and ensure regulatory compliance.

- Insurance Companies: Insurance companies also employ forensic accountants to investigate claims of insurance fraud and assess financial damage caused by fraudulent activities.

- Law Firms and Legal Consultancies: Forensic accountants often work as consultants for law firms involved in complex financial litigation. They provide expert testimony and assist in resolving financial disputes related to divorce, business valuation, or contractual breaches.

Challenges and Rewards

While forensic accounting can be highly rewarding, it does come with its challenges. Investigating financial fraud can be emotionally taxing, especially when uncovering deep levels of corruption or when legal proceedings stretch on for years. Moreover, forensic accountants often work under tight deadlines, particularly when their work is related to litigation or criminal investigations.

However, the rewards of a forensic accounting career are significant. The intellectual challenge of solving financial mysteries can be deeply fulfilling, and the opportunity to play a crucial role in preventing financial crimes offers a sense of purpose. Forensic accountants also enjoy a competitive salary, job stability, and the possibility of career advancement in both public and private sectors.

Conclusion

Forensic accounting is an exciting, challenging, and highly specialized career path. As businesses, governments, and individuals become more aware of the importance of financial transparency and accountability, the demand for skilled forensic accountants is expected to grow. If you are detail-oriented, enjoy problem-solving, and are interested in both accounting and law, forensic accounting might be the perfect career for you.

With the right qualifications, certifications, and skills, forensic accountants have the opportunity to make a significant impact in the fight against financial fraud while building a rewarding and dynamic career.

8.2.2 Environmental Accounting

Environmental accounting, often known as "green accounting" or "sustainability accounting," is a rapidly growing field within the broader accounting profession. As the world becomes increasingly aware of environmental issues and the need for sustainable business practices, environmental accounting has emerged as a crucial tool for organizations to measure, report, and manage their environmental impact. This specialization not only focuses on traditional financial aspects of accounting but also integrates environmental factors into business decision-making processes.

In this section, we will explore what environmental accounting is, why it is important, the skills required to succeed in this field, and the career opportunities it offers to young accountants.

What is Environmental Accounting?

Environmental accounting is a subset of accounting that deals with the identification, measurement, and reporting of an organization's environmental costs. It aims to incorporate environmental factors into financial decision-making, creating a more holistic picture of an organization's economic impact. This form of accounting provides insights into how a business interacts with the environment, tracks costs related to environmental management, and helps organizations implement sustainable practices.

Environmental accounting can be broken down into two main categories:

1. Environmental Cost Accounting: This involves tracking and reporting on the costs associated with environmental protection and compliance. These costs might include the expense of waste disposal, energy consumption, water usage, pollution control, and environmental remediation. Companies need to identify these costs to understand the financial impact of their environmental footprint.

2. Environmental Performance Reporting: This focuses on reporting an organization's environmental impact, often in the form of sustainability reports or environmental performance statements. These reports highlight energy usage, waste management practices, emissions levels, and other key environmental indicators. They provide stakeholders—investors, customers, regulatory agencies, and the public—with an understanding of how well the company is performing in terms of sustainability.

In practice, environmental accounting helps businesses develop strategies for reducing their environmental footprint, improve efficiency, and ensure compliance with environmental regulations.

Why is Environmental Accounting Important?

Environmental accounting is gaining importance for several reasons:

1. Increasing Regulatory Pressure:

Governments and regulatory bodies worldwide are imposing stricter environmental laws and regulations. From carbon emissions standards to waste management protocols, businesses are required to comply with a growing number of environmental policies. Environmental accounting plays a critical role in ensuring that companies stay compliant and avoid potential penalties.

2. Corporate Social Responsibility (CSR) and Reputation:

In today's competitive market, consumers and investors are increasingly favoring companies that demonstrate a commitment to sustainability. Businesses that fail to address environmental concerns risk damaging their reputation and losing customers. By implementing sound environmental accounting practices, companies can showcase their sustainability efforts, enhance their reputation, and attract environmentally-conscious consumers.

3. Cost Savings and Efficiency:

An often-overlooked benefit of environmental accounting is its ability to identify cost-saving opportunities. For example, tracking energy usage can reveal inefficiencies that can be addressed, such as upgrading to more energy-efficient equipment or changing operating practices. Similarly, better waste management can lead to reduced disposal costs and the possibility of reusing materials.

4. Investor and Stakeholder Demand:

Investors and stakeholders are increasingly interested in environmental, social, and governance (ESG) factors. They want to know how businesses are managing risks related to climate change, resource depletion, and environmental liabilities. By engaging in environmental accounting, companies can provide transparent reporting, making them more attractive to responsible investors.

5. Sustainability and the Future:

As businesses strive to reduce their impact on the planet, environmental accounting is a crucial tool in achieving long-term sustainability goals. It helps businesses integrate sustainability into their core strategy and operations, ensuring that environmental responsibility becomes part of the company's culture and decision-making processes.

The Skills Required for Environmental Accounting

Environmental accounting requires a unique set of skills. While it draws heavily from traditional accounting practices, it also requires knowledge of environmental issues, sustainability practices, and the regulatory environment. Some of the key skills needed for success in environmental accounting include:

1. Understanding of Environmental Regulations:

Environmental accountants need to stay up-to-date on laws and regulations that affect businesses' environmental practices. These include local, national, and international regulations on carbon emissions, waste management, energy efficiency, and environmental impact assessments.

2. Knowledge of Sustainability Practices:

In addition to accounting expertise, environmental accountants should have a good understanding of sustainability practices and how businesses can reduce their ecological footprint. This knowledge may include resource conservation, waste reduction strategies, and energy management techniques.

3. Data Analysis and Reporting:

Environmental accounting involves the collection and analysis of a large amount of environmental data. Accountants must be proficient in using data analysis tools and software to process environmental data and generate reports that communicate the organization's environmental impact to stakeholders.

4. Financial Accounting Skills:

Like all accountants, environmental accountants need a strong understanding of traditional financial accounting principles, such as cost accounting, asset management, and budgeting. The ability to combine this knowledge with environmental data is critical to the role.

5. Attention to Detail:

Environmental accounting requires great attention to detail, particularly when it comes to tracking environmental costs and ensuring compliance with regulations. Small errors or oversights can lead to significant financial or legal consequences.

6. Problem-Solving and Critical Thinking:

Environmental accountants must be able to identify environmental risks and inefficiencies within a business and propose solutions. This requires creative thinking, problem-solving skills, and the ability to analyze data from multiple perspectives.

7. Communication Skills:

The ability to communicate complex environmental data in a clear and concise manner is essential. Environmental accountants often have to prepare reports and present findings to senior management, government agencies, and other stakeholders. Clear communication helps ensure that environmental accounting practices are understood and acted upon.

Career Opportunities in Environmental Accounting

As environmental concerns continue to shape the business world, the demand for environmental accountants is expected to grow. Here are some potential career paths in environmental accounting:

1. Environmental Accountant:

This role involves managing environmental costs, tracking energy use, waste disposal, and other environmental expenditures. Environmental accountants help businesses identify opportunities for cost savings and compliance with environmental regulations.

2. Sustainability Consultant:

Some environmental accountants may choose to work as consultants, advising businesses on how to implement sustainability practices and improve their environmental performance. Consultants often work on a project basis, helping businesses design and execute environmental accounting strategies.

3. Environmental Auditor:

Environmental auditors focus on assessing the environmental practices of organizations to ensure they comply with environmental regulations. They conduct audits of environmental costs, policies, and practices, often working for governmental agencies, large corporations, or independent auditing firms.

4. Corporate Social Responsibility (CSR) Manager:

In larger organizations, CSR managers may oversee environmental accounting practices as part of broader corporate sustainability efforts. They work closely with financial and environmental teams to develop strategies for reducing environmental impact and reporting on sustainability performance.

5. Regulatory Compliance Specialist:

Companies need specialists who are knowledgeable about environmental regulations and can help them stay compliant. These specialists ensure that businesses follow the legal guidelines related to environmental reporting and risk management.

6. Environmental Finance Manager:

Environmental finance managers focus on managing the financial aspects of environmental projects, such as green investments, sustainable product development, and carbon trading. They help businesses assess the financial viability of sustainable practices and secure funding for environmental initiatives.

7. Government and NGO Roles:

Many governmental agencies and non-governmental organizations (NGOs) now have dedicated teams focused on sustainability and environmental protection. Environmental accountants in these roles may work on environmental policy, financial reporting for conservation efforts, or assessing the environmental impact of public projects.

How to Get Started in Environmental Accounting

To pursue a career in environmental accounting, it is essential to start with the right educational background and professional development. Here are some steps you can take:

1. Educational Foundation:

Start by obtaining a degree in accounting, environmental science, or a related field. Many universities now offer programs that combine accounting and environmental studies, providing students with a solid foundation in both areas.

2. Certifications:

Consider obtaining certifications such as the Certified Public Accountant (CPA) designation or the Certified Environmental Accountant (CEA) certification. These credentials demonstrate your expertise in both accounting and environmental issues.

3. Gain Practical Experience:

Look for internships or entry-level roles in companies with a focus on sustainability, environmental compliance, or green accounting practices. Hands-on experience is invaluable in this field.

4. Stay Current with Industry Trends:

Environmental accounting is a rapidly evolving field, and it is important to stay informed about new regulations, sustainability practices, and industry trends. Joining professional organizations such as the Environmental Accounting Network (EAN) can provide valuable networking opportunities and resources.

Conclusion

Environmental accounting is an exciting and impactful specialization within the accounting profession. As businesses and governments focus on sustainability, environmental accountants play a critical role in shaping strategies that balance economic growth with environmental responsibility. For young accountants passionate about both numbers and the environment, this field offers diverse career opportunities and the chance to make a real difference in the world.

By pursuing a career in environmental accounting, you will not only help companies comply with regulations and save money but also contribute to a sustainable future. Whether you choose to work in corporate settings, consulting, or public service, environmental accounting offers a fulfilling and rewarding career path for those committed to making a positive environmental impact.

8.3 Setting Long-Term Goals and Finding Fulfillment

In the journey to becoming an accomplished accountant, long-term goals serve as the blueprint for continued success and personal fulfillment. As you progress in your career, it's important to periodically evaluate your aspirations, adjust your career path, and ensure that your professional growth aligns with your values and interests. This section will explore how to set meaningful long-term goals, how to measure your progress, and how to find fulfillment in your accounting career, ensuring you stay motivated and passionate for years to come.

The Importance of Long-Term Goals

Setting long-term goals in your accounting career is crucial for several reasons. First, they provide direction and clarity. Without clear goals, it's easy to lose focus or feel like you're drifting. Having specific, measurable goals helps you stay on track, prioritize your time effectively, and ensure you're progressing in the right direction. Second, long-term goals help you maintain motivation, especially during challenging periods when the work might seem monotonous or when you're faced with setbacks. They act as reminders of the bigger picture, reigniting your passion and reminding you why you chose this career path in the first place.

Third, long-term goals provide a sense of accomplishment. Achieving these goals, whether it's securing a leadership position, becoming a recognized expert in a particular area of accounting, or running your own accounting firm, gives you a feeling of fulfillment and personal satisfaction. Lastly, they encourage continuous personal and professional growth. A stagnant career can lead to frustration, but by setting long-term goals, you are constantly striving to improve yourself, your skills, and your impact on the profession.

How to Set Meaningful Long-Term Goals

To set meaningful long-term goals in your accounting career, start by identifying what success looks like for you. While the traditional route for accountants may involve reaching a senior position such as Chief Financial Officer (CFO), success can mean different things for different people. It's important to define your personal and professional success based on your interests, passions, and life circumstances.

1. Reflect on Your Interests and Values

Before setting your long-term goals, take the time to reflect on what truly matters to you. Are you passionate about forensic accounting and uncovering financial fraud? Do you care about making a positive impact on the environment and want to specialize in environmental accounting? Perhaps you value work-life balance and envision a career in advisory or teaching. Knowing your personal interests and values will ensure that your goals are aligned with what will bring you true satisfaction.

2. Set SMART Goals

The SMART framework is a widely recognized method for setting clear, achievable goals. SMART stands for Specific, Measurable, Achievable, Relevant, and Time-bound. For example:

- Specific: Instead of vague goals like "become a better accountant," specify what exactly you want to achieve, such as "become a certified forensic accountant."

- Measurable: Make your goals measurable so that you can track your progress. For instance, "complete my CPA certification within 3 years."

- Achievable: Set goals that are challenging but realistic given your current resources, time, and expertise.

- Relevant: Ensure that your goals are relevant to your long-term career aspirations and personal values.

- Time-bound: Set a clear deadline or timeline for when you want to achieve each goal.

3. Break Goals into Milestones

Long-term goals can often seem overwhelming, but breaking them down into smaller, manageable milestones can make them more achievable. For example, if your ultimate goal is to become a partner at an accounting firm, break that down into smaller steps such as gaining diverse experience, building a client base, and pursuing relevant certifications. Each milestone achieved is a mini-victory that keeps you motivated and on track.

Common Long-Term Goals in Accounting

Here are some common long-term goals that accountants may set for themselves, along with strategies for achieving them:

1. Becoming a CPA (Certified Public Accountant)

One of the most widely recognized credentials in accounting, obtaining your CPA license is often a critical long-term goal for many accountants. To achieve this, you'll need to complete the required coursework, gain relevant experience, and pass the CPA exam. This may take several years of hard work, but it's an essential stepping stone to advancing your career in public accounting, corporate accounting, or tax advisory.

2. Specializing in a Niche Area of Accounting

As you gain experience, you might decide to specialize in a particular area of accounting. Whether it's tax accounting, auditing, forensic accounting, or environmental accounting, specialization can set you apart from other professionals in the field. Specializing allows you to become an expert in a specific area, giving you an edge in job opportunities and career advancement.

3. Leadership Roles in an Organization

Many accountants aspire to reach leadership positions such as Accounting Manager, Finance Director, or CFO. To reach this level, you'll need to develop strong management, communication, and strategic thinking skills. Building a strong professional network, gaining a broader understanding of the business, and taking on more responsibility will be crucial steps in reaching leadership positions.

4. Starting Your Own Accounting Firm

For some accountants, the long-term goal is to start their own firm. This may involve transitioning from an employee to a business owner, managing your own clients, and building a brand. Entrepreneurship requires a different set of skills, such as business development, client relationship management, and financial planning, but it can be an immensely rewarding career path.

5. Continual Professional Development

Accounting is a profession that requires ongoing learning and adaptation. As you set your long-term goals, consider committing to lifelong learning. This could involve pursuing certifications like the CMA (Certified Management Accountant) or attending industry seminars and workshops. Staying current with changes in accounting standards, tax laws, and technology will help you remain competitive in the field.

Finding Fulfillment in Your Accounting Career

Achieving long-term career goals is important, but finding fulfillment in your work is just as crucial. Fulfillment is what keeps you engaged, motivated, and passionate about your work over the long term. Here are some ways to ensure that your accounting career brings you satisfaction:

1. Pursue Passion Projects

Fulfillment in accounting comes when you can combine your professional skills with your personal interests. For example, if you're passionate about helping non-profits, consider specializing in nonprofit accounting. If you have an interest in sustainability, you might explore environmental accounting or corporate social responsibility.

2. Work-Life Balance

Achieving a healthy work-life balance is essential for long-term fulfillment. Set boundaries between your professional and personal life to avoid burnout. Make time for family, hobbies, travel, and relaxation, ensuring that you're not just thriving in your career but also enjoying life outside of work.

3. Seek Purposeful Work

Accounting, when done right, can be a highly impactful profession. Whether it's ensuring the financial health of a company, helping a small business grow, or uncovering fraud in forensic accounting, find purpose in the work you do. When your work contributes to a greater cause or aligns with your values, it becomes more meaningful and fulfilling.

4. Celebrate Your Achievements

As you achieve your long-term goals, take the time to reflect on and celebrate your progress. Whether it's passing an exam, getting promoted, or landing a key client, acknowledge your accomplishments and reward yourself for the hard work you've put in.

Celebrating milestones, big or small, will keep you motivated and focused on the journey ahead.

5. Contribute to the Profession

Finally, fulfillment in accounting can come from giving back to the profession. Consider mentoring young accountants, volunteering for accounting-related causes, or sharing your knowledge through writing or public speaking. Helping others succeed will not only bring fulfillment but also strengthen the accounting community as a whole.

Conclusion

Setting long-term goals and finding fulfillment in your accounting career go hand-in-hand. By establishing clear, meaningful goals and breaking them down into manageable steps, you can stay focused on your path to success. At the same time, by aligning your work with your passions and values, you ensure that your career remains fulfilling and rewarding. Whether you aim to reach leadership positions, specialize in a niche area, or achieve a perfect work-life balance, the key is to continually evaluate your goals and adjust them as needed. Your career in accounting is a journey of growth, learning, and self-discovery, and with the right mindset and goals, you can build a career that not only supports you financially but also brings you deep personal satisfaction.

CHAPTER IX
The Future of Accounting

9.1 Technology and Automation in Accounting

9.1.1 Artificial Intelligence in Accounting

In today's fast-paced and highly competitive business environment, technology is rapidly transforming industries worldwide, and accounting is no exception. One of the most influential innovations shaping the future of accounting is Artificial Intelligence (AI). AI refers to machines and software systems designed to mimic human intelligence and perform tasks that traditionally required human intervention, such as problem-solving, learning, and decision-making. AI is revolutionizing accounting by automating complex processes, enhancing data analysis, and improving decision-making capabilities.

This section explores the role of AI in accounting, how it works, its applications, and the profound impact it is having on the profession.

Understanding Artificial Intelligence in Accounting

At its core, Artificial Intelligence in accounting refers to the use of advanced algorithms, machine learning models, and natural language processing to automate routine accounting tasks and provide deeper insights into financial data. AI systems analyze vast amounts of data, recognize patterns, and make predictions, which helps accountants make more informed decisions, identify trends, and optimize financial operations.

One of the key elements of AI that makes it particularly valuable in accounting is its ability to continuously learn and improve. Unlike traditional software that follows pre-programmed instructions, AI systems are designed to improve their performance over time by learning from the data they process. This means AI tools are not static; they evolve, refine their understanding, and deliver better outcomes as they are exposed to more data.

Applications of AI in Accounting

The applications of AI in accounting are diverse and impactful. Below are some of the most prominent ways AI is being used in the field:

1. Automation of Routine Tasks

For years, accountants have spent significant time manually entering data, reconciling accounts, and processing invoices. AI has the potential to automate these repetitive and time-consuming tasks, freeing up accountants to focus on higher-value activities. Robotic Process Automation (RPA), powered by AI, can automatically perform tasks like data entry, invoice processing, and bank reconciliation. AI-driven systems can identify discrepancies in financial records, flagging issues for human review, which reduces errors and speeds up financial close processes.

By automating these routine tasks, AI helps improve efficiency, reduce human error, and accelerate accounting workflows, all while providing accountants with more time for strategic decision-making.

2. Predictive Analytics and Financial Forecasting

One of the most promising applications of AI in accounting is in predictive analytics and financial forecasting. AI-powered systems can analyze historical financial data and identify trends, allowing accountants to make more accurate predictions about future financial performance. For example, AI tools can help predict cash flow, project future revenues, and assess the potential impact of various economic scenarios on a company's bottom line.

By leveraging AI's ability to analyze vast amounts of data and identify patterns, accountants can make more informed decisions and provide valuable insights to management, enhancing strategic planning and business forecasting.

3. Fraud Detection and Risk Management

AI is also a powerful tool in detecting fraud and managing risk. In an era where financial fraud is increasingly sophisticated, AI can help organizations detect irregularities that may go unnoticed by human auditors. Machine learning algorithms are capable of monitoring transactions in real time and identifying suspicious patterns, such as unusual spending behaviors, inconsistent transactions, or patterns of financial misreporting.

For example, AI can detect anomalies in financial transactions, identify discrepancies in audit trails, and monitor employee access to sensitive financial data. AI systems can also evaluate the overall risk profile of an organization by analyzing market conditions, financial records, and external factors. This can help accountants assess risk more effectively and provide early warnings about potential financial threats.

4. Improved Accuracy and Efficiency in Auditing

Auditing is another area in accounting that is being transformed by AI. Traditionally, auditing is a time-intensive process, requiring accountants to manually review large volumes of financial transactions, tax records, and supporting documents. AI tools can now streamline this process by automatically analyzing data and identifying inconsistencies or discrepancies that might indicate errors, fraud, or non-compliance.

AI-driven audit tools can analyze 100% of transactions rather than just a sample, ensuring more comprehensive coverage and higher accuracy. This allows auditors to spot potential problems earlier and more accurately, making the audit process more effective and efficient. Additionally, AI can help reduce the time auditors spend on repetitive tasks like data extraction and analysis, allowing them to focus more on interpreting results and providing actionable recommendations to clients.

5. Intelligent Financial Reporting

AI is revolutionizing the way financial reports are generated. With the help of AI-driven tools, accountants can automate the creation of financial statements, balance sheets, and other reports, reducing the time it takes to generate accurate financial reports. AI algorithms can gather data from multiple sources, perform calculations, and prepare reports with minimal human intervention.

AI tools can also be programmed to tailor financial reports to meet specific needs. For instance, if a company needs a custom financial analysis report for a particular department or project, AI can quickly gather the necessary data, analyze it, and produce a report in a fraction of the time it would take a human accountant.

6. Enhanced Client Services and Advisory

As AI automates routine accounting tasks, accountants are able to take on a more advisory role. By leveraging AI tools to analyze data and generate insights, accountants can offer clients more personalized and strategic advice. For example, AI can help accountants identify tax-saving opportunities, recommend better budgeting strategies, or offer advice on improving cash flow management.

AI can also improve client communication by automating the preparation of reports and financial summaries, making it easier for accountants to share insights with clients in real time. This enhanced service level is becoming increasingly valuable to clients who expect timely and actionable financial guidance.

The Impact of AI on Accounting Professionals

While the adoption of AI in accounting brings numerous benefits, it also presents challenges and changes to the role of accounting professionals. AI is not here to replace accountants, but rather to enhance their capabilities and empower them to focus on higher-value tasks that require human judgment, creativity, and strategic thinking. However, this shift in responsibilities requires accountants to adapt to new technologies and stay updated on emerging trends.

1. Skill Development and Training

To remain relevant in an AI-driven accounting landscape, accountants will need to develop new skills and competencies. While technical accounting skills remain essential, accountants will also need to acquire proficiency in working with AI tools, interpreting data generated by AI systems, and integrating AI insights into their decision-making processes.

Accountants will increasingly need to be well-versed in technology and data analytics to complement their traditional accounting skills. The ability to collaborate with AI systems and use AI insights to drive business decisions will become a crucial part of the profession's skill set.

2. Changing Job Roles

As AI takes over more routine tasks, the role of accountants will evolve. Rather than spending time on data entry, reconciliation, and basic reporting, accountants will take on more complex responsibilities, such as interpreting AI-generated data, offering strategic advice, and making high-level decisions based on predictive analytics.

This change in job roles could lead to a shift in the types of skills and expertise employers seek when hiring accountants. Accountants with strong data analysis skills, AI proficiency, and the ability to interpret complex data will be in high demand. As AI continues to develop, we may also see the rise of new accounting roles focused on managing and optimizing AI systems within financial departments.

3. Ethical Considerations and Challenges

While AI offers many advantages, it also raises ethical questions about data privacy, security, and fairness. AI systems are only as good as the data they are trained on, and biased or incomplete data can lead to inaccurate conclusions and decisions. Accountants will need to play an essential role in ensuring that AI systems are used ethically and that the data being processed is accurate, unbiased, and compliant with legal standards.

Accountants will also need to remain vigilant about protecting sensitive client and company data when using AI tools, as the rise of AI could expose organizations to new cybersecurity risks.

Conclusion

Artificial Intelligence is undoubtedly transforming the accounting profession in profound ways. By automating routine tasks, improving data analysis, enhancing decision-making, and providing more personalized client services, AI is revolutionizing how accountants perform their work. However, the integration of AI also presents challenges that require accountants to stay ahead of technological trends and continuously adapt their skill sets.

While AI may change the nature of accounting roles, it will not replace the need for human accountants. Instead, it will empower them to focus on more strategic, high-level tasks, ultimately creating a more dynamic and valuable profession. As AI continues to evolve, it will be essential for accountants to embrace these technologies and leverage their potential to drive innovation, efficiency, and value within the field of accounting.

9.1.2 Blockchain and Data Analytics

In the ever-evolving landscape of accounting, technology continues to disrupt traditional practices, creating new opportunities for accountants and reshaping the way financial data is managed, stored, and analyzed. Two of the most transformative technologies driving these changes are blockchain and data analytics. For young professionals considering a career in accounting, understanding these technologies is crucial. In this section, we will explore how blockchain and data analytics are revolutionizing the accounting profession, their potential applications, and the skills accountants need to develop to stay ahead in this rapidly changing field.

Blockchain Technology: A Game Changer for Accounting

Blockchain is one of the most significant innovations in the digital era, and it holds immense potential for the accounting industry. At its core, blockchain is a decentralized, distributed ledger system that records transactions across many computers in such a way that the registered transactions cannot be altered retroactively. This technology offers several advantages, particularly in areas related to security, transparency, and the reduction of fraud.

Transparency and Security

One of the most crucial aspects of blockchain technology is its ability to ensure transparency. In traditional accounting systems, transactions are typically recorded in centralized ledgers, which can be prone to errors, fraud, and manipulation. Blockchain, however, creates a public record of transactions that all parties involved can access, ensuring that data is transparent, verifiable, and immutable.

For accountants, this means that financial records are more reliable and accurate, and the risk of fraud or errors is significantly reduced. Each block in the blockchain contains a timestamp and a cryptographic hash of the previous block, forming a chain of data that is secure and tamper-proof. This makes blockchain an ideal solution for financial reporting, auditing, and the overall management of financial transactions.

Auditability and Real-Time Reporting

The transparency and immutability of blockchain also revolutionize the auditing process. Traditionally, audits are time-consuming and prone to discrepancies, as auditors must manually reconcile records from different sources. With blockchain, every transaction is automatically recorded and visible in real time, making it easier for auditors to trace and verify financial data.

The ability to audit transactions in real time means that accountants and auditors can identify discrepancies and potential issues more quickly. This has the potential to reduce the time and cost associated with audits, improve the accuracy of financial reporting, and enable more proactive decision-making.

Smart Contracts: Automating Processes

Blockchain also supports the use of "smart contracts," which are self-executing contracts with the terms of the agreement directly written into code. These contracts automatically execute and enforce the terms when predefined conditions are met, removing the need for intermediaries or third-party verification.

For accountants, smart contracts have the potential to streamline a wide range of processes, from billing and payments to compliance and regulatory reporting. By automating routine tasks, accountants can focus more on strategic decision-making and add greater value to their organizations.

Data Analytics: Unlocking Insights from Financial Data

While blockchain provides the foundation for secure, transparent, and efficient financial transactions, data analytics plays an equally vital role in the accounting profession by helping accountants extract valuable insights from the vast amounts of financial data they handle. The rise of big data has created opportunities for accountants to leverage advanced analytics to improve decision-making, drive business performance, and enhance their advisory roles.

The Role of Big Data in Accounting

The concept of big data refers to the massive volumes of structured and unstructured data generated by businesses, customers, and financial markets. Accountants have traditionally worked with historical data, such as financial statements and balance sheets, to make decisions. However, with the availability of big data, accountants can now analyze real-time data from a wide variety of sources, including social media, transaction records, and even IoT (Internet of Things) devices.

By analyzing big data, accountants can identify trends, patterns, and correlations that would have been impossible to spot with traditional methods. For example, data analytics can be used to predict future cash flow, assess financial health, and even detect potential risks before they become major issues. This enables accountants to become more proactive in their roles, offering insights that can guide strategic business decisions.

Predictive Analytics and Forecasting

One of the most powerful applications of data analytics in accounting is predictive analytics. This involves using historical data and statistical algorithms to predict future outcomes. In the context of accounting, predictive analytics can be used to forecast financial performance, budget planning, and resource allocation.

For example, accountants can use predictive models to estimate future sales, cash flows, or expenses, helping businesses make more informed decisions about investments, cost-cutting measures, or expansion plans. Predictive analytics also helps accountants anticipate challenges and prepare for uncertainties, improving financial planning and risk management.

Data Visualization: Turning Data into Actionable Insights

Another key aspect of data analytics is data visualization. With advanced tools like Tableau, Power BI, and Google Data Studio, accountants can transform complex financial data into easy-to-understand visual representations, such as graphs, charts, and dashboards. These visual tools allow accountants to present data more effectively, making it easier for stakeholders to grasp financial information and take action.

Data visualization can help accountants communicate financial trends, performance metrics, and forecasts to non-financial professionals, such as executives or clients. This enhances the accountant's role as a strategic advisor, as they can now provide insights in a way that is clear and actionable, even to individuals without a financial background.

Automating Data Analysis and Reporting

Data analytics also enables accountants to automate much of the data analysis and reporting process. By using tools like Excel macros, machine learning algorithms, and artificial intelligence (AI), accountants can automate repetitive tasks, such as financial data entry, reconciliation, and reporting.

For instance, AI-driven software can analyze large datasets to detect anomalies, assess risks, and generate reports without the need for manual intervention. This automation not only saves time but also reduces the likelihood of errors, making the accounting process more efficient and accurate.

The Synergy Between Blockchain and Data Analytics

While blockchain and data analytics are powerful technologies on their own, their true potential is realized when they are integrated. Together, they can transform the accounting profession by improving transparency, security, efficiency, and decision-making.

For example, blockchain's ability to provide real-time, immutable transaction data can serve as a valuable input for data analytics. By analyzing data from the blockchain, accountants can gain deeper insights into financial trends, performance metrics, and potential risks. This integration enables accountants to work more efficiently and effectively, providing more value to clients and organizations.

Moreover, blockchain can enhance the data privacy and security of analytics processes. With blockchain's decentralized structure, sensitive financial data can be securely shared and analyzed without the risk of breaches or unauthorized access. This is particularly important in the context of financial reporting and auditing, where confidentiality and integrity are paramount.

Skills Accountants Need to Develop

As blockchain and data analytics continue to play an increasingly central role in accounting, it is essential for aspiring accountants to develop skills in both areas. Understanding blockchain technology and how to leverage data analytics tools will be critical for future accountants looking to remain competitive in the field.

Key skills to develop include:

- Blockchain Fundamentals: Understanding how blockchain works, its applications in accounting, and how it can be used to streamline financial processes.

- Data Analytics Tools: Familiarity with software like Excel, Tableau, Power BI, and AI-based platforms used to analyze and visualize data.

- Statistical Analysis: The ability to analyze large datasets using statistical techniques and predictive models.

- Financial Modeling: Understanding how to build and interpret financial models using both historical data and predictive analytics.

- Cybersecurity Knowledge: Since both blockchain and data analytics deal with sensitive financial data, having a solid understanding of cybersecurity principles will be essential.

Conclusion

Blockchain and data analytics are two of the most transformative forces in the accounting profession today. By embracing these technologies, accountants can unlock new opportunities for improving financial reporting, auditing, decision-making, and strategic advising. For young professionals entering the field, mastering blockchain and data analytics will not only enhance their technical expertise but also position them as forward-thinking professionals capable of driving the future of accounting.

As technology continues to evolve, accountants will play an increasingly vital role in integrating these innovations into business practices. By staying informed and adaptable, aspiring accountants can thrive in an industry that is becoming more technology-driven than   ever   before.

9.2 Emerging Roles and Opportunities

The accounting profession is no longer confined to the traditional roles of bookkeeping, financial reporting, and tax preparation. As the world evolves and technology advances, new roles and opportunities are arising, transforming the landscape of accounting. With the increasing demand for specialized skills, forward-thinking professionals will find exciting new areas to explore, while still leveraging the core principles of accounting.

This section will explore some of the emerging roles in accounting, which are being shaped by advancements in technology, changing business needs, and evolving global markets. As you embark on your accounting career, understanding these opportunities will allow you to better position yourself for a successful future.

1. Forensic Accounting: Investigating Financial Crimes

Forensic accounting is one of the most intriguing and rapidly growing fields in accounting. This specialized area involves investigating financial irregularities, fraud, and criminal activity related to financial transactions. Forensic accountants use their expertise to uncover hidden information, trace assets, and provide evidence for legal proceedings.

In today's increasingly complex business environment, fraud and financial crimes are becoming more sophisticated. As a result, forensic accountants are in high demand, particularly in industries such as banking, insurance, and government. They work closely with law enforcement, legal professionals, and organizations to ensure financial integrity and transparency.

Forensic accountants must possess strong investigative skills, analytical thinking, and a keen eye for detail. They also need to be well-versed in legal procedures, as their findings may be used in court cases. With the rise of white-collar crime and cybercrime, forensic accountants will continue to play a vital role in securing the financial sector.

2. Environmental and Sustainability Accounting

As sustainability becomes an increasingly important issue, the role of accountants in managing and reporting on environmental impacts has grown. Environmental accounting, also known as sustainability or green accounting, involves tracking and reporting a company's environmental costs and liabilities. This includes the costs associated with waste management, energy consumption, carbon emissions, and other environmental factors.

Environmental accountants help organizations assess their environmental footprint, make improvements, and comply with environmental regulations. They are also crucial in the growing area of corporate social responsibility (CSR) and sustainability reporting. Many businesses are recognizing the need to demonstrate their commitment to sustainability not just for legal reasons but also to appeal to customers, investors, and stakeholders who value environmental responsibility.

For those with a passion for both accounting and environmental issues, this career path offers a unique opportunity to make a positive impact on the planet while using your accounting skills to influence corporate practices. Environmental accountants work in various industries, including manufacturing, energy, and finance, as well as in non-profit organizations focused on sustainability.

3. Data Analytics and Business Intelligence (BI) Accounting

Data analytics has become a game-changer in accounting, allowing businesses to gather, analyze, and interpret vast amounts of data to make more informed decisions. As the amount of data available to companies continues to grow, accountants with expertise in data analytics and business intelligence (BI) are in high demand.

Business intelligence accountants utilize advanced software tools to process and analyze financial data, helping companies uncover trends, identify inefficiencies, and make data-driven strategic decisions. These professionals must possess a strong understanding of both accounting principles and data analytics tools like SQL, Python, Tableau, or Power BI.

The role of data analytics in accounting extends beyond traditional financial reporting; it is being integrated into budgeting, forecasting, risk management, and strategic planning. With businesses seeking a more comprehensive understanding of their financial health and performance, data-driven insights have become a vital part of modern accounting functions.

Accountants who specialize in data analytics and BI have the opportunity to work across industries, ranging from finance and healthcare to retail and technology. This role is not just about crunching numbers; it's about transforming data into actionable insights that drive business success.

4. Cloud Accounting and Remote Work

Cloud computing has revolutionized the way businesses manage their finances. Cloud accounting allows businesses to store and access financial data over the internet, offering real-time access, enhanced security, and greater flexibility. Accountants who are skilled in cloud-based accounting software, such as QuickBooks Online, Xero, and NetSuite, are well-positioned for the future of accounting.

The rise of cloud accounting has led to the emergence of a new role—cloud accountants. These professionals are responsible for managing financial data stored in the cloud, integrating cloud-based tools into the financial workflow, and ensuring that businesses take full advantage of the flexibility and efficiency cloud accounting offers.

Cloud accounting also plays a key role in the growing trend of remote work. With many businesses embracing flexible work arrangements, accountants can now perform their duties from anywhere with an internet connection. This shift offers greater opportunities for global collaboration and the ability to work with clients from various locations, all while ensuring that financial data is accessible and secure.

Cloud accountants are not only skilled in accounting software but also understand the implications of data security, privacy laws, and the best practices for managing cloud infrastructure. As businesses continue to transition to cloud-based systems, cloud accounting is set to become an integral part of the accounting profession.

5. Cybersecurity Accounting: Protecting Financial Data

With the increase in cyber threats, cybersecurity has become a critical concern for businesses across all industries. As accounting professionals handle sensitive financial data, accountants with expertise in cybersecurity are becoming increasingly valuable.

Cybersecurity accountants focus on ensuring that financial data is secure and protected from hacking, fraud, and other cyber threats. They work closely with IT professionals to develop security protocols, monitor for breaches, and respond to security incidents. They may also play a role in educating employees on cybersecurity best practices and ensuring compliance with data protection regulations.

Cybersecurity accountants need to have a strong understanding of both accounting and information technology. They should be familiar with encryption, firewalls, data backup strategies, and other cybersecurity measures. Given the importance of safeguarding financial data, professionals in this role will be in high demand as cyber threats continue to evolve.

6. Blockchain and Cryptocurrency Accounting

Blockchain technology, which underpins cryptocurrencies like Bitcoin and Ethereum, is gaining traction in the accounting world. Blockchain is a decentralized, secure, and transparent system that records transactions in a way that reduces the potential for fraud and errors. As blockchain continues to be adopted by businesses and financial institutions, the demand for accountants with expertise in blockchain technology is growing.

Blockchain accountants are responsible for ensuring the accuracy and integrity of financial records maintained on the blockchain. They may also be involved in auditing blockchain transactions, ensuring that cryptocurrency transactions comply with regulations, and advising companies on how to integrate blockchain into their accounting processes.

In addition to blockchain, cryptocurrency accounting is another emerging opportunity. Cryptocurrencies require specialized accounting treatment due to their volatility, lack of central regulation, and unique tax implications. Accountants in this field must be familiar with both the technical aspects of cryptocurrency and the regulatory landscape surrounding digital currencies.

For those interested in the intersection of technology and finance, blockchain and cryptocurrency accounting offer an exciting and rapidly growing field with immense potential.

7. Artificial Intelligence and Robotic Process Automation (RPA)

Artificial intelligence (AI) and robotic process automation (RPA) are transforming the accounting profession by automating routine tasks, such as data entry, invoice processing, and reconciliation. These technologies allow accountants to focus on more strategic aspects of the job, such as financial analysis, advisory services, and decision-making.

AI and RPA are expected to continue evolving, with applications in areas such as auditing, risk management, and fraud detection. AI-powered tools can analyze vast amounts of data in real-time, helping accountants detect anomalies and identify potential risks much faster than traditional methods.

While AI and RPA may reduce the need for manual data entry and repetitive tasks, they also create new opportunities for accountants to take on higher-level roles. Professionals who can manage AI systems, interpret AI-generated insights, and ensure the ethical use of automation will be well-positioned for the future of accounting.

8. Global and International Accounting Roles

As businesses expand globally, there is an increasing demand for accountants who understand international financial reporting standards (IFRS), cross-border tax regulations, and global financial markets. International accountants play a key role in helping companies navigate the complexities of operating in multiple countries, including managing currency fluctuations, complying with tax laws in different jurisdictions, and understanding the cultural nuances of business operations in various regions.

International accountants may work for multinational corporations, government agencies, or international organizations. The role often requires expertise in both accounting and international business, as well as proficiency in multiple languages and knowledge of global economic trends.

As the world becomes more interconnected, international accounting roles will continue to grow in importance, offering accountants the opportunity to work in diverse environments and gain a global perspective on finance.

Conclusion

The future of accounting is dynamic, with new technologies and specialized roles creating exciting opportunities for aspiring professionals. Whether you are interested in forensic accounting, sustainability, data analytics, or emerging fields like blockchain and AI, the accounting profession offers endless possibilities for growth and specialization. By staying informed about these emerging trends and developing relevant skills, you can position yourself for a successful and fulfilling career in the ever-evolving world of accounting.

9.3 Adapting to Changes in the Field

Accounting, like every profession, is subject to evolution. Whether it's due to technological advancements, shifts in economic trends, regulatory updates, or the changing nature of business itself, accountants must be agile in responding to new challenges and opportunities. In today's rapidly evolving business world, the ability to adapt is not just a choice; it's a necessity. Let's explore how accountants can best prepare for and adapt to the changes transforming the field of accounting.

The Growing Role of Technology in Accounting

Technology is undoubtedly one of the most influential factors reshaping the accounting profession. With the integration of artificial intelligence (AI), machine learning, and other advanced technologies, accountants are now able to automate repetitive tasks, streamline complex calculations, and analyze large sets of data in ways that were once unimaginable. This shift is not only increasing efficiency but is also allowing accountants to add more value in strategic decision-making.

To stay competitive in the field, accountants must become comfortable with the tools that are changing how they perform their duties. While some may fear that automation will replace human accountants, the reality is quite the opposite. Automation is helping accountants focus on higher-level tasks that require critical thinking, problem-solving, and interpersonal communication. For example, automated software can handle data entry, invoice processing, and payroll management, but the accountant still plays a key role in interpreting the data, offering financial advice, and ensuring compliance.

To adapt to this change, accountants should prioritize learning new technologies and embrace a mindset of continuous learning. Getting familiar with accounting software, cloud computing, AI, and data analytics tools will be crucial. Additionally, accountants should stay abreast of technological trends by attending industry conferences, joining professional organizations, and taking specialized courses to stay ahead.

Developing Analytical and Strategic Thinking

As automation takes over many routine tasks, the role of accountants is shifting towards more strategic involvement. The future accountant will need to possess strong analytical skills to interpret financial data, identify trends, and provide actionable insights to management. Data analytics has become one of the most valuable skills an accountant can possess, and it's essential to embrace this shift toward data-driven decision-making.

For example, rather than merely processing transactions, accountants are increasingly expected to evaluate financial data to advise on budgeting, forecasting, and business strategy. This requires a deeper understanding of not just numbers, but also of market conditions, business operations, and long-term financial goals. To adapt to this change, accountants should actively work on building their strategic thinking and analytical capabilities.

Educational institutions and online courses are increasingly offering specialized programs that focus on data analysis, predictive modeling, and forecasting. By gaining expertise in these areas, accountants can position themselves as business advisors and decision-makers within their organizations, not just number crunchers.

Shifting Towards Advisory Roles

As automation takes care of more transactional work, accountants are moving toward advisory roles, helping businesses navigate complex financial decisions, regulations, and compliance matters. Accountants are no longer just seen as back-office number crunchers but as strategic business partners. They are expected to offer insight into managing risk, maximizing profitability, and driving business growth.

This evolution in the role of accountants means that future professionals must possess strong communication and interpersonal skills. The ability to explain complex financial information in a clear and understandable way is becoming just as important as technical accounting skills. The accountant's ability to foster relationships, advise leadership, and collaborate with other departments will be central to their success in these advisory roles.

Accountants can adapt by honing their soft skills. Public speaking, client management, and the ability to present financial strategies effectively will all become vital. Accountants may also consider earning certifications or credentials that are geared toward advisory services, such as the Certified Management Accountant (CMA) or the Chartered Financial Analyst (CFA) designation, to expand their expertise.

Embracing the Remote Work Environment

The global pandemic has irrevocably altered the work environment, with remote and hybrid work becoming a permanent feature of many industries, including accounting.

While remote work has presented challenges, it has also created opportunities for accountants to work more flexibly and with clients across the globe. As accounting software and cloud platforms allow for seamless collaboration and access to financial data from anywhere, remote work is likely to continue being an integral part of the accounting profession.

Adapting to this change means that accountants must become adept at using digital tools for collaboration, communication, and project management. Being comfortable with cloud-based accounting platforms, virtual communication tools, and digital document management systems will be crucial. Moreover, remote accountants need to manage their time effectively, work independently, and stay organized to meet deadlines.

For those who aspire to work in a global context, remote accounting also provides the chance to collaborate with diverse teams, gain exposure to international markets, and serve clients from different countries. For future accountants, adaptability in a remote or hybrid work environment will be a key skill to develop.

Staying Informed about Regulatory Changes

Accounting is a profession that is highly regulated. With changing tax laws, evolving financial reporting standards, and new regulations emerging regularly, staying up-to-date on these legal requirements is essential for accountants. In fact, one of the most important aspects of adapting to changes in the field is ensuring that accountants are continuously educating themselves on the regulatory landscape.

For example, the implementation of new accounting standards like the International Financial Reporting Standards (IFRS) or updates to the Generally Accepted Accounting Principles (GAAP) require accountants to adjust their practices to remain compliant. The shift toward tax reforms or updates in international financial regulations requires constant vigilance.

Accountants must stay informed through industry news, attending training sessions, and regularly reading updates from professional bodies and regulatory authorities. Additionally, investing in ongoing education, such as certification courses and webinars offered by organizations like the American Institute of CPAs (AICPA), can help accountants stay ahead of regulatory changes and maintain their expertise.

Building Resilience in the Face of Change

The future of accounting is filled with change, and the ability to adapt to new challenges will be the defining trait of successful professionals. Resilience is essential for navigating the inevitable disruptions that occur in any industry. Accountants who are resilient will be able to adjust their strategies and workflows in response to technological innovations, market shifts, and changes in client needs.

Building resilience involves developing a proactive mindset, staying flexible in your approach to work, and being open to learning new skills. Accountants should be prepared to face challenges head-on and embrace opportunities for growth. In addition, creating a network of mentors, colleagues, and professional communities can help build emotional and professional resilience, providing support and guidance as needed.

As the accounting profession continues to evolve, those who embrace change and adapt effectively will not only stay relevant but thrive in an increasingly dynamic field.

Conclusion

Adapting to changes in the accounting field is an ongoing journey that requires flexibility, continuous learning, and a willingness to embrace new technologies and practices. Accountants must be prepared to stay ahead of technological innovations, develop analytical and strategic thinking skills, transition into advisory roles, and navigate the complexities of remote work and regulatory shifts. By fostering a growth mindset and staying informed, future accountants will not just survive but excel in the ever-changing landscape of the profession.

Adapting to these changes is more than just a career survival strategy; it is an opportunity to redefine the role of accountants in the modern business world. Those who can successfully adapt will find themselves at the forefront of the profession, shaping the future of accounting in ways that were once unimaginable.

Conclusion

10.1 Final Thoughts and Encouragement

Embarking on a career in accounting is not just about mastering numbers; it's about shaping your future, solving problems, and contributing meaningfully to the success of businesses, organizations, and communities. Whether you are drawn to the logical precision of financial statements, the thrill of tax planning, or the satisfaction of auditing and ensuring compliance, accounting offers a diverse range of opportunities that can suit your interests and strengths.

A Career Full of Potential

From the very first moment you decide to pursue accounting as a career, you step into a world full of potential and growth. What many young people don't realize is that accounting is more than just a job—it is the backbone of all businesses. Without accounting, no company could manage its finances, strategize for growth, or ensure compliance with tax laws and regulations. By choosing this path, you are entering a profession that plays a central role in the financial health of every organization, big or small.

But accounting is not static. It is a dynamic, evolving field that is continually influenced by changes in laws, technology, and business practices. As an accountant, you will have the chance to grow and adapt along with these changes. New software tools, emerging regulations, and the increasing importance of data analytics are transforming the way accounting is done, opening up even more opportunities for accountants to innovate and drive change. So, when you enter the field, you're not just choosing a job—you're choosing a lifelong learning journey.

The Journey Ahead

While this guide has equipped you with the foundational knowledge to understand the world of accounting, your journey has only just begun. The next steps in your path— whether it's furthering your education, landing your first job, or obtaining your professional certifications—will require commitment, discipline, and a strong work ethic. But remember, every successful accountant started with a single step, just like you.

It's important to recognize that challenges are inevitable along the way. Whether you're struggling with an accounting problem in school, facing the uncertainty of a tough job market, or grappling with difficult clients at work, you will encounter moments of doubt and frustration. These moments are part of the process, not the end of the road. They're opportunities to learn and grow stronger. Every difficulty you face is a building block in the development of your skills and your character. Embrace these challenges, knowing that they will make you better, wiser, and more prepared for the next phase of your career.

One of the greatest strengths you can cultivate as an accountant is resilience. This doesn't just mean working through challenges; it means approaching every task with a mindset of continuous improvement. In accounting, there's always more to learn—new tax laws, new accounting standards, and new technology. Those who are constantly learning and evolving will find their careers advancing faster than those who stagnate.

The Importance of Passion and Purpose

While it's essential to focus on developing your technical skills, it's equally important to connect your work to something greater than just numbers. Accounting is a profession that thrives on purpose and value. It's about understanding the broader picture of the businesses and clients you work with and making a tangible difference in their success. You may be helping a small business navigate its financial statements or ensuring that a multinational corporation adheres to international tax laws. In each case, your role will have a lasting impact on the people you serve.

To sustain a long and successful career in accounting, you'll need to be passionate about the work you do. Passion drives motivation, creativity, and dedication. It fuels your desire to continue learning and improving, even when things get tough. Find areas of accounting that you are particularly interested in—whether that's forensic accounting, international taxation, or nonprofit management—and dive deep into them. Specializing in an area that excites you will make the work more enjoyable and fulfilling, and it will also open up new career possibilities.

Building Strong Relationships

One aspect of accounting that often gets overlooked is the importance of building relationships. Whether you're working with clients, your team, or other professionals, the ability to communicate effectively and build trust is critical to your success. Accounting may be seen as a solitary profession, with accountants working behind the scenes on numbers and reports, but the truth is that accountants are trusted advisors who often guide businesses and individuals through complex decisions.

Good communication skills are an asset in every area of accounting. Whether it's explaining financial data to clients who may not have a background in numbers or collaborating with colleagues on a large audit, the ability to articulate complex information in a clear and concise manner is invaluable. Don't be afraid to develop your soft skills—your ability to communicate, collaborate, and solve problems will be just as important as your technical skills.

Investing in Your Growth

The road ahead will require you to continuously invest in your personal and professional growth. In a world that is increasingly fast-paced and technology-driven, the most successful accountants are those who take charge of their development. This means staying on top of industry trends, earning professional certifications, and participating in networking opportunities. It also means being open to feedback and seeking mentorship from those who have more experience.

While formal education is the foundation, your growth as an accountant is a lifelong endeavor. The accounting field is constantly evolving, and so should you. As you gain experience, you'll encounter new areas of expertise, and you'll have the opportunity to diversify your skill set. This flexibility and adaptability are key factors that will keep you motivated and help you thrive in your career.

Believe in Yourself

One of the most important pieces of advice I can offer you is to believe in yourself. The path to success in accounting—just like in any career—is rarely linear. You will face setbacks, but how you respond to those setbacks will determine your success. Be confident in your abilities and know that you have the potential to achieve your career goals. Hard work, determination, and a positive attitude will take you far.

As you continue your journey, remember that everyone's path to success is unique. Some may progress quickly, while others may take a bit longer to find their footing. What matters is your dedication and persistence. Don't be discouraged by setbacks; they are simply stepping stones to greater success. Keep your eyes on the long-term goals, stay focused, and enjoy the process of becoming the professional you aspire to be.

The Impact of Your Career

As an accountant, you will have a direct and significant impact on the organizations you work for and the people you serve. The role you play in managing finances, ensuring compliance, and providing strategic financial guidance is invaluable. Your work will help shape the future of businesses, whether you're working in a small startup or a multinational corporation.

Moreover, your work as an accountant is essential to the stability of economies. Proper financial management and ethical accounting practices prevent fraud, mismanagement, and financial collapse. In a world where financial transparency and accountability are vital, you will be at the forefront of ensuring that businesses operate ethically and efficiently.

This sense of purpose and responsibility will be your guiding light throughout your career. No matter where your path takes you, remember that you are part of something much bigger than yourself. Accounting is a profession that requires integrity, precision, and a commitment to the greater good. Keep these values at the core of your work, and you will find fulfillment and success in ways you never imagined.

Conclusion: Your Future in Accounting

As we close this chapter, I want to leave you with one final thought: your future as an accountant is bright. The skills you develop, the experiences you gain, and the relationships you build will shape your career and provide you with countless opportunities to succeed. Whether you decide to specialize in a niche area, work your way up the corporate ladder, or branch out on your own, the possibilities are endless.

So, take what you've learned in this book, apply it to your journey, and continue to seek out opportunities for growth. No matter where you are in your career, always remember that you are capable of achieving great things. Your dedication, passion, and resilience will be the keys to unlocking your potential in the world of accounting.

The future is waiting, and it's yours to shape.

10.2 A Look Forward: Making Your Career Count

As you look toward the future of your accounting career, it's important to remember that a career in accounting is not just about numbers; it's about making an impact, both personally and professionally. Accounting is a field with a wealth of opportunities, and the choices you make today will shape your career tomorrow. The future of accounting is dynamic, and it offers endless opportunities for growth and fulfillment. In this chapter, we'll explore how to make your career count, ensuring that your journey through accounting will not only be successful but also meaningful.

1. Setting Meaningful Career Goals

When embarking on any career, it's crucial to set goals that are not only achievable but also meaningful. Rather than simply focusing on promotions or financial success, think about what you want to accomplish in your career in a way that aligns with your values and passions. Start by asking yourself questions like:

- What impact do I want to make in the world through accounting?

- How can I use my accounting skills to help businesses, communities, or individuals?

- What kind of work environment will make me the happiest and most fulfilled?

The answers to these questions will provide a framework for the career path you choose. You might discover that you are particularly passionate about helping small businesses thrive through sound financial advice, or perhaps you have an interest in using your accounting expertise to advocate for environmental sustainability. Setting meaningful career goals that are aligned with your personal passions will give you a sense of purpose and motivation that will carry you through both the highs and lows of your career journey.

2. Lifelong Learning and Professional Development

Accounting is a profession that is constantly evolving. New regulations, technologies, and industry trends emerge regularly, and it's essential to stay updated to remain competitive and effective in your work. One of the best ways to ensure that your career continues to thrive is by committing to lifelong learning and professional development.

Continuous education doesn't necessarily mean going back to school for another degree (though that could be an option in some cases), but it does mean actively pursuing opportunities to learn. This could involve:

- Pursuing certifications: Certifications such as the CPA (Certified Public Accountant), CMA (Certified Management Accountant), and CISA (Certified Information Systems Auditor) can boost your credibility and open doors to higher-paying, more specialized roles. Each certification has its own set of requirements, but achieving these qualifications will provide you with an edge in the job market.

- Attending conferences and workshops: Whether it's an accounting conference, a workshop on new tax laws, or an online course about the latest accounting software, attending events like these keeps you informed about the latest trends in the industry. These events are also fantastic opportunities to network with like-minded professionals and learn from industry leaders.

- Staying current on technology: Accounting is increasingly driven by technology, and staying informed about new tools, software, and innovations is essential. From cloud-based accounting platforms like QuickBooks to cutting-edge AI-driven accounting technologies, understanding how to leverage these tools will make you more efficient and open up new career opportunities.

The ability to adapt and grow in response to new trends is a key trait of successful accountants. In fact, in today's rapidly changing world, those who stop learning and growing risk falling behind.

3. Specializing in a Niche Area

While general accounting skills are highly valuable, specializing in a niche area of accounting can significantly increase your marketability and allow you to pursue your true interests. Consider exploring fields like:

- Forensic Accounting: If you have a knack for problem-solving and investigative work, forensic accounting might be a great fit. Forensic accountants work on cases involving fraud, financial disputes, and other criminal activities, using their accounting skills to uncover the truth behind financial irregularities.

- Environmental Accounting: With the growing focus on sustainability and corporate responsibility, environmental accounting has become a highly relevant niche. This specialty involves accounting for the costs associated with environmental impacts, helping companies measure and manage their carbon footprint and adhere to sustainability regulations.

- Management Accounting: If you're interested in working closely with a company's internal operations, management accounting focuses on providing financial insights to help businesses make informed decisions. This role requires a deep understanding of cost behavior, budgeting, and financial analysis.

- Tax Accounting: If you enjoy solving complex puzzles and working with laws and regulations, tax accounting might be the path for you. Tax accountants help individuals and organizations navigate the complex world of tax laws, ensuring they meet legal requirements while minimizing their tax liability.

Specializing in one of these areas can make you an expert in a specific field, increasing your earning potential and providing opportunities for career advancement. Specialization allows you to become highly valuable to your clients or employer and creates a career that feels personally fulfilling.

4. Making a Difference Through Ethical Practices

As an accountant, you are in a unique position to influence the success and reputation of businesses and individuals. One of the most important ways to make your career count is by committing to ethical practices that reflect integrity, transparency, and responsibility.

- Upholding the integrity of financial reporting: Accurate and honest financial reporting is at the core of accounting. By ensuring that financial statements and reports are reliable and truthful, you can help businesses make informed decisions and maintain the trust of investors, regulators, and clients.

- Supporting corporate social responsibility (CSR): Many businesses today are looking for ways to contribute to their communities and the environment. As an accountant, you can help companies measure their CSR efforts, implement sustainable practices, and report on their social and environmental impact.

- Fighting financial fraud: In addition to general accounting practices, ethical accountants also play a role in preventing and detecting fraud. Whether you work in forensic accounting or are simply vigilant in your day-to-day responsibilities, fighting fraud and ensuring compliance with laws and regulations can help make a significant impact.

By following a path of ethical accounting, you not only contribute to the well-being of your clients and employers but also help to build a stronger, more trustworthy industry overall.

5. Mentoring the Next Generation of Accountants

As you gain experience and expertise, it's important to give back to the profession by mentoring the next generation of accountants. Mentorship is one of the most rewarding aspects of a long-term career. By sharing your knowledge and guidance, you can inspire young professionals, help them avoid common mistakes, and encourage them to pursue their own passions within the field.

Mentorship also helps build a strong professional network and community. Whether you mentor through formal programs, through your workplace, or through professional associations, offering advice and support to newer accountants not only strengthens the profession but also enhances your own career satisfaction.

6. Finding Balance Between Work and Life

While making your career count is important, it's equally vital to maintain a healthy work-life balance. Accounting can be demanding, with long hours and high-pressure deadlines, especially during busy seasons like tax time or year-end reporting. However, achieving a balance between your professional and personal life is crucial for long-term success and happiness.

- Setting boundaries: Learn to set clear boundaries between work and personal time. If possible, take advantage of flexible working arrangements or work-from-home options that allow you to manage your time more effectively.

- Taking breaks and vacations: Don't neglect your physical and mental well-being. Taking regular breaks, taking time off for vacations, and engaging in hobbies or activities outside of work can help you recharge and prevent burnout.

- Fostering relationships: Remember to nurture relationships with family, friends, and loved ones. A strong support network will help you stay grounded and motivated as you navigate the ups and downs of your accounting career.

Ultimately, making your career count isn't just about professional achievements; it's also about creating a balanced and fulfilling life that supports your personal well-being.

Conclusion

A career in accounting offers many paths and opportunities, and as you look forward, you have the chance to create a meaningful and impactful future. By setting clear goals, committing to lifelong learning, specializing in areas that ignite your passion, adhering to ethical practices, mentoring others, and maintaining a healthy work-life balance, you can ensure that your accounting career is not only successful but also deeply fulfilling.

Remember, the journey ahead is uniquely yours. As an accountant, you have the power to shape your career in a way that aligns with your values and aspirations. The world of accounting is full of potential—embrace it, and let your career make a lasting impact.

10.3 Acknowledgements

*First and foremost, I would like to express my deepest gratitude to you, the reader, for choosing **"So You Want to Be an Accountant? A Youth Career Guide"**. Your interest in this book marks the first step on a potentially life-changing journey toward a rewarding career in accounting. I am truly honored that you have decided to embark on this exploration of the accounting profession with me.*

This book was written with you in mind – the curious young mind who is ready to understand the dynamic and essential role that accountants play in our world. Whether you're still deciding on your future career or already beginning your studies, I hope this guide provides you with valuable insights and inspires you to take the next steps with confidence.

I would also like to extend my sincere appreciation to my mentors, peers, and the professionals who shared their knowledge and experiences, making this book a more comprehensive and authentic resource. Your generosity with your time and wisdom has been invaluable.

Finally, I want to thank my family and friends for their unwavering support throughout this process. Your encouragement has kept me motivated and focused on completing this project.

I wish you all the best as you begin your career journey. May you find fulfillment, growth, and success as you navigate the exciting world of accounting. Remember, every great journey starts with a single step—and you've just taken yours.

Thank you again for your support!

Warmest regards,

www.ingramcontent.com/pod-product-compliance
Lightning Source LLC
Chambersburg PA
CBHW062349220526
45472CB00008B/1748